BANISHED

BANISHED

COMMON LAW AND
THE RHETORIC OF SOCIAL EXCLUSION
IN EARLY NEW ENGLAND

NAN GOODMAN

PENN

UNIVERSITY OF PENNSYLVANIA PRESS

PHILADELPHIA

Published by
University of Pennsylvania Press
Philadelphia, Pennsylvania 19104-4112
www.upenn.edu/pennpress

Printed in the United States of America on acid-free paper

10 9 8 7 6 5 4 3 2 1

Library of Congress Cataloging-in-Publication Data
Goodman, Nan, 1957–
    Banished : common law and the rhetoric of social exclusion in early New England
/ Nan Goodman. — 1st ed.
        p. cm.
    ncludes bibliographical references and index.
    ISBN 978-0-8122-4427-4 (hardcover : alk. paper)
    1. New England—History—Colonial period, ca. 1600–1775. 2. Exile (Punishment)—
New England—History—17th century. 3. Common law—New England—
History—17th century. 4. Puritans—New England—History—17th century.
5. New England—Civilization—17th century. I. Title.
F7.G65 2012
974'.02—dc23

                                                                                                2012002921

For Sam and Q,
canlarım

Contents

A Banishment Primer

Presume not that I am the thing I was,
For God doth know, so shall the world perceive,
That I have turn'd away my former self;
So will I those that kept me company. . . .
. . . I banish thee, on pain of death.
—William Shakespeare, *Henry IV, Part 2*, 5.5

COMMUNITIES MAKE MEMBERS. Working from the principles articulated in contracts, constitutions, or even simple screeds, communities create a sense of belonging among their inhabitants that draws people in, binds them together, and fosters a collective identity. This sense of membership has been a commonplace in the history of communities from the city-states of ancient Greece to the incipient nation-states of Europe in the seventeenth century and beyond. Without holding out the possibility of inclusion—in the form of shared principles—few communities would have been established, and fewer still would have endured. Less obvious in the formation of community, however, are those negative principles that facilitate the exclusion of people who do not "belong" and yet work, paradoxically, to reinforce the bonds among those who do. As the legal scholar Peter Goodrich explains, a community's ability to exclude not only strengthens the connections between insiders but also casts the membership of the community in the form of a Manichean struggle. "The establishment of an identity, the constitution of a community, and the capture of subjectivity," he writes, "are first a matter of establishing a collective . . . identity whose virtue will be matched only by the evil of those who do not belong to it."[1] In this way inclusion and exclusion are paired, or as Charles Tilly puts it: "Every act of . . . inclusion consists of creating, activating, or transforming an us-them boundary, and thus inevitably twins with an act of . . . exclusion."[2]

If inclusion and exclusion are twinned, however, there are certain times and certain places where one twin assumes primacy over the other, and where inclusion or exclusion appears to take precedence as a means of producing community. Such a time and place was seventeenth-century New England—from 1620, when the first Puritan colony, Plymouth Plantation, was established, to 1684, when the charter of the Massachusetts Bay Colony, the biggest and most powerful of the colonies, was revoked and administrative power was ceded to the Crown. Exercised ruthlessly and obsessively in this period, banishment, by which undesirable individuals and groups were forcibly removed from the colonies, overpowered the ways and means of inclusion—contractual, constitutional, or otherwise—and became a central, and yet up to this point almost entirely unrecognized, way of defining the place and the people within it.

This book is about that period and its banishments.[3] From the moment they first set foot in the New World, the Puritans, banished or in flight from persecution themselves, banished hundreds if not thousands of others.[4] Between 1620 and 1630, the first decade of the Plymouth Colony's existence, Governor William Bradford banished dozens of people, including John Lyford and John Oldham, for sending letters "full of slanders and false accusations" about the colonists back to England.[5] More notably between 1630 and 1631, the first year of the founding of the Massachusetts Bay Colony, out of fewer than a thousand people in Salem, Charlestown, and Boston combined, between six and ten people were banished, an astonishing 0.6 to 1 percent of the population.[6] Nor did the percentage of those "sent out of the lymitts of the patent" dwindle much in subsequent years as the theocracies in Plymouth and the Bay Colony continued to attract and to banish traders, visitors, and aspiring members who were deemed to have insufficiently conformed to the Puritans' ways.[7]

Admittedly most of those banished escaped all but the most cursory notice. Their names are enshrined in legal casebooks from the period, but few have paid attention to their stories, and in most cases little of their stories is known. In 1640, for example, the otherwise obscure Hugh Bewett was banished for claiming he was free of original sin, and in 1642 William Collins was banished for seeking sexual favors under a false promise of marriage.[8] During the same period Thomas Walford and Philip Ratcliffe were banished for declaring their "contempt of authorities and confrontinge officers etc," and Captain Stone for calling the magistrate Ludlow "not a justice but a 'just-ass.'"[9] In addition, starting in 1672 records confirm that banishment was imposed in one case of adultery and in another of "adulterous behavior," as well as in one case for prostitution, another for contempt of authority, and two others for unspecified crimes.[10] To this list can be added a banishment in Connecticut for contempt of authority and another in New Haven for lascivious behavior, an indication that while the Bay Colony and Plymouth may have been the most avid of the banishing colonies, other colonies engaged in the practice as well.[11]

In contrast to the Bewetts, Stones, and Walfords of the world, however, many of the banished were and continue to be well known, though for reasons discussed below, the true significance of their banishments has been obscured. In this category are the stories of the Anglican renegade Thomas Morton, banished by Plymouth in 1635 and memorialized by Nathaniel Hawthorne for unlawfully erecting a Maypole in the settlement of Merry-mount, and the controversial minister and founder of Rhode Island, Roger Williams, who was banished by the Bay Colony that same year. In 1637 the Bay Colony also banished the infamous heretic and "antinomian" Anne Hutchinson,[12] after whose banishment the colony enacted a series of laws banishing whole groups of so-called heretics, including the Anabaptists in 1645 and the Jesuits in 1647. In the 1650s the Bay Colony went on to banish numerous Quakers,[13] including the illustrious Mary Dyer, and throughout the 1660s and 1670s authorities expelled hundreds of Christianized Indians, whose removal to Deer Island in the Boston harbor was banishment in everything but name.[14]

Not Religion

Unsurprisingly those among the banished whose names still resonate today made their banishments memorable by complaining loudly about them. If their names are known, however, the accounts of their punishments and of the consequences that followed in the wake of their banishments have been neglected. Two factors account for this neglect. The first is that their stories—like most of the stories that have come down to us from Puritan America—have been read by scholars almost exclusively for the light they shed on the Puritans' religion and religious practices. In their focus on religion, scholars of history and literature have done no more than follow the Puritans' lead. The initial colonies of Plymouth and Massachusetts Bay as well as the subsequent colonies of New Haven and Connecticut were founded on the principle of religious congregationalism, and the communities that were established in these places were structured to serve that end. If an individual qualified for church membership—a qualification that was based on the church's judgment about the candidate's conversion experience—then the candidate also qualified for membership in the colony, and in this way religion provided an undeniably strong basis for social cohesion.

One of the results of the scholarly focus on religion has been to emphasize religion's role in building this social cohesion. Histories of the period, both literary and social, are replete with references to the founding documents—preeminent among them John Winthrop's lay sermon "A Model of Christian Charity"—that not only emphasize the connections between people that religion enabled but also help us think through the principle of community membership in this light. For Winthrop, the Puritan community was "knit together" in "the body of Christ," by which it formed "a city on the hill" for all to emulate, if not to enter.[15] In terms of the popular history of inclusion in America, the line that runs from Winthrop to the universal welcome—"Give me your tired, your poor, your huddled masses"—inscribed on the Statue of Liberty's pedestal remains virtually uninterrupted.

I say "virtually" because, as most of us are aware, the line has been broken many times. As a nation we have witnessed the erection of countless impediments to inclusion from the quotas imposed on Italian, Irish, and Jewish immigrants of the mid-nineteenth century, to the Chinese Exclusion Act at the end of that century, to the torturous policy on Mexican immigrants in our own day. However, long before these more recent debates over inclusion and exclusion, passionate debates over banishment occurred in seventeenth-century New England. These debates were played out in the numerous pamphlets, trial testimonies, histories, and affidavits concerning banishment that are newly examined in this study. According to most scholars of the banished, the debates about banishment were strictly religious and gave way in their ostensible resolution to the development of a coherent, religiously based foundation for membership in the Puritan communities. To be sure, social exclusion as an ideological component or mechanism for community coherence is as central to religious community coherence as it is to the law; René Girard describes the religious, even superstitious, turn of many communities to the figure of the scapegoat—that "one individual" who has been designated by community members as bearing all the fault for their ills and "who can be easily disposed of."[16] There can be no question that the Puritans engaged in scapegoating. Michel de Certeau describes the need for purification or cleansing that accompanies many forms of religious communities, which he recognizes as the creation of "clean space" in utopian discourse and which almost certainly played a part in the creation of the Puritan church-state.[17] The more traditional story of social exclusion told about the Puritans dwells on just such rituals, including different forms of shaming, such as wearing placards—the penalty inflicted on Hester Prynne in *The Scarlet Letter*, Nathaniel Hawthorne's version of seventeenth-century New England—or being thrown into the stocks and pillory, a common penalty for all sorts of disruptive behavior. In addition, of course, there were excommunication and execution, penalties suffered by countless people, including perhaps most famously the so-called witches of Salem in 1692.

For scholars from Perry Miller to Matt Cohen, however, the banishments of celebrated figures such as Hutchinson, Morton, and Williams proved not that religiously motivated social exclusion was one among many reasons for the frenzied banishments but that it was the only one.[18] Thus the stories they tell about the banished assume the centrality of their heresies. For Philip Gura, for example, Hutchinson and Morton were significant for the radical impact they had on "the doctrinal and ecclesiastical . . . development of American Puritanism," while for Janice Knight, Hutchinson and fellow antinomians such as John Wheelwright and Henry Vane were expelled for the disruption they introduced in the church hierarchy.[19] For Louise Breen, Hutchinson's problem was her "prophetic voice," while for Jonathan Field, Hutchinson, Williams, and the Quakers alike still figure as "*religious*," not legal dissidents.[20] Even Martha Nussbaum's reading of Williams in the context of his civil defense and leadership returns him in the end to a religious context. The "common political life" envisioned by Williams, she writes, was to be based "on ethical principles [of mutual respect and dignity, for example] that, for many of us, also have a religious meaning and a religious justification."[21]

Still, it is not my point to challenge these statements here. They are accurate and illuminating as far as they go, and there is no denying that religious conceptions of social exclusion were central to the Puritans' community making. Rather my point is to put these religious conceptions into dialogue with the legal ones that have traditionally been left out of the equation. After all, even if Morton's, Williams's, and Hutchinson's alleged religious violations set the exclusionary mechanisms available to the Puritans in motion, it is crucial to remember that they were all banished for nonreligious reasons. Though she was considered a heretic, Hutchinson, for example, was banished not for heresy but for "holding meetings" in her house that were not sanctioned by the civil law. Roger Williams, who defied the principles of congregationalism and was long a thorn in the side of the Bay Colony ministry, was banished for "disturbing the peace," an infraction that was, as the Puritans knew well from having endured the same accusation in England, a secular, not a religious, offense. Moreover to speak of the religious notions that guided the Puritans in their decisions about who could participate in their communities as members without at the same time speaking of the legal notions that were so often in tension with them is to tell only one side of their story; and to tell only that side—the religious side—is to reinforce certain stereotypes about the Puritans that have for too long had a stranglehold on our understanding of this period. If the Puritans were strict and absolute in their imposition of religious rules for membership and engaged in frequent rituals of religious purification or exclusion, they were equal in their devotion to the more ambiguous rules set forth in the common law—uncovered often only in the infliction of and resistance to banishment—driven ultimately to admit people who would not have qualified under the stricter religious rules alone.

Banishment, in short, in contrast to the many forms of religious exclusion favored by the Puritans, proved to be a limit case for social exclusion, a point at which the excluded were sent beyond the typical or traditional limits involved in ostracism or shaming, to name just two alternatives. The question at the heart of banishment, in other words, was not whether it was legitimate to inflict social exclusion on certain undesirable members of the community, but whether it was legitimate to inflict a form of social exclusion that undid their membership altogether. Unlike shunning or shaming or even imprisoning or killing (victims of which the community could mourn and thus reincorporate), banishment provided no semblance of or opportunity for social reintegration. It used the law to create a zone outside the law, and so it tested the limits of the law more than its counterparts tested those of religion. For readers familiar with the work of Carl Schmitt and Giorgio Agamben, moreover, this formulation will resonate, for both have wrestled with the ways in which the law occasionally transcends its own boundaries and makes exceptions to itself. Schmitt and Agamben discuss this legal paradox within the context of the rise of fascism in mid-twentieth-century Europe.[22] In spite of that distance, their theories and those of several other contemporary political theorists inform the analysis of banishment throughout this book. I invoke Schmitt and Agamben as well as Alan Badiou, Jacques Derrida, Jacques Rancière, and others on the theory that (1) many of the banishment narratives reveal ideas about political and legal communities that share affinities with more recent ones, and (2) the standard stories told about many of these historical figures and texts have been unnecessarily conditioned by limited scholarly approaches that refuse to put them into the transhistorical and transnational contexts they deserve. These texts, despite their distance from us in time, continue to be part of an ongoing conversation about community and social exclusion within the Anglo-America common-law tradition. Moreover this conversation, as we cannot help but observe, has taken on an urgency in recent years that has in part given rise to relevant theories about space, borders, and boundaries that can help us shed light on earlier concerns as well as better understand our own.

For Schmitt, for example, the exception to the law was just that—an irregular condition, called into being by an emergency and creating a special, suspended relation between the sovereign, who called it into being, and the law.[23] Schmitt's work, then, provides a paradigm for thinking about banishment in colonial New England as a law that went beyond the law only in individual, exceptional cases; this of course was a kind of law that was problematic in and of itself but could still be seen as an anomaly. For Agamben, however, the operation of banishment or the "ban," as he calls it, is no longer the exception that proves the rule but the rule itself, a state of being in which the law is defined by what is outside or excluded from it.[24] For Agamben, exclusion from the law is the norm and is called into being not by an emergency, as it is for Schmitt, but by any and every circumstance. The law, then, for Agamben *is* the exception, the suspension of law itself, and taking this as his starting point, he describes contemporary society as a bare zone and contemporary life as "bare life" that is always lived on the margins. That Agamben's theory of the ban is extreme can be seen in his use of the concentration camps of World War II as a model for contemporary law and politics, so I want to be clear that I am not drawing a parallel between the world of Puritan New England and the world he depicts today. Rather, I invoke him to raise the possibility that the banishments that characterized seventeenth-century New England, extreme and frequent as they were, might share some of the structural features he ascribes to the law in a state of exception. When Roger Williams, for instance, referred to John Cotton's desire that he (Williams) be "denied the common aire to breath in," he seems to have been thinking of a place beyond which the law applied. When the Puritan authorities found themselves unable to contemplate a place outside either their own or the Indians' territorial possessions, they too seemed to be thinking of a metatopical place in which neither law, Puritan nor Indian, seemed to exist. Could the arguments about banishment made by these and other figures studied here amount to some version of Agamben's state of suspension?

I return to this and other similar questions more explicitly in the book's conclusion, but for now it is enough to bear in mind that in sending people outside the bounds of the law, even the Puritans saw themselves as doing something controversial, as setting up communities that put pressure on the very notion of the law as they understood it. Not surprisingly, then, the stories that the subjects of banishment tell about themselves as well as the stories told by contemporary detractors and supporters of them revolve less around religious principles than around the validity of the legal principles that enabled the creation of communities in which banishment became a regular practice. While religion and the law informed each other, in other words, it was the legal punishment of banishment and not the religious grounds that may have precipitated it that became one of the major catalysts for defining what the Puritan community could and should look like. This study gives voice to these legal stories.

Not a Nation

This brings us to the second reason that aspects of the story and the significance of banishment have been neglected: even among studies of the period that are legally, and not religiously, oriented, most concern the notion of the nation and are thus driven by a "nationalist teleology."[25] While these studies, many of which have been enormously influential and have provided invaluable models for my own, offer nuanced explanations for certain specific legal developments, such as the implementation of Puritan legal reforms, they have tended to gloss over the extent to which, in the exercise of banishment, the Puritan colonies contemplated all kinds of nonstandard and nonnational directions for themselves. These directions have been occluded by the nation-building point of view common to most legal scholarship, the major features of which—territory or jurisdiction and power or sovereignty—have for too long been seen as combining in predictable and even invisible ways.

Put another way, legal, social, and literary studies written in the light, if not in the service, of this nationalism have fallen prey to a notion of community that aligns with the maddeningly vague, almost ineffable sense of coherence that defines nationalism—a sense in which belonging and membership are somehow inextricably and inexplicably linked to territory and the process by which an "us" takes shape against a "them." As the legal geographer David Delaney suggests, what people understand about the rise of the nation tends to remain at the level of the us/them divide. "'We' [the members] simply are who we are," he writes, "and 'they' [the nonmembers] are obviously not 'us.'"[26] This tautological understanding of the idea of national belonging and membership offers a sense of national territory as fixed and inelastic—a border or boundary between "us" and "them"—on the one hand, and a sense of membership in the community as homogenous—whatever "we" are, it is nothing like what makes them "them"—on the other.

A focus on this divide prevails even when those studies differ on precisely how the nation came into being.[27] For a social scientist such as Liah Greenfield, for example, the us/them divide is a function of different individual relations and collective dispositions. According to Greenfield, there is a moment in which an awareness of a shared community spreads *among* people to make them *a* people, a community with a coherent membership, but that moment, conveniently, escapes definition.[28] Benedict Anderson's model of the nation as an "imagined community" shares features with Greenfield's, as do those of Peter Sahlins and Anthony Smith.[29] Taking issue with this dispositional model, Charles Tilly has offered a more materialist approach that nevertheless reinforces the ineffability of national bonds. He comes at the subject through an analysis of transactions. "Strictly speaking, we observe transactions," he writes, "not relations. Transactions between social sites transfer energy from one to another . . . [and] from a series of transactions we infer a relation between the sites: a friendship, a rivalry, an alliance, or something else."[30] Though his examples here—friendship, rivalry—suggest a community on a relatively small scale, for Tilly these transactions provide the "ties" that make up the membership of a nation as well.

The sociologist Saskia Sassen speaks in similar, albeit far more critical, ways about the methods of inclusion and exclusion that comprise the nation. They are a "bundling," a term that for her conjures the strange and ostensibly unassailable mixture of territory, on the one hand, and authority or sovereignty, on the other, to which Sassen adds a third component, which she calls "rights."[31] Exasperated with this bundling, which she repeatedly calls "a challenge" and insists we "decode," Sassen has begun the project of disambiguating or "unbundling" in order to provide a template for the spread of denationalization and globalization.[32] But if Sassen sees her task as future oriented—she imagines a new, global order—she turns to the past to begin her engagement with this future, rereading the history of a number of different kinds of communities or "assemblages" from the medieval period forward.[33] For Sassen, these early communities were neither necessarily protonational nor based on rigid and unexamined assumptions about how territory, sovereignty, and rights should combine. Rather they were variable, trying on new understandings of community, of membership and belonging, by responding to historical and material conditions in unexpected ways and by altering the way people understood territory, authority, and rights.

Like Sassen, I turn to communities in the making, not yet bound by the predetermined territorial lines that we associate with the nation and yet, unlike those studied by Sassen, not completely free of them either. I turn, in other words, to a particular moment in time, to the formation of communities that began as companies, turned into colonies, found themselves alternately with and without charters, sympathized at times with kings and at others with regicides, and were, finally, attracted to and yet defiant of the pressure to identify themselves as and with nations. Like others, that is, the communities studied here were in constant flux, but the terms of that flux revolved around the specific poles of separation and incorporation, monarchy and its alternatives, that marked their relationship with early modern England and altered their ideas about community in turn. In addition the communities in question here were marked by their own social and material changes. During the span of time covered by this study, roughly 1620 to 1684, the communities of Plymouth and Massachusetts Bay, for example, underwent transformations that included varying levels of immigration (as well as different kinds of immigrants), changing ideas about religious practice and Puritanism, and changing ideas about self-rule and internal government, all of which informed their exercise of banishment and their sense of community. As many scholars have pointed out, the first five or six decades of Puritan rule in New England can be divided neatly into generational phases, revealing dramatic differences between how the first (from the 1620s through the 1630s), second (from the 1640s through the 1650s), and third (from the 1660s through the 1670s) generations set some events in motion and responded to still others.[34] Last but not least, we note the changing notions of law that were intimately tied to but not entirely encompassed by changes in sovereignty in these years.

Banished, which proceeds chronologically, attempts, like Sassen's work, "to register the complexity" of these changes, and yet in its description of banishment, it also suppresses some of the chronological details in order to open up other ways of telling the story and other ways of asking questions about it. Thus the book focuses in its description of banishment on changes in the law up to 1684 because the legal order defined by the period of the first charter, regardless of how internally changeable it was, provides us with distinct parameters. During this period the law was particularly fraught and fluid; the common law vied for and ultimately achieved supremacy over other kinds of law in England and yet was subject to reworking in the colonies. More significantly, in this period the very tenets of the common law—its dependence on negotiation and precedent, among others—were on people's minds in a way that was unparalleled, and thus under the leadership of Sir Edward Coke and others, the law became a kind of lingua franca for thinking about community and membership. Subsequent periods, especially those decades immediately following the revocation of the charter, in the 1680s and 1690s, were also involved in many of these same discussions. Indeed in the years between the revocation of the charter in 1684 and the creation of the Province of New England in 1693 there were legal complexities as power shifted from Joseph Dudley, the president of a temporary council established in the Bay Colony, to Edmund Andros, the first royal governor, to Simon Bradstreet, the second. However, the issue of how to form a community in those years did not revolve around the peculiar operations of the common law or its understanding of social exclusion, as it did in the earlier period.

The Common Law and Rhetoric

What do we mean when we refer to "those peculiar operations of the common law"—the negotiation and precedent cited above—and how did they come to play a role in the exercise of banishment and the understanding of community on which it relied? The answer lies largely in their rhetorical form. The product of judge-made law that was rooted in the "customs of the people," the common law, as opposed to legislation or royal fiat, evolved through a process of precedent in which a previous decision was both applied to and if need be altered by a subsequent one. This treatment of precedent created a unique rhetorical context for lawmaking, entering into a dialogue with previous legal actors while at the same time speaking to present legal actors and enacting changes on their behalf. Still in effect, the common-law system set in motion by Sir Edward Coke and his immediate heirs was also arguably different from our own in its strict adherence to the principles of responsiveness and reciprocity—of a negotiation between past and present with lawyers for both sides arguing the merits of their cases and in so doing hoping to be persuasive.[35] These arguments or negotiations are essentially rhetorical performances, examples of rhetoric or the art of persuasion. As all seventeenth-century lawyers would have known, rhetoric as Aristotle defined it is a way of getting at the truth through the persuasive interactions of speaker and audience.[36] Cicero, who followed Aristotle in this regard, clarified the rhetorical essence of the law by explaining that legal truth was similarly produced through speakers who could "win people over."[37]

The link I am making here between the law and rhetoric is at once obvious and subtle: obvious because anyone who has been to court or seen a courtroom drama knows that judge-made law is a process of question and answer or give and take; subtle because an acquaintance with the law, especially in its television incarnation, fails to reveal that in rhetorical terms this legal give and take, this "winning of people over," is also what structures community creation and is thus central to the inquiry into territory, jurisdiction, and membership undertaken here. James Boyd White has observed that this "aspect of legal rhetoric is what might be called its ethical or communal character, or its socially constitutive nature. Every time one speaks as a lawyer, one establishes for the moment a character—an ethical identity, or what the Greeks called an *ethos*—for oneself, for one's audience, and for those one talks about. . . . The law is an art of persuasion that creates the objects of its persuasion, for it constitutes both the community and the culture it commends."[38] Building on White's ideas, Francis Mootz raises the possibility that rhetoric is not simply a constitutive feature of law but also "a way of knowing." Rhetorical knowledge, which Mootz describes as the knowledge we acquire from arguing with each other, "is a *constitutive* feature of legal practice."[39] Using Mootz to examine the law of banishment allows us to draw from our reading of the banishment narratives a sense not only of what issues were at stake in the creation of community through the us/them or inside/outside divides, but also how Puritans in both majority and minority positions came to know their world and their laws.

To see the law in rhetorical terms, then, is to depart to some degree from the rubric of law and literature that may be familiar to readers of studies such as this. To be sure, *Banished* would not have been possible without the work of the law and literature scholars who first insisted that both "law and literature structure reality through language."[40] But the readings offered here do not see the law as a form of language, a genre of literature, or even as one of many normative discourses, as Robert Cover suggests, as much as a specific way of talking worlds and their members into existence.[41] *Banished* explores these new worlds through an examination of the arguments over banishment, that is, over the terms of jurisdiction, sovereignty, and rights that were central to banishment, not simply because boundaries and membership were at stake in these decisions but because the law provided a language in which the Puritans came to know themselves and to make themselves known to others. That the banished found a voice at all was due in part to the rhetorical structure provided by the law. Thus while many have noted that banishment ends in silence— think of the long line of exiles who, like Mowbry in *Richard II*, experienced banishment as a "loss of language"—*Banished* moves in a different direction, still Shakespearean in many ways but more like the Shakespeare of *Henry IV* than the Shakespeare of *Richard II*. It demonstrates how, far from imposing silence on the banished, banishment opened up a way of talking about and thinking through how communities were formed in the seventeenth-century transatlantic world and how territory, authority, and rights might combine in new ways to form new kinds of members among them.[42]

In some ways, then, *Banished* does its own banishing: it takes up the story of banishment as told by the "Henrys" of the colonial world while excluding that of the "Mowbrys," even though the "Mowbrys" clearly had their own story to tell. In some cases, of course, the problem is simply practical; the stories of the Bewetts, Walfords, and Stones who were banished along with their more famous counterparts were either lost or never written. All we have in the case of many of these figures is a brief entry in the record books of the General Court indicating that they were "sent away." Such sparse records are naturally less revealing than the extensive narratives studied here, and yet they do tell us something: that banishment, for instance, was not reserved for celebrated political upstarts but was widely deployed and accepted as a means of ridding the colony of criminals. Indeed it is this feature of banishment that motivates the analysis here, for it is only because it was a commonly inflicted punishment that banishment figured so significantly in the larger debates over how the Puritans' community was and should be constructed. But the stories of the silent may suggest even more: that banishment cut across class lines, targeting the well-to-do as well as the illiterate and those without access to print technology. This figures prominently in the banishment debate, as will be demonstrated in Chapter 2. In addition silence suggests that banishment may have been seen by some, as the Puritan authorities hoped it would be, as the lesser of two evils. For some of the banished, in other words, silence may have indicated gratitude, either for escaping the death penalty or, alternatively, for being forced to return to England, which so many of the early colonists longed to do.

While there are numerous lessons to be learned from the banished who, regardless of the reasons, did not speak, there is a way in which their banishments do not strictly fit the bill of the topic studied here, for to be banished without responding to the banishment is in some ways not to be banished at all. To the extent that banishment depends on a rhetorical relationship to the law, that is, it demands a response; without it, the individual targeted by the law is, arguably, excluded from the community but not exactly banished. Indeed the need for a reciprocal, even dialogical relationship between banished and banisher is at the very heart of what banishment means: it is precisely to be excluded and yet not excluded—to continue to speak across jurisdictional boundaries and in so doing to challenge their very existence. The quality of the speech matters as well; the speech of the banished must be carried on within the terms of the law by which the exclusion was put in place, and it must attempt, like the arguments put forward for the banishment to begin with, to be persuasive, albeit to opposite ends.

This distinguishing characteristic of banishment and of the banishment narratives taken as sources here begins to explain what else has been banished from these pages. Edward Said has observed that there are two primary responses to exile: exiles either assimilate with remarkable zeal to their new surroundings or they fetishize their displacement and refuse to adapt.[43] *Banished* does not tell the story of either of these types, for neither one gives voice to the question of community membership that proves to be so central here. In the former category, of assimilationists, we might include stories by successful immigrants and asylum seekers or the autobiographies of professionals, who manifest an immediate allegiance to their new country. In the latter category, of fetishists, we might include the stories of people who spoke eloquently about their banishments even as their subject is, like Mowbry's, the loss of their ability to speak at all. Indeed the stories of these people are far more frequently studied than the ones I tell here; they are the stories of exile and of loss, of nostalgia for the homeland and of a longing to return that have increasingly come to our attention as more and more people are displaced.

There were stories like these in the ancient past as well as in our period, and they form the source material for several excellent books, including Paul Tabori's *Anatomy of Exile* and Christopher D'Addario's *Exile and Journey in Seventeenth-Century Literature.*[44] However, the approach to these stories is, not surprisingly, different from my own. In keeping with the sentimental nature of his sources, for example, D'Addario takes as his task a description of "the formative psychological, social, affective and literary experience of exile in the lives of these divergent groups."[45] *Banished* is not about these kinds of exile and so does not explore the psychological, affective, or literary experience of the banished, if by literary we mean the plaintive or celebratory narratives of affiliation under consideration by Tabor, D'Addario, and others.[46] It does, however, explore the literary in terms of the legal, an aspect of literature not often considered in the context of exile and yet central to all of the banishment narratives examined here. That is, the banished in these pages take up the story of banishment as a political and legal affair and remake the law as they argue with it, delve into its purpose, contemplate its future, and consider its past, without which their arguments for or against it would make no sense within the terms of the common law.

A Brief History

A mode of punishment that is, according to *Black's Law Dictionary*, "inflicted upon criminals, by compelling them to quit a city, place, or country for a specified period of time, or for life," banishment in England was from the twelfth through the fourteenth centuries associated with the practice of giving religious sanctuary to criminals who, if they agreed to confess or, to use the contemporary legal term, abjure their guilt, would be sent out of the kingdom rather than killed or imprisoned. Related to this was the legendary system of outlawry, which differed from banishment in being imposed on subjects who were typically not present when sentenced and who tended to remain, like Robin Hood, within reach of the territory from which they were cast out.

Increasing in popularity over time, by the middle of the fifteenth century banishment, or eviction, as it was then often called, began to be used, like outlawry, to punish a variety of offenses committed outside of a religious context, and it was this turn in the history of banishment that has been overlooked in the New English context.[47] As Marjorie McIntosh notes, in these years banishment was used as a punishment for hedge-breakers, subtenants, and gamers, among others.[48] Often invoked as an alternative to other sentences, including imprisonment, corporal punishment, and shaming rituals such as the stocks and pillory, banishment was also often seen as a form of local police control, which could be used to bar certain individuals from the parish or from small areas within it, such as the town square.[49] In this incarnation banishment bears a striking resemblance to the far more familiar vagrancy laws, which proliferated in the seventeenth century as poverty became more widespread and the poor became more mobile.[50] Unlike banishment, however, vagrancy laws, as well as a closely related New England variant known as "warning out," targeted the poor for financial, not criminal, reasons. It was, in short, only because communities were obligated to support their poor that vagrants, so called, were sent away.[51]

At the end of the sixteenth century, as the power to banish was removed from the jurisdiction of the English local courts, these more local instances of banishment occurred less frequently, and banishment became associated with the larger territory of the "nation." As Edward Coke observed at the time, "[b]y law, no subject can be exiled or banished his countrie, whereby he shall perdere patriam, but by authoritie of parliament, [in consultation with the king]."[52] Surpassing the number of local orders of banishment were orders issued by Parliament and by the monarch—at first by Queen Elizabeth I (although she was not much given to issuing banishment orders) and then by her successors, James I and Charles I. These orders, including the 1592–93 act banishing English recusants as well as other acts banishing Egyptians, the Irish, Anabaptists, and Negroes, not only targeted larger groups of people than ever before but also mandated that these groups leave not the parish or the town but the nation conceived as a whole.[53]

It is, then, partly in light of this history that we can begin to appreciate how oppositional a gesture the Puritan New World banishments really were. Despite the authority extended to them in their charters, the Puritans' frenzied recourse to banishment in those first decades of settlement represented an approach to banishment that was no longer current in England and thus could be construed, as it often was, as a challenge to England's sovereignty. (Even as we recognize this, however, we need also to bear in mind that from a practical point of view, banishment was probably inflicted more in the New World than in the Old because of a lack of prison space in the colonies, at least in the early years.) As the authority of a state to govern itself or other states, sovereignty is inextricably linked to territory in what the law calls "jurisdiction," the power to make and administer justice in a given area.[54] To be sure, there are jurisdictions that are governed by nonterritorial criteria, such as subject matter—for example whether the action is civil or criminal—or subject—for example whether the defendant is a resident or nonresident of a certain place.[55] But in the vast majority of cases, in the seventeenth century as well as today, jurisdiction revolves around whether the issue in question—the crime or civil injury—occurred in the specific geographic area over which the court has the power to rule. Even more telling of sovereignty than the power to govern those within the jurisdiction, however, is the power of the sovereign to throw people out and thus to rob them of their membership within it. As Hannah Arendt has observed, "[t]heoretically . . . it ha[s] always been true that sovereignty is nowhere more absolute than in matters of emigration, naturalization, nationality and expulsion."[56] The question of sovereignty at stake in these early banishments, then, was as much a contest over who was in charge of drawing territorial lines and defining membership within them as it was about how to interpret the common law and whether Parliament, the king, or the common-law courts were the ultimate arbiters "in matters of emigration, naturalization, nationality and expulsion."[57]

These and other, similar questions were further complicated by the often-contradictory positions adopted by the colonists themselves toward the territory and government encompassed by the colonies as well as and sometimes in contrast to the territory and government encompassed by the island by which England was still circumscribed. Persecuted by Archbishop Laud and others in the royal government, the Puritans who left for New England clearly felt a need to sever some, if not all, ties with the jurisdiction into which they were born. Thus from the very beginning of their New World settlements, there were conflicts between the settlers and their authorizing entities, which included, as Richard Ross has explained, a dizzying array of charters, letters patent, trading companies, and royal proclamations that gave them and their inhabitants an uncertain status in the law.[58] Plymouth Plantation, for example, though granted a degree of communal coherence by the Mayflower Compact of 1620, was long considered a trading post, not a colony, and existed without any authority to make laws or declare its own status until 1629, nine years after the first white settlers arrived. Even the Bay Colony, whose initial settlers arrived with a charter that gave them the authority to make laws and, specifically, to banish people from their settlement, suffered from a long period of jurisdictional uncertainty, which included threats of charter revocation by the king.

If they were at times inclined to sever ties with England, however, the Puritans also felt compelled to maintain them. Indeed in leaving England under the threat of banishment, the Puritans insisted that they were denying not their Englishness but only the association between their Englishness and England's church; thus it was often said at the time that "it was for England's sake that they were going from England."[59] Nor was their leaving necessarily intended to be permanent or absolute. In fact when it became clear that social conditions were often better for the Puritans in England than they were in the New World, many Puritans engaged in what David Cressy has called a reverse migration.[60] During the 1630s and 1640s alone, several thousand people left the New World for the Old, including two hundred people from Governor John Winthrop's original fleet.[61] Even though there were attempts by the New England leadership to portray those who returned to England as defectors, Andrew Delbanco has noted that "the reverse emigration was much more than a winnowing of chaff, and everyone in New England knew it."[62] Even such a stalwart and devoted New Englander as Increase Mather indulged in a period of "reverse migration," returning to live in England during Cromwell's Protectorate in order to reclaim ancestral lands.[63] The maintenance of these connections with England the country in contradistinction to England the church has almost certainly been one of the major factors leading so many scholars to think about the Puritans' banishments of others in predominantly religious terms.

The complications brought on by the uncertainty of the Puritans' affiliation with England, as opposed to the Anglican Church, were only aggravated by the uncertainty of their status as colonists and by England's project of New World colonization. Colonization, together with annexation, became a source of friction in early modern understandings of community and, not surprisingly, a catalyst of change. With colonization and annexation, even the principle of birthright, which was the most fundamental assumption about community and community membership within the law, was challenged. Birthright, or jus solis, to use the contemporary legal term, declared that if you were born in England, you were ipso facto English (with the significant exception, of course, of slaves). Despite the apparent elegance and simplicity of the principle, however, the claim to birthright came under attack by those with a more complex birthright than the principle presupposed. For the first time there were large numbers of people born outside the original territory or jurisdiction to which membership had been confined but who were nevertheless making claims for inclusion. What, for example, did it mean to be born in England and then forced to leave it? Or, to take the version of this question that was being raised at the time, what did it mean to be born in Scotland before it was absorbed by England under the rule of James I? This question, which occupied some of the greatest legal minds in the early part of the seventeenth century and which found no easy answer, forms the core of *Calvin's Case* (1603), a landmark decision authored by Sir Edward Coke (and discussed in Chapter 2) that was at the very center of jurisdictional disputes in seventeenth-century England.

The complexity of the territorial affiliation at issue in *Calvin's Case*—in which one's place of birth and one's place of residence were redefined as a result of a consolidation of England's and Scotland's sovereignty—was only compounded in New England by the indeterminate legal status of the colonies and of their inhabitants. What did it mean to live in a colony three thousand miles away from the metropolis, and how far could the theory of jus solis be pushed? If you were English born, did that qualify you for membership in any English jurisdiction? Or, to put it in terms more common to banishment, if you were English born, could another Englishman exclude you from an English jurisdiction, no matter where that jurisdiction was? Moreover what, if anything, did it mean that unlike the laws about deportation today, in which only noncitizens are threatened with expulsion, both the banished and the banisher shared a territorial origin?

Because territories were expanding, borders became more permeable and jurisdictions more difficult to identify. But the jurisdictional complexities that occupy us here go beyond the problem of permeable or shifting borders. In addition to colonization and annexation, that is, other forces were at work in the disruption of the simple, nearly isomorphic relationship between person and place posited by jus solis. Cultural factors, such as the merging of customs and habits among people that resulted from their increased mobility, created new ideas about community that may have pushed the early moderns to go, as David Delaney puts it, "beyond the paradigm of territory as discretely bounded spaces" altogether.[64] For Delaney, as for many other scholars working in the newly invigorated fields of human and legal geography, territory is not so much a geographical location as a geographically informed manifestation of social order—a social imaginary, to use Charles Taylor's term, in which people think about and act upon versions of "how they fit together with others."[65]

Space, Place, Territory, Jurisdiction

This understanding of territory is indebted to a number of recent developments in space, place, and territory studies that though rarely seen as such were nevertheless at work in the debates about banishment in the seventeenth century and thus inform the use of the concepts here. I invoke contemporary space and place theorists, however, to suggest not that certain recent developments under examination in their works—in particular, developments brought about by twentieth- and twenty-first-century technological innovations such as computers, cell phones, and the Internet—bear any resemblance to perceptions of space by the early moderns, but rather to tease out some of the perceptions that *were* shared and yet not theorized as clearly in their day as in our own. In particular *Banished*'s examination of the kinds of spaces thrown into question by banishment includes an experiential or phenomenological component that has been central to scholars of space such as Yi-Fu Tuan, Edward Soja, and Edward Casey, among others.[66] For these scholars, adding a phenomenological component to a "space" turns it into a "place." If "space" denotes an undifferentiated or geometric area, in other words, "place" denotes that same area after it has been visited, inhabited, or experienced by people. Even the most cursory reading of some of the banishment narratives under scrutiny here suggests that it was just such a transformation of space into place that played a part in the arguments against banishment. In their description of hospitality, for example, both Hutchinson and Morton imply that their experiences of life in the community of the colonies, understood in abstract terms, had been changed irrevocably by their experiences of life within their homes, understood in personal terms, and that given their personal experiences, they could no longer tolerate the notion that the doors of the colony would not, like the doors of their homes, be thrown open to "all comers."

However, the phenomenological component goes beyond the comparison of colony to home. Tim Cresswell clarifies the primacy of human experience within even the most traditional of geographical paradigms. "The history of geography," he writes, "has taken as one of its central objects the common-sense experienced difference between portions of the Earth's surface."[67] That the colonists experienced the portion of Earth's surface they called New England as different from that of England is, of course, a commonplace of scholarship on this period, but Cresswell's observation helps us clarify how that experience might have entered into the colonists' sense of community and jurisdiction. Using Cresswell helps us appreciate the new alignments between inside and outside that informed the Puritans' early settlements, and their changing notions of the frontier, in particular. At the highest level of generalization, for example, the New World, because its flora and fauna were so different from England's and because it was so far away, was experienced as the frontier, an outside beyond which no one would ever dream of going. Yet almost as soon as they established their settlements, the English made smaller and smaller distinctions, according to how the larger space—the New World—was naturally divided. Where there were rivers or impenetrable forests, for example, the Puritans drew legal, political, and sometimes even religious lines until such time as they learned how to transcend them, at which point they were forced to redraw them all over again.

This reconfiguration of space often had the effect of turning places into territories. Indeed this emphasis on human experience is central as well to the investigation into territories, which are defined as places in which the issue at stake is not so much the experience of geography as such but the experience of sovereignty or control. "Territory," Delaney explains, should be "understood as implicating and being implicated in ways of thinking, acting, and being in the world, ways of world-making informed by beliefs, desires, and culturally and historically contingent ways of knowing."[68] Like territory, the concept of jurisdiction also goes far beyond the question of geographic range to engage the specific question of legal membership and meaning. Jurisdiction, as Bradin Cormack writes, "merges the making of meaning with the creation of bounded space, a meaning that emerges from the etymological root of the word—juris—law—and dictio—speaking. As a speaking of the law . . . jurisdiction thus grounds the activity of producing normative meaning."[69] The ways of thinking and making the world are legal (and thus normative) insofar as "they merge the making of meaning with a bounded space." Jurisdictional decisions about who can stay within a territory (and vote, pay taxes, or walk the streets, for example) as well as who can or should be thrown out of it—all of which are entailed in banishment—are at the heart of membership decisions examined in this book.

Implicit in all of the recent work on territory, space, and place, however, is the concept of nationalism. For Sassen and Delaney, it is a central concern, but even for theorists of space and place, such as Soja and Casey, it is the elephant in the room or, to return to Sassen's formulation, the bundle that needs unbundling. However, it was, importantly, not yet a given in the period covered by *Banished*, and that in itself contributed to the uncertainty and ambiguity that arose in discussions of banishment. The concept of the nation-state was in the air, but it was still very much a work in progress, and banishment, I argue, was central to fleshing out its details. Not protonational exactly, the territories encompassed by England and its colonies, taken together or on their own, were far more malleable than the territory of a nation, as was the concept of membership within them. In particular the significance of speaking of a membership that was not yet considered a form of citizenship—which accompanied the rise of the nation-state—is that the criteria for membership tended to be more expansive, and not confined, as they became in most cases of citizenship, to property ownership or offered, as the attributes of citizenship usually are, as a package set. Indeed the citizen-subjects, as Sassen calls them, of the early modern period did not necessarily have what Sassen calls "rights" at all; for the Puritans, for example, they were considered "liberties," which, unlike rights, attached at times to the person and at others to the place and variously offered large entitlements, such as permission to vote, as well as totally mundane ones, such as permission to store one's grain in the common granary. Moreover the variability within the idea of liberties made the idea of membership more malleable than in communities based on rights, an idea I return to in the Conclusion.

Admittedly the *Body of Liberties* for the Massachusetts Bay Colony, a list of ninety-eight "liberties" drafted over the course of several years but finally published and distributed in 1641, made the nature of these liberties clearer. But the common law or case law of the colony continued to add to and detract from them, rewriting them as it rewrote its understanding of territory and sovereignty over time. Indeed the common law was tailor-made for the reorganization of the elements that comprised communities and membership within them. Traditionally understood as judge-made law determined on a case by case basis, the common law was said to have derived from "the ancient constitution," an unwritten body of laws that emerged as doctrine in the fifteenth century but did not achieve widespread acceptance until the early seventeenth, when it was defined, as J. G. A. Pocock puts it, as "common custom, originating in the usages of the people and declared, interpreted and applied in the courts."[70] Of course the common law was only one of several different types of law in the early modern period. Royal law, equity, and canon law, among others, acting in concert created a domain of legal pluralism and jurisdictional competition.[71] If all these different types of law and law courts were competing for supremacy, however, the common law was at the same time emerging as victorious, a fact that led the Puritans, who were naturally ill disposed toward the king's law, to embrace it as their own. During the drafting of the colony's *Body of Liberties* in the late 1630s, the General Court of the Bay Colony specified "that there shalbe these [famous common law] books following procured for the use of the Courte from time to time: Two of Sir Edward Cooke [*sic*] upon Littleton; two of the Books of Entryes; two of Sir Edward Cooke upon Magna Charta; two of the Newe Tearmes of the Lawe, two Daltons Justice of Peace; two of Sir Edward Cooks Reports."[72]

If the Puritans consulted books of common law for wisdom in constructing their own legal codes, they diverged from them as well, holding fast to the parts that suited them and remaking others.[73] The question of how the Puritan settlers in New England remade the common law in their own image has been the subject of many invaluable legal histories.[74] The first generation of these histories tends to confirm that the common law survived the transatlantic voyage largely intact and suffered only minor revisions. This conclusion has produced interest in colonial legal reform. More recently, however, research into the colonial and English versions of the common law has suggested a greater degree of interplay between England's version of the common law and that of the colonies, yielding a theory of what one scholar has called a "transatlantic constitution."[75] This theory has opened up new avenues for legal research and has made it possible to see colonial common law as existing in a reciprocal relation with that of England. Nevertheless this reciprocity has its own drawbacks insofar as it tends, like earlier theories, to associate the mother country with an older, more entrenched version of the common law and the colonies with legal reform or innovation—producing a model that does not capture the changes that characterized the Puritan recourse to banishment. By targeting individuals for banishment, the Puritans were not making new laws or even reforming old ones but reviving a common-law tradition that had largely been abandoned in England at that time.

The version of colonial common law that emerges in the light of banishment, then, adds a new wrinkle to the history of the common law's transatlantic move. More specifically, this version makes it clear exactly how flexible and fluid the common law was, for it was capable not only of adapting to unprecedented conditions in the New World but also of returning under new conditions to older versions of itself, ultimately taking on a new direction in the land of its birth and following an old direction in the land of its adoption. But the question remains: how exactly did the common-law rhetoric of banishment come to alter the prevailing relationship between person and place, community and member? This question prompts the following four chapters as they examine the challenges to the banishment law and to everything it implied about fixed boundaries, birthright, unambiguous sovereignty, and homogenous populations. Moreover, while all of the chapters share overlapping concerns, each one has a different story to tell and thus sheds a different light on the way standard assumptions about community and membership were being dismantled and reassembled through the debates over banishment.

Chapter Summaries

In Chapter 1 the challenge to banishment takes the form of a reconceptualization of territory and jurisdiction as a potential place of inclusion as opposed to exclusion. This chapter takes up the stories of Anne Hutchinson
and Thomas Morton, whose banishments were proximate in time but have
otherwise been seen as unrelated. Anne Hutchinson, as is commonly known,
was a pious Puritan whose membership in the Bay Colony was not, at least at
first, in question, whereas Thomas Morton, a successful trader and religious
renegade, was unwelcome (in Plymouth and the Bay Colony) from the start.
In my reading, however, both figures are united in their protest strategies,
strategies that go far beyond a repudiation of the Puritans' authority to banish them to find its roots in a rival reading of the common law, one based on
the custom of hospitality. Under the mandate provided by hospitality, which
was not coincidentally a religious and legal mandate all at once, Hutchinson
and Morton argued that the community was bound not only to let people in,
as opposed to throwing them out, but also to adapt itself to an increasingly
transient population.

In Hutchinson's trial testimony (given during her civil trial) and in Morton's *New English Canaan*, together with Governor Bradford's lengthy response
to him in his *Of Plymouth Plantation*, we see a new narrative of community
emerge in which members, under the transitory engine of hospitality, formed
bonds and affiliations through the very means that struck the Puritan magistrates as antithetical, namely through boundary crossings and cross-border relations. To be welcomed into the community, for Hutchinson and Morton, in
other words, did not mean that one had to stay forever in a certain fixed place.

Embedded within the arguments put forward by Hutchinson and Morton about a more transient population was an exhortation for the community to accept greater diversity among its members. This emphasis is at the
heart of Chapter 2, which reengages the banishment of Roger Williams. While
other scholars have written about the extent and importance of Williams's
legal vocabulary, few have examined the full range of his commitment to
common-law precepts about the diversity of the earthly and temporal realm
in its relation to Christendom. This focus on diversity emerges most clearly in
his fifteen-year-long pamphlet war with his primary banisher, John Cotton.
In these writings, as Chapter 2 argues, what most people read as a commitment to religious tolerance in Williams's thought is more accurately seen as a

commitment to what he saw as the common law's willingness to disarticulate "person" from a temporal, as opposed to a spiritual, place. For Williams, the magistrates' notion of creating a community on earth with a homogenous population was tantamount to a usurpation of God's realm—the only place, according to Williams, where such a thing was possible. Indeed it was Williams's belief in and familiarity with certain strands within the common law that drove him to advocate the virtues of heterogeneity in the context of civic belonging and thus to confront his fellow Puritans on the difference between the secular and spiritual realms.

The benefits of a diverse rather than homogenous population are also engaged by the story of the Quakers' banishments in Chapter 3. In contrast to the argument made by Williams, the Quaker argument for diversity emerges in the context of a new understanding of what it meant to be present in, or conversely to be absent from, a given territory or jurisdiction. In returning time and again to the Bay Colony in defiance of a law banishing them "on pain of death," the Quakers ultimately forced the Puritans to turn banishment—one way but not the only way to remove people from the jurisdiction—into execution, banishment's evil twin. When the magistrates of the Bay Colony hanged four of the returning Quakers, the extent to which banishment had been masquerading as a more lenient alternative to death—a social death rather than a physical one—was revealed. Moreover, in forcing the Puritan authorities to confront the hidden violence behind banishment, the Quakers introduced a notion of partial allegiance that has resurfaced in the context of an emerging global sphere. What the Quakers urged, in other words, was a community bound together by members who accepted some but not all of the community's rules, regulations, or ideologies, demonstrating that it was political and legal contentiousness that could create regularities between people and make community members of them.

The even greater significance of the Quakers' actions in this regard was to call attention to the way in which banishment presupposed a space that could be emptied in the first place—a space, in other words, that could be separated from the bodies of its members through physical or social means. As Robert Sack has observed, "territoriality . . . helps create the idea of a socially emptiable place," but as the Quakers suggested through their persistence, even in death, this notion remains something of a fiction.[76] Banished or killed, the Quakers seemed to say, the Bay Colony could not help but turn them into permanent members.

At stake in Chapter 4 is a new expression of territorial belonging that comes into being through its negation. More specifically, this chapter argues that for some individuals, specifically those for whom membership has traditionally been restricted to a territorial affiliation, such as the Indians, membership can emerge only when the members are deterritorialized, when their affiliations with any portion of land, no matter how small, have been severed entirely. The discussion in this chapter focuses on the internal banishment of nearly five hundred praying Indians to Deer Island in the Boston harbor during King Philip's War. During this banishment the Indians were for the first and arguably only time in the history of their relations with the white settlers unaffiliated with any land, since Deer Island was a place over which the Indians had no semblance of ownership. As further argued in Chapter 4, it was only because of this loss of affiliation that the Indians began to take up a new kind of identity within the community that was based not on their relationship to the land but on their personal agency. This made them subjects of the common law in ways that had not been available to them before and suggested that what counted for membership was not birthright or any form of ethnic or religious identity that might have been tied to it, but rather actions that furthered the public good. These actions, I argue, become the evidence for and source of their membership in the depositions and affidavits that surrounded their performance as soldiers for the English in King Philip's War.

The Puritan frenzy to banish came to a halt with the revocation of the Bay Colony's charter in 1684. Even so, banishment lived on. Although the Puritans were no longer allowed to indulge their obsession with banishment, other nations, including England, continued to banish, and the impulse behind banishment—the desire to define communities through exclusion rather than inclusion—found new expression in altered forms such as deportation. The Conclusion to *Banished* provides an overview of these forms, including information on those few remaining states in the Union that still have banishment laws on the books, but it resists providing any prescription for membership or formula for community formation. Rather the hope is that in coming to understand the flux that characterized community membership and exclusion in early modern America, we can think through and possibly past the rigid notions that have clouded our reading of the past and put up impediments for our thinking about the future.

CHAPTER I

"To Entertain Strangers"

It is worse for a common-wealth to receive a man whom they must
cast out againe, than to deny him admittance.

—John Winthrop, *Journal*

GOVERNOR WINTHROP'S STATEMENT in the epigraph above
reminds us that while banishment was popular among the Puritans, it
was not the only nor even the most sensible means of ridding the community
of undesirables. For one thing, it was arduous and time-consuming. All the
legal actors and instruments required for a trial had to be marshaled—at least
in those cases where trials were made available—and the punishment itself
had to be enforced. When Roger Williams was banished, for example, guards
were summoned to his house to insure that he was not hiding, and when
Thomas Morton was banished, he had to be sequestered until a ship willing
to take him on board arrived from England. Hence Winthrop's belief that it
was better to exclude people by preventing them from entering the colony in
the first place than to go through all the motions of having to throw them out.

This chapter is concerned with some of these prophylactic measures for
defining community and thus addresses the use and development of banishment somewhat obliquely. Moreover, as with each chapter, the notions
developed here about community within the debate over banishment are determined in part by the specific versions of Puritanism and of the common
law that were in place at the time. In these early years, when both Morton
and Hutchinson were banished, Plymouth and the Massachusetts Bay Colony
were in their infancy, and the nature of the religious provocations that led to
their banishments was in some sense much clearer than it was in later years.

These religious principles thus were in tension with the legal notions of community creation in slightly different ways than they were, say, in the case of
the Quakers. By the same token, the common law's conception of community
was much less settled in these early years (although much less embattled as
well) and so lent itself to greater manipulation. Yet the argument set forth here
about the successes and failures of these measures sets the stage for the rapid
rise of banishment and for the argument developed in the following chapters
about the importance of the banishment narrative as a rhetorical device for
shaping community. In particular this chapter tells the story of a split within
the common law between its contradictory tendencies for peopling a place—
one toward exclusion and one toward inclusion—and between those in the
colonies who favored one version over the other.

Scholars have emphasized what are commonly seen as the colonies' strict
membership requirements. In the absence of a principle such as jurs solis,
which had little relevance for the first generation of colonists, none of whom
had been born in the colonies, there was an initial push toward strict admission standards. The most rigorous of these revolved around religious conversion, which when delivered in the form of a conversion narrative and voted
on by the elders of a given Puritan church guaranteed full membership in
the church (and in the Lord's Supper) as well as in the community. However,
while the conversion narrative was intellectually and emotionally daunting, it
was also formulaic, familiar, and in many ways superfluous since, contrary to
popular opinion, the vast majority of colonists who applied for membership
in the Puritan churches and colonies had been thinking about their religious
experiences for a long time and were poised to pass the test. Additional criteria
were imposed on aspiring church members, including evidence of financial
self-sufficiency, but this too proved a relatively easy bar to reach since most
early colonists, at least those in Winthrop's colony, came from the middle
classes and had already amassed sufficient funds to establish themselves.[1]

This gap between the theory and the practice of the Puritans' admission
standards created an uncertainty within their law. As one legal historian noted
in a disarmingly simple formulation, "the covenants by which the pilgrims
formed their churches would have doubtless been sufficient to their needs
except for the presence of persons not members of the church."[2] Put in terms
of a membership paradigm and the language of social exclusion, it seemed as
if the Puritans were incapable of imagining a population for their communities consisting of anyone but members and thus had no apparatus for dealing
with those who did not fall into this category. Of course, there were many

"persons not members of the church" who were considered to be legitimate settlers; as Samuel Morison has remarked, included in this designation were individuals who were "unknown to the Leyden Pilgrims or to their friends, who had to be taken along to . . . increase the number of colonists."[3] Indeed the legendary Miles Standish was in this category. But as it turns out, not all were as distinguished as he, and the first community included rabble-rousers, spies, Indians (at least at first), short-term visitors, and the shipwrecked—all of whom because of a taxonomic failure of the law figured simply as nonmembers or "strangers," that is to say, people who were not part of the Puritan "us," in Charles Tilly's terms, but also not yet "them."[4]

The absence of a more nuanced taxonomy for these "strangers" created social boundary issues that would begin to test the Puritans' sense of community as a whole. Stories of encounters with "strangers" permeate the earliest descriptions of the new settlements, including Edward Winslow's *Good Newes from New England* (1624), William Wood's *New England's Prospect* (1634), William Bradford's *Of Plymouth Plantation* (1630–50), and John Winthrop's *Journal* (1630–49). In the case of strangers whose less-than-stellar reputations preceded them, of course, the Puritan welcome was understandably lukewarm. Bradford's account of the arrival of Sir Christopher Gardiner, "who was so great a persecutor of God's Saints in Queen Mary's days," is a perfect example of this kind of description.[5] But the tendency to consider everyone who was not a member as a "stranger" became a problem when the "stranger" showed no obvious signs of hostility, raised no suspicions, and yet chose for whatever reason not to undergo the conversion procedures.

In these cases the pressing question was, what obligation did the Puritans have toward strangers?, or to put it in Jacques Derrida's terms, "to who or what turns up before any identification?"[6] The most general mandate of the common law was to treat strangers with hospitality. Variously referred to as a "matrix of beliefs," a "facility" or "institution," an "obligation," a "ministry," or a "right," hospitality, while not confined to strangers, had organized relations with strangers in Western and non-Western societies for centuries.[7] A definition from the late seventeenth century is illuminating in this regard: "Hospitality," George Wheler wrote, was "a Liberal Entertainment of all sorts of Men, at ones house, whether Neighbours or Strangers, with kindness, especially with Meat, Drink and Lodgings."[8] As English people, of course, the Puritans would have been steeped in the tradition of hospitality; they prided themselves on demonstrations of hospitality and had long considered them cultural practices that set them above neighboring nationalities. In his hagiography of John Winthrop, Cotton Mather rendered him with the highest praise by ascribing to him "the liberallity and hospitality of a gentleman."[9] Additionally, as devout Christians, the Puritans would have been especially sensitive to the many exhortations toward hospitality in the Bible, such as Hebrews 13:2, from which this chapter derives its title: "Be not forgetful to entertain strangers: for thereby some have entertained angels unawares."

If the common law (and the Bible) seemed to mandate hospitality in the general case, however, they were less clear about what to do with strangers who proved unworthy of their welcome. This was the problem, for example, with John Oldham and John Lyford, visitors to Plymouth in 1624. Governor Bradford observed of Lyford: "When this man first came ashore, he saluted them [the Pilgrims] with that reverence and humility as is seldom to be seen," and so the Pilgrims "gave him the best entertainment they could, in all simplicity, and a larger allowance of food out of the store than any other had." On discovering that Lyford and Oldham had grown "very perverse, and showed a spirit of great malignancy," the Pilgrims were in the uncomfortable position of not only having to rescind their offer of hospitality but also taking measures that would designate them both as unwelcome in the future, for which the only appropriate expression was banishment.[10]

For Derrida, to offer and then withdraw hospitality would not necessarily have seemed out of place, since for him hospitality was not an entirely friendly act. There is, Derrida wrote, "a moment of great indecision about the arrival of the stranger on another's shores" that reveals how hospitality is "interlaced with hostility."[11] Indeed, as J. Hillis Miller has pointed out, the concept of what it means to be a host is fraught at the etymological level. Miller notes, "The relation of household master offering hospitality to a guest and the guest receiving it, of host and parasite in the original sense of 'fellow guest,' is inclosed within the word 'host' itself. A host in the sense of a guest, moreover, is both a friendly visitor in the house and at the same time an alien presence who turns the home into a hotel, a neutral territory."[12] Still, for a number of contemporary commentators on hospitality, to banish strangers, even after discovering some wrongdoing on their part, was a direct affront to the common-law mandate of hospitality. For these individuals, hospitality was driven by a spirit of inclusiveness that did not, like the requirements for residency and church membership, revolve around a process of selectivity but demanded to be played out in its absence through a sustained interaction between host and guest until some sort of understanding had been reached or a zone of cultural contact in the form of an alternative kind of community had been formed. Indeed in teasing out some of the ways in which the common law inscribed the concept of hospitality within its structure, we can begin to appreciate how it contained within it the seeds of many varied types of communities, all legal, and yet not often thought of in those terms. Indeed the kinds of communities imagined within the terms of hospitality are more easily understood in anthropological and sociological terms, and so we turn to the language of these disciplines later in the chapter for clarification.

The following discussion takes up the story of the struggle in the early years of the Bay Colony and Plymouth Plantation between those who, like Winthrop, as hospitable as he was, thought of hospitality as a limited endeavor and thus a means of giving the community definition through exclusion, and those who, like Anne Hutchinson and Thomas Morton, promoted a version of hospitality that opposed the exercise of such authority. Though Morton and Hutchinson are rarely if ever spoken of in the same breath—one was a renegade Anglican trader, the other an ostensibly pious Puritan—Morton's *New English Canaan* (1637), Bradford's *Of Plymouth Plantation*, Hutchinson's trial testimony (1636), John Winthrop's "Short History of the Rise and Ruine of Antinomianism" (1644), and Winthrop's pamphlet debate with Henry Vane, the antinomian and onetime governor of the Bay Colony, reveal that their struggles against banishment—for both were famously banished in the end—were preceded and in many ways linked by a similar focus on hospitality. Hutchinson opened her house to strangers, sometimes hosting several hundred people, while Morton in setting up his community at Mare Mount styled himself "Mine Host" and welcomed people from all walks of life, including Indians. In both cases it was their hospitality more than anything else that was put on trial and led to their banishments.

Hospitality and Charity

Hospitality became a source of friction in the law of the Puritan colonies in part because of the political controversy it had already stirred in England. In her survey of the uses of hospitality, Felicity Heal suggests that while hospitality was still part of the belief system in England in the early modern period, it was on the wane in part as a result of the Protestant Reformation. According to Heal, the material aspects of hospitality—specifically the offer of food and lodging—that had been essential features of the practice since ancient times and were particularly significant during the Middle Ages came to be viewed by Protestants as yet another expression of the material pomp of the Catholic Church and began to be looked on with disfavor. As a result, starting in the late sixteenth to early seventeenth centuries, the kind of hospitality associated with household giving declined.[13] So troubling was this decline that in 1623 it spurred King James I to issue a proclamation "commanding noblemen, knights, and gentlemen of quality, to repayre to their mansion houses in the country, to attend to their services, and keepe hospitality, according to the ancient and laudable customs of England."[14]

That the king's proclamation specifically directed his subjects to return to their "mansions" and to "keep hospitality" there speaks to another one of the changes wrought in the ritual of hospitality by the Protestant Reformation: a growing aversion to the household as a site of interacting with guests, or more specifically the poor. Along with a growing Protestant dislike for what was seen as the material excess of hospitable giving came a distinction, long noted in the scholarship on this period, between the worthy poor and the unworthy poor. Although what made a poor person worthy or unworthy was never entirely clear, the convention at the time was to consider officers, minstrels, and what were euphemistically called the "life cycle" poor to be worthy of aid, while rejecting the claims of "vagrants, beggars and idlers."[15] To the extent that one feature of traditional household hospitality encouraged the opening of one's doors to the poor who, in seeking alms from householders, were by definition "vagrants" or "beggars," it was seen as favoring the unworthy poor and was discouraged. As Steve Hindle points out, "condemnations of hospitality for its encouragement of begging undoubtedly derive from a literature whose rhetorical agenda (the encouragement of greater discrimination in the giving of alms) must be acknowledged."[16]

One aspect of this newfound Protestant aversion to household giving that was of particular relevance to the Puritans' response to Morton and Hutchinson was the disaggregation of the discourse of hospitality from the discourse of charity. By distinguishing between the worthy poor and the unworthy poor, the Protestant church made it clear that it was not abandoning the poor but merely replacing the conduit by which they were aided; specifically the church aimed to replace customary household giving with a more institutionalized form of giving to be administered under exclusively religious auspices. We might think of this as hospitality minus the host as well as the home, which in the end is what the church called charity. The virtue of charity over hospitality was obvious from a social point of view: church-based charity helped the needy without making them part of the community. "The virtues of conviviality and care for the helpless continued to be related," Heal writes, "but were juxta-posed rather than integrated: good neighborhood was increasingly separated from the active doing of Christian good."[17]

Given the growing religious emphasis on charity in relation to the com-munity in colonial New England, tensions between the advocates of hospital-ity and the advocates of charity ran high. Indeed the stories of Hutchinson's and Morton's banishments are in part about how far the law could be stretched in one or the other direction: toward charity or back toward hospitality. Not surprisingly some of these tensions are visible in the founding documents of the New England colonies, and preeminent among them is John Winthrop's "Model of Christian Charity." When seen in the light of hospitality, Win-throp's concept of charity appears to be less the principle of selfless sacrifice that so many have taken it to be and more a mechanism that just as surely as it held people together—"bonded" them, in Winthrop's words—also kept them apart. In the "Model" we note that charity "knits the body" together, but only insofar as the body is understood as the already-assembled society of Puritans.[18] In Winthrop's idiom, in other words, charity serves to strengthen preexisting bonds, among those en route to the New World, rather than mak-ing room for new ones, among "strangers" soon to arrive.[19] Worth noting in this context is the similar work performed by the compact—the associational conceit in the Mayflower Compact—signed by the first English settlers in Plymouth Plantation. Although the Mayflower Compact does not explicitly mention charity, it is like Winthrop's "Model" in that it calls into being a confraternity that conspicuously does not extend a welcome to those outside it but merely reinforces ties among individuals who had, in a previous context, already pledged to help each other.[20] In light of this politicization of hospital-ity with respect to charity, we can begin to see that if Anne Hutchinson had seen herself as performing a traditional duty in offering hospitality to her fel-low colonists—in the form of household giving and instruction—she might also have been seen by others, namely the leading magistrates and ministers of the Bay Colony, as interfering with the newer Protestant reforms in hospitality that were emerging in England and New England alike.

Religion, Custom, Law

If the relatively closed model of charity and the relatively open one of hospital-ity offered different ways of dealing with strangers and in particular the poor,

that difference was magnified by the way in which the divide between charity
and hospitality also mirrored a growing historical divide between religious
precepts and the law. To be sure, hospitality was, like charity, rooted in Christian doctrine. Yet of the two, hospitality was understood not only as more
open but also as more secular and thus more understandable in the terms of
the law.[21] That it had its roots in the practices of the rural gentry—to which,
not coincidentally, both Hutchinson and Morton belonged—linked hospitality to custom and thus to what the common lawyers called "the ancient
constitution," which was nothing less than the body of English common law.

The link between hospitality and the common law made it, like banishment, a key site within the struggle in New England over what kind of law—
legislative, customary, king's, canon—the colonists were ultimately bound by.
But hospitality differed from banishment in adding to this struggle a question
not only about what kind of law was at stake in its exercise but also about the
source from which its directives derived. Hospitality put the home into the
mix of church, law courts, the royal court, and Parliament, and the home was
a venue that challenged traditional distinctions between public and private
realms and raised the possibility that ordinary people in ordinary places might
contribute to the lawmaking process. Hutchinson emerges as a major figure
in this regard, for it was under the rubric of the antinomians' hospitality that
New England, in the earliest years of English settlement, became engaged in
a debate about the law as a practice, as Michel de Certeau has famously called
it, of everyday life.

Even more significant to the association of hospitality with the common
law and custom was the growing connection made by common lawyers in
England and in other countries between custom and certain facets of international law—a growing area of legal interest and practice that has played an as-
yet-understudied role in the formation of the Puritan colonies. Indeed to read
Morton and Hutchinson in terms of hospitality is to see them not as lone dissenters in a sectioned-off Puritan world—as they were so often seen by mid-
twentieth-century literary and legal historians—or even as voices of a newly
reconfigured transatlantic world—as they are increasingly seen by scholars
today—but as products of an emerging global community whose offers of
hospitality gesture toward the opening of cultural, political, and legal boundaries not only between England and New England but also between England,
New England, and a range of European countries. In Plymouth, in particular,
where settlers did not acquire the authority to make laws for themselves until
1629, international law would have been as good a guide as any and one with

which the colonists, having already lived abroad, in Holland, would have been more familiar than most. Numbering several among their first generation, such as John Winthrop and Roger Williams, who were specifically trained in the law, the first Bay colonists would have been familiar with international law as well. If nowhere else, evidence of their familiarity with international law is visible in their reports on the status of the Indians, which were guided by discussions about indigenous peoples that originated with Francisco de Vitoria, one of the founders of international law in sixteenth-century Spain.

Based on a shared heritage of welcoming strangers to the shores of European countries, international law stemmed in large part from the rituals of hospitality. In the language of much early modern political theory, hospitality emerges as a right or liberty that stands in stark contrast to its previous status as a social virtue or biblical injunction. For Vitoria, hospitality was not simply a matter of benevolence or goodwill on the part of the natives of a given country—a social virtue, in other words—but a right that foreigners or strangers could demand and enforce. In his *De Indis*, a treatise on Spain's conquest of the Indies and their questionable right to claim ownership of their land, Vitoria developed his theory of hospitality. "[I]n the beginning of the world," he wrote, "when all things were held in common, everyone was allowed to visit and travel through any land he wished. This right was clearly not taken away by the division of property."[22] Under the rubric of hospitality, Vitoria also included a right in the countries visited to dwell, to trade, to use common property, and perhaps most interestingly from the point of view of banishment and exclusion in general, to resist expulsion without just cause.

Building on the work of Vitoria, even as they drew back from his all-inclusive attitude toward hospitality, later political thinkers, including Hugo Grotius and Samuel Pufendorf, contributed much to the development of international law and to hospitality as an individual right. In his *De Indis*, for example, Grotius subsumed under hospitality an individual's right to free access to other people's countries—a claim that was directly at odds with Winthrop's preference for a "denial of admittance." No "state or prince," Grotius wrote, "has the power to issue a general prohibition forbidding others to enjoy access to or trade with the subjects of that state or prince. This doctrine is the source of the sacrosanct law of hospitality."[23] While he took issue with Grotius's designation of international law as distinct from natural law, Pufendorf spoke of a freedom to travel and to be received hospitably by other countries as well. "Another duty of Humanity," wrote Pufendorf, "is the admission of strangers, and the kind reception and Entertainment of travellers." Like Grotius, although in more tempered terms, Pufendorf went so far as to say that denying strangers admission because of a fear of corruption from foreigners was not legal. "The Spartans," he wrote, "to justify themselves in driving all Strangers from their Coasts thought this one Reason [fear of corruption] sufficient. . . . In answer to which it is well urged by some, that what we practise at home is not always the best, nor what others do abroad the worst; if then a foreign Custom be really better, it is absurd to despise, and to reject it on the Score of its being foreign."[24] Hospitality between states, then, emerges from the arena of international law as a way of talking not only about an individual host's duty to entertain guests but also of an individual guest's right to be entertained in or travel to a foreign place or country. This endows both Morton and Hutchinson, though hardly foreigners from a national point of view, with a platform from which to claim the protections of hospitality as a defense against their banishments.

Even from this brief account of certain elements of the work of Grotius and Pufendorf, we can begin to see why hospitality became a source not only of international law but also crucially of human rights law.[25] In recognizing a person's right to be welcomed into another's dominion—be it house, colony, or country—hospitality became a right that was, in contrast to most others, tied not to a geographically bounded sense of cultural, ethnic, or religious belonging but to a shared understanding of what it meant to be human no matter where one was from. As Micheline Ishay has written, "human rights are rights held by individuals simply because they are part of the human species."[26] An Englishman, then, could claim a right to travel and be entertained elsewhere, not because he was English—from which he derived a right to own English land, for example—but because he was human.[27] Given these roots, it is not surprising that hospitality has in recent years enjoyed a new prominence in discussions about human rights. In addition to Vitoria, Grotius, and Pufendorf, scholars now often cite Kant, who, long after the early modern period and in a place far removed from the New England colonies, elaborated on how hospitality could and should operate. Though he was writing about a global context that did not yet obtain in the seventeenth century, and though he took issue with many of the natural law claims Grotius made, it is nevertheless useful for us to refer back to Kant for his definition of hospitality as a right, for he connected it not only to the condition of being human but also to the way in which humans came to occupy the earth.[28] Men can claim a right to hospitality, Kant wrote, "by virtue of their common possession of the surface of the earth, where, as a globe, they cannot infinitely disperse and hence must tolerate the presence of each other."[29]

Hospitality and Tolerance

While not current at the time, Kant's definition of hospitality, which foregrounds the concept of tolerance, would nevertheless have resonated with the Pilgrims (by which I mean the people who settled Plymouth as distinct from those, more commonly referred to as Puritans, who settled the Massachusetts Bay Colony). The Pilgrims left England initially for Holland, where tolerance on the part of an already-established people—the Dutch—played a crucial role. To understand how the Pilgrims and their Bay Colony successors responded to Morton and Hutchinson, it is necessary to put their attitudes about hospitality in the light of Dutch tolerance. The Puritans' process of applying to the Netherlands for refuge was complicated and included a protracted correspondence between the Pilgrims in England and the authorities in Leyden, based on a shared notion of hospitality. Dated December 2, 1609, the Puritans' official request read as follows:

> To the Honourable the Burgomasters and court of the City of Leyden,
> With due submission and respect Ian Robarthse [John Robinson], Minister of the Divine Word, and some members of the Christian Reformed Religion, born in the Kingdom of Great Britain, to the number of one hundred persons or thereabouts, men and women, represent that they desire to come to live in this city "by the first" day of May next; and to have the freedom thereof in carrying on their trades, without being a burden in the least to any one. They therefore address themselves to your Honours, humbly praying that Your Honours will be pleased to grant them free consent to betake themselves, as aforesaid, This doing, etc.[30]

Although the passage makes no explicit reference to tolerance, no one could have mistaken the Pilgrims' request for it since it was well known that they intended not only to carry "on their trades without being . . . a burden . . . to any one" but also to "carry on" their religion without anyone else being "a burden" to them. Indeed it was the absence of tolerance on the part of the

English authorities that was, in the minds of John Robinson's congregants at least, driving them out of England and to another part of the globe. Thus, not surprisingly, it was to the issue of tolerance that Jan van Hout, the secretary of the city of Leyden, responded when he wrote, "[We] refuse no honest persons ingress to come and have their residence in this city, provided that such persons behave themselves honestly, and submit to all the laws and ordinances here."[31] In making this statement, van Hout was not only reiterating the Dutch adherence to the principle of tolerance in the practice of religion but also reinforcing the significance of the principle in the development of international law, for the statement was made in direct defiance of a communication from King James asking that Holland not admit the Pilgrims because they had been banished from England and should therefore be considered international outlaws. Regardless of the fact that the claim was not true—the king was only *thinking* about banishing the Pilgrims but had not yet published an edict to that effect—Holland's subsequent admission of them was a blow to England's hopes to trump hospitality with banishment as a tenet of international law.

That the Pilgrims appreciated Dutch tolerance and hospitality from a more personal point of view is indicated in Bradford's *Of Plymouth Plantations* and in Nathaniel Morton's *New England Memorial* (1669), where Morton wrote at length of their "being courteously entertained and lovingly respected by the Dutch, amongst whom they were strangers."[32] In the end, however, it may be that the hospitality shown to the Puritans by the Dutch also determined their own refusal to offer it to others, for the tolerance that lay at the heart of Dutch hospitality also drove the Dutch to welcome all sorts of people, including the poor, and gave rise to satirical descriptions of Holland as a refuge for everyone from heretics to vagabonds. "You may be what devil you will there," a contemporary English writer noted, "so you be but peaceable."[33] Indeed it did not escape the Pilgrims even at the time that the hospitality they enjoyed in Holland went above and beyond the temporary welcome mandated by the Bible. Nathaniel Morton, for example, was careful to point out that the separatists, contrary to popular opinion, were not thrown out of Leyden but rather chose to leave. "The state," he stressed, "did not grow weary of them." As it turns out, it was paradoxically the very absence of restrictions on their presence in Leyden that ultimately drove the Pilgrims away. Morton went on to address this paradox by reiterating that while the separatists *chose* to leave, it was not in the end much of a choice because the only alternative was complete assimilation. Had they stayed, "[t]heir posterity would in few generations become Dutch," he wrote, and for people who prided themselves on being Puritan and English at the same time, this was not an option.[34]

"All Comers"

The Pilgrims having learned this, from their perspective, rather negative lesson about an all-inclusive and open-ended version of hospitality, it was perhaps inevitable that they would clash with others, specifically other Englishmen, such as Thomas Morton, who had experienced hospitality in a much more positive light. Morton, who had been raised in the West Country of England, where the customs of hospitality were especially strong, was of a very different mind about it than his separatist contemporaries. Other differences in position and faith—in addition to being Anglican, Morton was an attorney for the Council of New England, which was run by Ferdinand Gorges, the Pilgrims' rival in trade—no doubt exacerbated the conflict between him and the Plymouth settlers.[35] The separatists found Morton so objectionable that they banished him three times in three consecutive years, from 1628 to 1630, each time on a different charge: selling guns to the Indians; creating disturbances in the country; and trading irregularities.[36]

But if the multiplicity of charges leveled against Morton attests to the extent of the Pilgrims' rancor against him, their diversity attests to the Pilgrims' desperation in finding a legal basis on which to hang their accusations, for each charge was more trumped up than the last, and as Morton's favorable reception back in England suggests, the Pilgrims were ultimately unsuccessful. To be sure, Morton was no angel—his settlement at Mare Mount even by his own report was raucous and profane—but the claims made against him were so contrived that scholars have long been preoccupied with finding the real cause of the Pilgrims' antipathy toward him. One scholar blames Morton's "erotic mode" for creating such antagonism, while others suspect it had to do either with his connection to Gorges or with his commercial success.[37] However, no scholar to date has identified what to my mind is the far more plausible source of hostility between the Pilgrims and Morton: his replication in Mare Mount of the kind of hospitality the Pilgrims had experienced in Holland—the all-inclusive kind—and the similar threat of cultural domination and assimilation it posed. As Bradford and Winthrop put it, the danger was that Morton "welcomed all comers."

The idea of welcoming all comers or of nonselectivity, to put it in terms that more clearly reveal the contrast between this policy and that of the Pilgrims, was so deeply rooted in Morton's worldview that it colored his descriptions of the New World. In contrast to the first accounts produced by noted Pilgrim settlers, which described the land variously as "rank," "harsh," and "infertile," Morton saw New England as a "Zona Temperata," a middle zone where cold and heat mingle and form "the most perfect and wholesomest" site for a new commonwealth.[38] "So that for the temperature of the Climate, sweetness of the Air, fertility of the Soil, and small number of Salvages," he wrote, "this country of New England is by all judicious men accounted the principal part of all America, for habitation and the commodiousness of the Sea."[39] Given this and other similar pronouncements about how "commodious" New England was, Michelle Burnham goes so far as to characterize Morton's descriptions of New England as constituting a new literary genre— what she calls a New World pastoral—in which the land is depicted as yielding wealth on its own as opposed to needing people to elicit that wealth. For Burnham, this description of the land distinguishes Morton's writing from other forms of New World promotional literature, which repeatedly characterized the land as "difficult" and called on the English to send laborers over to mine its riches. Morton, by contrast, urged his countrymen to come for reasons of their own and while there to enjoy what the land offered up without prodding.[40] The significance of this claim from the perspective of hospitality is clear. The land was so hospitable, Morton seems to have said, that it would provide a generous welcome for all, an attitude that surely irked the Puritans for whom population was considered not a resource but something to tame and control.

In promoting the colonization of the New World with this open-ended view of the land in mind, not only did Morton make promises about the New World's all-inclusive hospitality, but he also made good on those promises by peopling the colony of Mare Mount with men of questionable rank and ambition. Originally a member of a trading party to Massachusetts led by the English merchant Thomas Weston and consisting of a few officers and more than twice that many servants, Morton found himself alone when in the spring of 1624 Weston abandoned his hopes for trade in New England and set sail for Virginia. Taking some but not all of his servants with him, Weston soon sent for the rest, finding that he could sell them profitably to others. Committed to giving trade in the area one more try, Morton, by contrast, asked the remaining men in Weston's party to join him instead, and in exchange for their services he promised to give them their freedom. Hearing this, Bradford recounted the speech he imagined Morton, the "pettifogger from Furnival's Inn," as he called him, gave to this end. "'You see,' saith he, 'that many of your fellows are carried to Virginia, and if you stay . . . you will also be carried away and sold for slaves with the rest. Therefore I would advise you to thrust out this Lieutenant Fitcher [the man Weston had employed to send the servants to Virginia], and I, having a part in the Plantation, will receive you as my partners and consociates; so may you be free from service, and we will converse, plant, trade, and live together as equals and support and protect one another.'"[41]

The tone of Bradford's passage is unquestionably sarcastic—one could even say mock epic—but even if we dismiss the prejudice inherent in a scene imagined from his point of view, the radical nature of Morton's gesture cannot be missed. His hospitality was so broad as to put people from an inferior rank on an equal par with others, a prospect that made Bradford write that Morton "would entertain any, how vile soever."[42] But Bradford's disapproval of Morton was rooted not only in Morton's violation of strict notions of class hierarchy but also in the recognition that Morton's policy of indiscriminate inclusiveness would almost certainly mean that Mare-Mount would soon overtake his own plantation in size and number and thus pose an additional threat to the Pilgrims. In a letter to a friend Bradford wrote: "That which further presseth us to send this [Morton's] party [away], is the fear we have of the growing of him and his consorts to that strength and height, by the access of loose persons, his house as a receptacle for such, as we would not be able to restrain his inordinariness when we would, they living without all fear of God or common honesty, some of them abusing Indian women most filthily, as it is notorious."[43]

The language Bradford used here to disparage Morton speaks to more than his antipathy for Morton; he hid little of his scorn with the use of words such as "loose," "filthily," and "abusing," but even more noteworthy is his use of the organic metaphor of "growing" that links Bradford's view of Morton's hospitality to the Puritans' view of heresy in general, implying that hospitality could, like heresy, spread like a virus. Indeed the language of contagion is widespread in Puritan descriptions of heresy, which was said to travel by means of "infection" like the "Plague."[44] Given that no more than six of Weston's original men could possibly have joined Morton in his plantation, as Charles Adams and Jack Dempsey point out, this sense of Morton's power seems wildly exaggerated. But time soon proved the soundness of the Puritans' suspicions when, by force of reputation alone, as Adams wrote, Morton "drew as many as fifty sail a year to his establishment for barter and refreshment."[45]

To be sure, Morton's reputation as a host was not merely a result of his opening his home and by extension his community to "loose persons." We know from the detailed report of his activities in the *New English Canaan* that he worked hard to make his community a comfortable place and took his role as host seriously—a fact that proved especially threatening to the Pilgrims for what it said about a host's identity. For one thing, Morton understood the importance of providing not just food and lodging but also entertainment for his guests. After naming the settlement Mare Mount, for example, Morton decided to memorialize the name with "Revels, and merriment after the old English custom." This, as we know not only from Morton but also from subsequent accounts of Morton's plantation by Washington Irving, Nathaniel Hawthorne, and Robert Lowell, among others, included the erection of a Maypole around which the English and natives could dance. "And upon May Day," Morton wrote, "they brought the maypole to the place appointed, with drums, guns, pistols, and other fitting instruments for that purpose," and "a goodly pine tree of 80 foot long was reared up, with [a poem affixed to it and] a pair of buck's horns nailed on somewhat near unto the top of it; where it stood as a fair sea-mark for directions, how to find out the way to Mine Host of Ma-re Mount."[46]

From this account we see just how clever and dynamic a host Morton was, for in marking the way to Mare-Mount with a Maypole, Morton aligned himself and his plantation with the English and the Indians simultaneously and made the boundaries between them more porous in the process. In deploying a Maypole, of course, Morton declared his allegiance to one of the oldest of all English symbols, pagan though it was.[47] He also revealed an essential intelligence about how to appeal to and include the natives in his model of community. While the old English custom of May Day dancing would not have been familiar to the Indians, the idea of dancing around a totem would have been, and this, as Morton no doubt knew, proved a strong interethnic connection. In addition, as Matt Cohen points out, in affixing a poem as well as a buck's horns to the Maypole, Morton created a network that deliberately mixed Indian and English genres of communication.[48] Morton contrasted the inhabitants of Mare Mount to the Pilgrims and thus designated a new civic model, which included the Indians and excluded the separatists. "And this the whole company of the Revellers at Ma-re Mount," he wrote, "knew to be the true sence of and exposition of the riddle: that was fixed to the Maypole, which the Separatists [*sic*] were at defiance with."[49] Adding to the extraordinary draw constituted by Morton's revels-based hospitality was the male-only atmosphere of his plantation, which, according to Morton, proved a magnet for native women. Needless to say, the mingling of the two races—anathema to the Pilgrims, who, unlike their counterparts in Virginia, had thought to bring their wives and daughters with them to prevent this very thing—was yet another element of Morton's hospitality that drove a wedge between him and the Pilgrims.

Despite his unusual talent for hospitality and the unorthodox venue in which he offered it, Morton was not alone in capitalizing on the identity available to him as a host. His contemporary Anne Hutchinson, though far less flamboyant and far more entrenched in the community of Puritans, was also viewed suspiciously in this regard. Like Morton, Hutchinson had been raised in an area of rural England that continued to practice traditional forms of hospitality, and so she may have been more used than others to opening her home to strangers. But there were other reasons why she was more inclined to be hospitable as well: she was the wife of one of the most prominent men in the Bay Colony and the owner of the largest house in town, which was built to accommodate a family of between fourteen and nineteen people and was, not coincidentally, right across the street from Winthrop's. As such she was often called upon to open her house for lectures and study groups. Henry Vane, her neighbor, friend, and the provisional governor, was perhaps most vocal in this regard.[50]

Like Morton, Hutchinson seemed to have had an open-door policy for her conventicles, in which she debriefed her fellow inhabitants about the previous week's sermon. As we know from statistical data on most of the men who made up what Emery Battis referred to as Hutchinson's support group, Hutchinson drew untold numbers of people to her way of thinking and to her home to instruct them in the error of the ministers' ways.[51] For Hutchinson, famously, the ministers of the Bay Colony had gone astray by preaching a doctrine of works that indicated that sanctification—the state of being chosen or blessed by God—might come about as a result of one's good deeds and visible demeanor as opposed to a doctrine of grace, which was at the root of the Puritan religion and importantly gave no indication of how or even whether one might achieve sanctification at all. Needless to say, this description provides only the briefest and most general idea of what was at stake in Hutchinson's so-called antinomian views. The theological debate alone defies summary and included questions about whether personal revelations of the sort Hutchinson finally claimed as her own were allowable and whether expressions of faith were best captured by imitable forms or inimitable affect.[52] The political implications of antinomianism were also at issue. Among other things, especially in these early years before the Puritan Revolution, the antinomians threatened the supremacy of the Puritans' more orthodox form of the reformed religion and so threatened their chances for establishing a reformed church in England.

While Hutchinson did not make as much of the open-endedness of her hospitality as Morton did, it did not escape the attention of the Bay Colony ministers and magistrates that she welcomed everyone, from any walk of life, into her home. To her meetings, Winthrop remarked, "resorted sundry of Boston, and other Townes."[53] It is worth noting too that like Morton, Hutchinson was said to draw people to her as though her hospitality were "contagious." At first, as one historian observed, only five or six women came to her house, but soon her meetings became so popular that "shee kept open house for *all comers* and set up two Lecture days in the week, when they usually met at her house, three or fourscore persons."[54] The indiscriminate nature of her welcome and the ensuing popularity of her meetings reinforced the accusation that Hutchinson had demonstrated an improper degree of hospitality. When the church synod in 1637 ruled that having a few women to her house was permissible but entertaining sixty was not, the number of Hutchinson's adherents and the nature of her hospitality proved determinative.[55]

Action or Inaction

In pursuing the charge that Hutchinson displayed an improper level of hospitality in welcoming strangers to her home, the Puritans of the Bay Colony unwittingly revealed another aspect of hospitality that they saw as threatening—not the intangible appeal of hosts or the indiscriminate manner of their hosting but the way in which the act of hospitality was in some ways not an act at all. Winthrop famously began Hutchinson's examination not with a question but with a long litany of her offenses. Among other things she had, he said, "troubled the peace of the commonweath," "promot[ed] and divulg[ed] of those opinions that are causes of this trouble," and "maintained a meeting and an assembly in your house that hath been condemned by the general assembly as a thing not tolerable nor comely in the sight of God."[56] To this long and otherwise daunting list, Hutchinson responded as if Winthrop had said nothing at all. Later in the examination, she invoked the biblical rule of Titus in her defense, which ordered older women to instruct younger women, but at this earlier point she was categorically dismissive of the accusation. "I am called here to answer before you," she said, "but I hear no things laid to my charge" (312). Confounded, Winthrop noted, "I have told you some already and more I can tell you." But Hutchinson persisted. "Name one Sir," she said.

Baffling to her contemporary audience, this particular moment in Hutchinson's examination remains opaque to modern students of the antinomian controversy as well. When attended to at all, it is typically and, I would argue, mistakenly read as an expression of spite or of deliberate obtuseness on Hutchinson's part. However, the clue to its logic lies not in her attitude but in her understanding of what, by law, a legal accusation of the type Winthrop is making requires. Thus to Winthrop's subsequent question, "Have I not named some already?," Hutchinson asked in more precise legal terms, "What have I said or done?" Not satisfied with the charge that she had violated the law by maintaining a meeting in her house, Hutchinson pointed the governor toward the well-known requirement that a violation of the law must be based on a specific act or, in legal terms, an actus reus. Not spelled out until centuries later when it became the subject of some controversy, the actus reus was nevertheless a central feature of criminal law from its inception. In his *Institute* on the criminal-law category of English common law, Hutchinson's contemporary Sir Edward Coke implied that the actus reus consists of bodily movements that produce a result. "Whether the movements will result in liability for the person making them," as one modern-day legal theorist and political philosopher explains, "will then depend upon the mental state that accompanied his act."[57] The actus reus, in other words, is necessary but not sufficient for criminal liability; it must be accompanied by a mens rea—a mental attitude that can be associated with intentional wrongdoing.

Like the actus reus, the mens rea is necessary but not sufficient for criminal liability because the common law, even in its earliest incarnations, did not punish people for their thoughts. In addition the mens rea is traditionally a much more difficult element of the criminal law to prove. This is why most criminal accusations start with the act, which is exactly what Winthrop tried to do in his interrogation. But the problem with the acts Winthrop identified—the meetings in Hutchinson's house—is that they amounted to no more than offers of hospitality, which under normal circumstances were not criminally blameworthy. Thus Winthrop explained that it was not simply the act of opening her house for which Hutchinson stood accused but also the nature of those she let in. "Why, for your doings," he explained, "this you did harbour and countenance those that are parties in this faction that you have heard of."[58]

A reading of Hutchinson's various responses to this accusation reinforces our sense that she understood and intended to capitalize on the difference between act and attitude. Her first response was that "harbouring" and countenancing" people is a private affair or, in her words, a "matter of conscience, Sir." In this Hutchinson dematerialized the so-called act of hospitality and put it in the realm of mental attitude or belief. In so doing Hutchinson did not deny that she might have had the mens rea for the accusation but merely reminded Winthrop that he still lacked evidence of an act. At first Winthrop could do no more than agree, but he cautioned her with a preview of how "a matter of conscience" could easily become an action. "Say that one brother should commit felony or treason and come to his other brother's house," he said. "It is his conscience to entertain him, but if his conscience comes into *act* in giving countenance and entertainment to him that hath broken the law he is guilty too."[59] Again Hutchinson demurred, pointing to yet another legal distinction—between act and omission—that Winthrop also seemed to overlook. "Will it please you to answer me this," Hutchinson asked: "If any come to my house to be instructed in the ways of God what rule have I to put them away?"[60]

A brilliant rhetorical flourish in the face of which Winthrop found himself temporarily speechless, the question Hutchinson asked by way of answer identifies yet another sense in which hospitality seemed to defy categorization and escape the clutches of Winthrop's notion of criminality. In her formulation here, hospitality appears not as an activity but rather as a manifestation of passivity, as if having once opened her door, there was little else Hutchinson could do. Indeed this understanding of hospitality or more specifically of "entertaining and harbouring"—the words Winthrop employed—comports with the etymology and usage of those terms at the time. The *Oxford English Dictionary* defines the verb "to entertain" as "To keep (a person, country, etc.) in a certain state or condition [or] to retain in use (a custom, law, etc.)." To entertain or to be hospitable, in other words, is merely to keep things at the status quo ante or to do nothing at all. It was not until some years after Hutchinson's trial, when he was reflecting on her responsibility and wrongdoing, that Winthrop found words to associate with her hospitality—words such as "sleights" "salutes," and "invitements," which, though they come closer to resembling acts in the common understanding of the term, still fall short of criminal action. He wrote:

> Consider the sleights they used in fomenting their Opinions. They labored much to acquaint themselves with as many, as possibly they could, that so they might have the better opportunity to communicate their new light unto them. Being once acquainted with them, they would strangely labour to insinuate themselves into their affections, by loving salutes, humble carriage, kind invitements, friendly visits. . . . Yea, as soone as any new-commers . . . were landed, they would be sure to welcome them, shew them all courtesie, and offer them roome in their owne houses.[61]

Even in the course of her trial, Hutchinson was not content to let the question of her action go unexamined, so she diverted Winthrop's attention from the ostensible act of maintaining a meeting—which constituted no act for her at all—to her failure to act as the only possible source of her wrongdoing. In asking the question "If any come to my house . . . what rule have I to put them away?" she implicitly reminded Winthrop that except in rare instances—for example the paying of taxes—Anglo-American common law did not require one to act affirmatively but rather only to refrain from certain actions, such as the doing of harm. By extension Hutchinson's question also drew on the truism that the law did not hold people responsible for failing to act or for remaining neutral in the face of another's wrongdoing. Later to become officially divorced from the realm of misconduct, Hutchinson's inaction here proved that in the absence of any explicit law against it, her hospitality did not rise to the level of an act and therefore could not be the basis for a criminal charge.[62]

Hutchinson's last question to Winthrop before he, no doubt sensing defeat, moved away from the issue of her hospitality altogether changed the course of the colony's legal history and its notions about community formation and membership forever. "In entertaining those," Hutchinson pointedly asked, "did I entertain them against any act (for there is the thing) or what god hath appointed?"[63] Knowing that there was no law he could point to at the moment, Winthrop nevertheless lost no time in getting one passed, much to Hutchinson's chagrin. Winthrop's order, known as the Act of Exclusion, was passed by the General Court of the Bay Colony in 1637 and ruled that "none should be received to inhabit within this Jurisdiction but such as should be allowed by some of the Magistrates." That the Act of Exclusion, despite the generality of its language, was precipitated by Hutchinson's hospitality and directed against the antinomians as opposed to any other group was hard to miss. In addition to the direct provocation of Hutchinson's question at her trial, the Act of Exclusion was passed just as a group of Hutchinson's friends and relatives, having made the journey from Boston, England, to Boston, New England, were within sight of the colony's harbor.[64]

Lest this coincidence not be enough to stop the antinomians from entering the colony, the Act of Exclusion added a provision to its otherwise general language that directly criminalized hospitality, imposing a penalty on those already within the colony who offered food and lodging to strangers for longer than three weeks.[65] In this provision the law addressed the gap between the inclusive nature of hospitality, which governed visits and short stays, and the colony's aspiration for a restrictive policy for permanent membership. Not surprisingly, given the length of the journey from England to the New World and the difficulty of traveling within or between colonies, most people considered three weeks an unreasonably short period of time, and the act provoked a good deal of public outrage.[66]

As the target of much of that outrage, Winthrop felt compelled to publish a defense of the act in which he did an end run around the question of hospitality by diverting attention away from the future of the colony and toward the moment of its founding. "No common weale," he wrote, "can be founded but by free consent," from which it followed that "if we here be a corporation established by free consent, if the place of our cohabitation be our owne, then no man hath right to come into us &c. without our consent."[67] Seemingly airtight at first glance, the argument Winthrop employed here has as many twists and turns as does his "Model of Christian Charity," for having made the assertion that the commonwealth was founded on consent—which served as a shared principle of inclusion—he then took it as a given and turned the meaning of consent on its head, from an instrument securing the freedom of a "common weale" to an instrument of force and exclusion. The consent that initially enabled the formation of a free community, in other words, was now being put to work to bar others from enjoying that same freedom, inhibiting the influx of strangers and freezing the community in time. Needless to say, this is a perfect example of what Charles Tilly meant when he said that inclusion and exclusion were inevitably twinned. Having subordinated the issue of hospitality to that of consent, Winthrop went on to marginalize it even further, suggesting that it could never be the source of any permanent legal change. Hospitality, he wrote, "doth not bind further than for some present occasion" and was thus best left to a judge's discretion.[68]

For Winthrop's rival Henry Vane, who not only sympathized with the antinomians but also had wrested the governorship away from Winthrop, albeit only for a year, hospitality had a different provenance and a different legal standing.[69] In his "Briefe Answer to a certaine declaration, made of the intent and equitye of the order of the court," Vane reminded Winthrop that while the colony was a private corporation authorized by private subscribers (as Winthrop's notion of consent and discretionary justice implied), it nevertheless remained under the authority of the Crown and was thus subject to the broader, traditionally English, understanding of hospitality. "Such may the stranger be," Vane wrote, "as have true right of cohabitation, and sojourning with us, as hath been shewed . . . by his majesties patent, for they are fellow subjects to one and the same prince, they are also of the same nation, and if they be christians [sic] they are in a farre nearer relation than all these."[70]

Vane's emphasis on the authority of the king's patent indicates that while he may not have looked to international law for his understanding of hospitality, he did see it as a principle of the common law that pertained not only to him and Winthrop but also to all Englishmen alike. For Vane, hospitality was an English custom that required the accommodation of all Englishmen in English territories, colonial or otherwise. In the debate between Winthrop and Vane over the Act of Exclusion, we see just how central hospitality had become in the formation of the colonial community, for it was on the basis of the colony's inhospitable stance toward other Englishmen that both Vane and Morton urged the Crown to revoke its charter. Vane argued that by turning English strangers away—particularly the boatload of Hutchinson's followers then anchored in the Boston harbor—the Puritans were illicitly rewriting the patent, which had made hospitality an essential element of England's and New England's shared law.[71]

Role Reversal

According to Morton and Vane, the extent to which a version of the English custom of hospitality should have served as a constraint on the Puritans' welcome of others was not the only way in which hospitality threatened the Puritans' increasingly unwelcoming community. It is easy to forget in analyzing Morton and Hutchinson in terms of the scope and level of their welcome that one of the most insidious aspects of their hospitality was that in assuming the role of host in the first place, they upset the power balance inherent between host (the Puritans) and guest (the stranger).[72] Morton, after all, entered the jurisdiction of the Plymouth Colony as a guest or nonmember, or so the separatists claimed, while Hutchinson, though affiliated with the Puritan faith and therefore more a member than Morton ever was, entered the Bay Colony as a faithful follower, not as the potential leader she soon proved to be. But in neither case was Morton's or Hutchinson's relationship to hospitality primarily a question of how or even whether the colony should welcome them; as a Puritan, Hutchinson was initially welcomed with open arms, and as an Anglican and trader, Morton not at all. Rather the question was how, after establishing themselves in the colonies, Morton and Hutchinson went on to welcome others. In this regard the cases of Morton and Hutchinson reveal the way in which hospitality was not simply a singular or unique event in the lives of its participants, host or guest, but by its very nature a series of events that were repeated as the former guest became, in yet another iteration of the ritual, the host of others. As Conrad Lashley wrote, "when a guest settles and becomes rooted, he can become a host; and when a host leaves home to travel, he transforms into a guest (though each carries with them traces of their former identity)."[73]

Central to this role reversal was the expectation of reciprocity that was at the heart of early modern hospitality and perceived as a threat to colonial sovereignty; in agreeing to be the beneficiary of someone's hospitality, in other words, one was at the same time agreeing to return it, either to the same person or to another person at a different time. Unlike hospitality, charity—the principle on which Winthrop founded the Bay Colony—did not have this feature and was for that reason almost certainly less threatening to the Puritans. As Maria Moisa wrote, charity was a practice "for which benefactors could expect no return."[74] The expectation of reciprocity and of social reorganization increased as hospitality became more widespread toward the end of the Elizabethan era, when it was no longer confined to noble households and the aristocracy but a regular practice among all householders, including those of average means. As Steve Hindle has written, "Both status differentiation and social distance between donor and recipient were diminished (or perhaps even temporarily effaced) when hospitality became more widely practised throughout the social order."[75] To reciprocate an offer of hospitality, in other words, was to indicate that host and guest were at least to some extent equal.

In most cases in the early years of the Plymouth and Bay Colonies, the potential for this kind of reciprocity and role reversal was limited. The vast majority of residents settled quietly into homes of their own, and if they served as hosts for others, they did so infrequently and with little fanfare. However, in the case of Morton, who, like Falstaff, referred to himself in the third person as "Mine Host," and of Hutchinson, who less obviously but no less meaningfully invited large numbers of people into her home for entertainment and instruction, the issue of role reversal was preeminent.

Driven by this expectation of reciprocity, the uses to which Hutchinson and Morton put the dynamic of role reversal came to highlight nothing less than the crucial question of how communal identities could and would be formed outside the bounds of official religious, legal, or political organization. Defined as they were by this kind of subject status reversal—from guest to host and somewhat less often from host to guest again—Morton, Hutchinson, and their friends and neighbors would have experienced a fluidity of identities unavailable in any other Puritan ritual. Indeed hospitality allowed for a kind of freedom or play in the realm of identity that was not otherwise available in the early modern period—except perhaps on specially designated days of carnival—and that posed an obvious threat to the Puritans' society, where roles were strictly prescribed and intended to last a lifetime.

What went on inside the home under the rubric of hospitality is the kind of behavior that Erving Goffman might have described as a "focused gathering" or "interaction ritual." For Goffman, the essence of a focused gathering is fluidity and context: people, he noted "take turns at talking" and experience what he called "face time," in which a person "must take into consideration the impression they have possibly formed of him."[76] Following Goffman, Clifford Geertz identified several other crucial features of interactive rituals and focused gatherings. "Such gatherings," he wrote, "meet and disperse; the participants in them fluctuate; the activity that focuses them is discrete—a particulate process that reoccurs rather than a continuous one that endures."[77] Not surprisingly, given this description, the model most commonly invoked by Goffman and Geertz for a focused gathering is a game—for Geertz, famously, a cockfight—a performance in which roles are assumed, often reversed, and yet have lingering social and legal consequences.

Hospitality, especially the kind associated with Morton and Hutchinson in early seventeenth-century New England, is a perfect example of the kind of game or performance that could lead to social and legal change as concerned communities and their memberships. Many have commented on the performative aspects of Morton's hospitality—in particular the feasting around the

Maypole—making the point that it represented his nostalgia for the masques and antimasques of Elizabethan England, among other things.[78] But Morton's version of hospitality went far beyond this in mimicking the revels and feasting that were so central to the lessons learned by lawyers at the Inns of Court—Clifford's Inn, not Furnival's as Bradford carelessly noted—where Morton, not coincidentally, was trained. At the Inns of Court, as Paul Raffield has observed, revels were used to provide "evocative images of the ideal state and its constitutional mechanisms." Indeed during Elizabethan times revels included the frequent staging of masques and antimasques for which law students rehearsed for weeks, creating in effect "an artificial state . . . in which the functions of executive, legislative and judiciary were enacted by members of the Inns [and] enabled the legal profession to explore and develop the political concepts of constitutionalism and limited monarchy." In addition to providing a mechanism for experimenting with models of state, revels and hospitality became a form of reinforcing the customary nature of English common law that was "considered to be of equal, if not greater, importance than knowledge of substantive law."[79] In this regard Morton's revels reveal him as killing two birds with one stone: alerting the Pilgrims to his familiarity with and mastery of the law as well as to his knowledge of and belief in the priority of ancient community forming customs, such as hospitality, within it.

With the construction of the Maypole, Morton turned hospitality into a process of civic interpellation. The community that gathers around the Maypole is by definition a community that agrees to the supremacy of that particular icon.[80] That the icon in this case was pagan and visual—both anathema to the Pilgrims—only added to the complications brought on by Morton's acts, which reached new heights of violation when Morton added a poem to the Maypole and blended verbal with visual community.[81] That the poem was offered in the form of a riddle, moreover, which remained largely impenetrable to the separatists, may also explain why it was seen as such a provocation. In the poem, as Edith Murphy explains, Oedipus is invoked, in the manner of a classical Muse, to solve the riddle of why Scilla, who has apparently been newly widowed, is provided with a new husband in whom "no signe / Can be found of vertue masculine."[82] Scilla, in short, has a new man who nevertheless lacks manhood, and in order to make her feel better—she is described as "sick with greife [sic]"—a more manly man must be found. According to Murphy, this new man is none other than Morton, while the men who lack masculinity are the separatists, who have tried to settle the new land (Scilla) in a fruitful way but have failed. Murphy goes on to draw a parallel between the dead husband and the Indians, whom Morton described in the way that did not denigrate them but simply acknowledged the decimation they suffered in the plague epidemic of 1616–18. Indeed, Jack Dempsey reinforces this feature of Murphy's reading of the poem in drawing out the use of classical and Renaissance allusions to document events in Native American history in his own gloss on the poem.[83]

Whether or not Murphy and Dempsey are right about the details of the poem or the drift of its allegory, we can profit from their analyses by noting the role that gender plays in their readings. The problem: the New World is a woman who needs a (real) man; the solution: find a real man and enjoy his hospitality. Needless to say, this is where Morton and his phallic Maypole come in. Without belaboring the point, we note that hospitality was not simply an ancient custom embedded in the common law but a requirement of manhood: to be hospitable was to reinforce one's position as lord of the manor (husband and father all rolled into one), and Morton would certainly have been alive to this. More specifically, by affixing a poem about manhood to the phallic Maypole, Morton in effect offered not only a rival constitution that served to bind Mare Mount's inhabitants together, just as the Mayflower Compact and the "Model of Christian Charity" bound the Puritans, but also a rival notion of what it meant to reconstitute a community as only a real man could.[84]

But what then do we make of Hutchinson's hospitality?[85] That Hutchinson, a woman and by the time of her civil trial a visibly pregnant woman at that, was seen in part as usurping a man's role in challenging the ministerial authorities on the issue of grace versus works has not escaped the attention of countless critics. Yet few have examined its relevance to her role as host, for there again it played a part, albeit in a minor rather than a major key. Despite her being instructed to obey the rule of Titus, that is, and invite women into her home, her assumption of the role of host, especially insofar as it extended to members of both genders, would certainly have aggravated those who still thought of the home as essentially a male domain. (It goes without saying that in a world in which women were denied legal rights except as they attached to them as daughters or wives, the household, though domestic, was not yet a woman's sphere.) It is against the backdrop of the gender violation implicit in her offer of hospitality, then, that we can begin to gauge Hutchinson's violation of other usurpations of authority. For one thing, what Hutchinson said in the conventicles held in her home bore an obvious parallel to what was being said in church and so took on the trappings of the church's authority—also male. This was the primary charge leveled against her in her church trial, which took place some months after her secular one. In the secular examination the substance of Hutchinson's heresy took a backseat to questions about the context in which she was said to have delivered it. This took the form of questions that acknowledged the extent to which Hutchinson's home and other homes might serve as additional or alternative forums for the making of law. That her home could have become such a public forum did not rise to the level of an official recognition, and yet the expression of the magistrates' and ministers' fear about Hutchinson's "influence" was proof enough that her home had the potential to rival the courts or legislature as a place for the expression and dissemination of power.

Among other things this had the effect of confusing the public and private spheres and making the authority to determine matters of inclusion and exclusion more problematic. Under cover of hospitality, the home became a new and potentially ungovernable jurisdiction in which affairs of the colony could be concealed as private, domestic matters. Of course the venue in which Morton offered his hospitality had already confused the categories of public and private for the Pilgrims. In referring to Morton's homestead as a "nest"—a metaphor that for Bradford could have had only negative associations, as in a "nest of vipers"—Bradford nevertheless ascribed to it certain domestic qualities that it might otherwise be thought to lack. In the Old World, of course, a few rude houses and a Maypole would hardly have counted as a community of any kind, but in the New World, where everyone was starting over, houses were hard to come by, and a show of hospitality could turn even the simplest and most open-framed dwellings into bastions of generosity and privacy. Robert Blair St. George has referred to the early structures in colonial New England as "hybrid houses," and as David Flaherty has noted, "the social pressures to provide hospitality to strangers were perhaps greater in the seventeenth century, or at least until a newly settled area lost some of its roughness, inns were built, and life became more formalized."[86] Morton, not surprisingly, encouraged and supported this association, going so far as to imply that the Maypole itself was a home. "Then drink and be merry, merry, merry my boys / Let all your delight be in Hymen's joys; Io! To Hymen, now the day is come, / about the merry Maypole take a room," he wrote.[87]

A Little Commonwealth Hospitality

Ramshackle though their houses were, there was precedent for thinking of early Puritan homes as legal spaces. As John Demos has reminded us, the Puritans had a fondness for thinking of the family and by analogy the family home as a "little commonwealth." In his pathbreaking work *A Little Commonwealth*, Demos reveals the widespread nature of this metaphorical link.[88] But as Demos explains, the "little commonwealth" constituted by the average Puritan home was a place where the law as handed down from on high was replicated, not revised. The family home, according to Demos, served as a "school" for the inculcation of proper social values, a "church" for the dissemination of the approved faith, and a "house of correction" for character reformation, among other things. But the home as a venue for hospitality and for the trying on of roles of host in some cases and guest in others was not the same kind of "little commonwealth" Demos had in mind. Indeed what went on in the home in the name of hospitality did not necessarily mimic but often countered what went on in the state, if only temporarily.

In their struggle over hospitality, in other words, the colonists came face-to-face with the fact that law not only penetrates a multitude of social domains—as in the model of the little commonwealth—but can be forged and revised there as well. As one legal scholar has written, "Law is not a distinctly bounded 'thing' that belongs exclusively to the state. It is a continuum of normative orders."[89] Given the prominence of the conflicts over the letters patent and charters of the New England colonies, which were constantly in dispute and under threat of revocation, historians have tended to neglect this aspect of lawmaking in early New England. Even so, it played a large part in helping the colonies define their sense of collective identity as preliminary to the exercise of banishment, a punishment that was leveled on others with a far heavier hand. What the colonists learned from Hutchinson and Morton was that everyday life could provide a potential template for the construction of norms and procedures for inclusion and exclusion that could vie with official pronouncements from the state.

Keeping this in mind, it is particularly important to note that what occurred in the name of hospitality in both Morton and Hutchinson's "homes" was a slightly different kind of law than that traditionally displayed by the "state"; we might see it as an even more fluid version of what was an already fluid common law. For one thing, it was less adversarial and more constitutive of interests. As we know from the Mayflower Compact and the "Model of Christian Charity," as well as from the countless judicial decisions that have been preserved from the time, the colony's official legal machinery was deployed largely to solidify the existing community and to adjudicate disputes between its members. But as this examination of the ritual of hospitality has shown, this was just one very limited kind of lawmaking. By contrast what went on in Hutchinson's home and around Morton's Maypole seemed to have more to do with creating bonds that may not have existed before and with discovering mutual interests between inhabitants and strangers. We could even say that for Morton and Hutchinson, the stranger was, as Georg Simmel wrote, not the wanderer who "comes today and goes tomorrow"—which was almost certainly the stranger whom the Puritan magistrates would have preferred—"but rather . . . the person who comes today and stays tomorrow."[90] The stranger for Morton and Hutchinson was someone who should have been accommodated within the law in ways that went beyond or existed alongside the membership requirements. This was especially true in Hutchinson's case, where neighbors who, if not new to the community of the colony, were new to the community of her home and her ostensible heresy were initially figured as strangers or guests and then reconfigured as neighbors once again, after they had experienced the power of her teachings. Indeed the community of neighbors who gathered in Hutchinson's home was famously composed of the most eminent and orthodox men and women in Boston—including deputies to the General Court and prominent merchants and selectmen—whose openness to antinomianism seemed to be only one aspect of their lives in the colony and not, as Winthrop and the other magistrates feared, the determinative one. As Geertz has reminded us, in a focused gathering such as one might find in a hospitable home, people "meet and disperse." Thus hospitality served as a site for making law that was based on interactions and the contingencies of the circumstances at hand—a kind of law, or "legality," as Patricia Ewick and Susan Silbey have written, "that emerges out of and continually shapes those roles and relationships."[91]

In this chapter we have seen some of the ways in which hospitality functioned as a threshold issue for the Puritans in thinking about the languages and practices of identity formation and by extension practices of social exclusion. But hospitality was just one manifestation of the ongoing debate over and experimentation with different ways of ordering social space, determining the boundaries of jurisdictions, and defining members within them. In the next chapter we encounter a similar nexus of problems—between law and religion and between law and custom—in their relation to the question of a homogenous community to which the Puritans aspired. As Richard Ross explains, there were a variety of ways of construing the first plantations—as corporations, as free states, as colonies, to name just a few—and, not surprisingly, a variety of legal and paralegal sources for those constructions, including charters, letters patent, Scripture, custom, and legislation.[92]

CHAPTER 2

The "Predicament of Ubi"

Thence it is that you stand on tip-toe, to stretch yourselves beyond
your bounds.
> —Samuel Gorton, "The First Letter of Samuel Gorton and His
> Accomplices," in *Hypocrisie Unmasked*

IN BANISHING MORTON and Hutchinson, the Puritans made it clear
that they would not tolerate people who entered their jurisdiction only to
turn around and make offers to others to do the same—people who came
in as guests, in other words, but turned into hosts in short order. They said
little, however, about strangers who did not take up these identities. In prohibiting people from welcoming others into their homes—or around their
Maypoles—the Puritans not only failed to stem the flow of strangers into their
communities but also actually contributed to it, becoming part of a trend in
England toward a decline in hospitality that led to a greater mobility among
the population. With fewer places available in which to take shelter or to find
the comforts of home—provisional though they might be—more and more
people found themselves on the move between parishes, towns, and counties.
A trickle at first, the number of these "wanderers" increased steadily throughout the first half of the seventeenth century, spurred on in part by population
growth and unemployment until the association of jurisdiction with a fixed
demographic was no longer manageable. To put it in slightly different terms,
people who moved from place to place introduced difference into an existing
locale and disrupted the prevailing sense of sameness within it.

Banishment, a punishment intended to reinforce sameness by casting out
those who differed from the norm, was implicated in this process and surfaced

as a focal point for the sorting out of many of the issues associated with no-tions of sameness and difference within a bounded territory. Homogeneity not only characterized but also functioned as a criterion for the establish-ment of legal jurisdictions from their inception. The earliest sense of juris-diction revolved around a bounded space inhabited by like-minded people over whom a jurisdictional authority would rule in a way that was informed by and reflected that like-mindedness. Part if not most of the force of law behind the court of any given jurisdiction was the notion of community co-herence. The connections provided by kin in a period when extended families still lived in relatively close proximity were often enough to shape the same-ness of a community. In addition neighborly relations, labor guilds, and other social organizations whose memberships were coincident with the jurisdic-tion often induced a sense of sameness among residents. In his treatise on the lower branches of the legal profession in early modern England, C. W. Brooks quotes a contemporary commentator who touts the virtues of local courts for the homogenous venues they offer. They "doe serve rather for men that can be content to be ordered by their neighbors," he writes, "and which love their quiet and profit in their husbandrie, more than to be busie in the lawe."[1]

A Culture of Homogeneity

To be sure, jurisdictions tended to be more homogeneous in theory than in practice—there were demographic divisions within civil jurisdictions long be-fore hospitality began to wane—but the idea maintained a strong hold on the public imagination, and the facts suggest a change from relative homogeneity throughout the sixteenth century to relative heterogeneity at the beginning of the seventeenth as a result of these "wanderers."[2] Though their interest does not extend to the concept of jurisdiction, Patricia Fumerton and other schol-ars of this phenomenon speak in terms of the sameness and difference of pop-ulations, referring to the newly mobile, for example, as introducing a certain "heterogeneity" into the community and causing old forms of allegiance and affiliation to fall away. Among those creating this new heterogeneity was an influx of itinerant laborers who came from different places looking for work. This, Fumerton notes, contributed to "a newly emergent economy character-ized by mobility, diversity, alienation, freedom, and tactical . . . craft."[3] These individuals, moreover, were joined by growing numbers of beggars and other vagrants who, though law-abiding, merged with a criminal population that increased the diversity of the population in turn. Bryan Reynolds observes that "early modern England's criminal culture of gypsies, rogues, vagabonds, beggars, cony-catchers, cutpurses, and prostitutes was defiantly and transversally mobile" and that "its criminal practice was heterogeneous, discursive, elusive, and performative."[4]

Further complicating the intrusion of such individuals into an otherwise homogenous population was the homogenizing impulse of the nation-state. Though the nation-state was not formally introduced as a civil entity until the treaty of Westphalia in 1648, England and other European powers had been moving for some time toward the kind of consolidation of culture that would help bring it into being. Nations began to define themselves by identifying cultural traits that differed from those of other nations in a simultaneously burgeoning international regime. Many political theorists addressed themselves to the field of international relations in the early modern period, but no one spoke more directly to the concerns of England's jurisdiction in relation to foreign jurisdictions than Hugo Grotius. In his *On the Law of War and Peace* (1625), Grotius reasoned that the warfare that raged throughout the Europe of his day had less to do with overarching or global differences between countries than with local conflicts that stemmed from different systems of "national" law. Thus in Grotius's model people living in different countries were recognizably different because of their behavior: people in Spain, that is, behaved differently from people in England, and so on. Not only did people in different countries abide by different local or customary laws, but they also served different monarchs and called themselves by different names. Jane Newman describes this theory of Grotius's as creating a bridge between countries through the recognition of "abstract principles of sameness and realities of difference."[5]

If Grotius's belief in "abstract principles of sameness," however, provided a long-sought-after ground on which warring nations could make peace, it also hinted at the controversial proposition long associated with the homogenous nation: that place and person were isomorphic. This in turn contributed to the confusion that prevailed between nations and their newfound colonies. A necessary corollary to Grotius's theory of international heterogeneity was the assumption of intranational homogeneity. Extending the homogeneity previously attributed to local communities to the entire country, however, flew in the face of colonialism, whose agenda in part was to establish outposts of the mother country in far-flung places. In Stuart England, for example, whose colonial expansion took in parts of America and of the West Indies, relations between the mother country and the colonies were particularly fraught. And because they did not fall neatly into either the intranational or international paradigms Grotius provided, they ended up driving further jurisdictional reform. Specifically, when confronted with colonialism, Grotius's assumption of sameness within a country formerly constituted by a particular land mass and difference outside it had to be revised. In relatively isolated areas cut off geographically and socially from others, a population homogeneous in terms of worldview and behavior might safely be assumed. But with the increased geographical reach and the concomitant interactions and crossings it encouraged came an increased diversity of inhabitants whose difference from each other forced a revision of older notions of jurisdictional sameness—from the parish to the precinct to the kingdom to the nation. The establishment of colonies such as Massachusetts Bay, which was three thousand miles from the mother country, made such a complication concrete. How could one characterize populations abroad that—like those of the colonists in New England—shared the customs and customary law of all Englishmen but were physically removed from the seat of England's authority and thus had added to the set of traditional English customs a number of different customs from which they derived a number of new laws?[6] Put another way, what kind of connections could be made between jurisdiction and identity if English colonists in the Bay Colony or elsewhere retained their liberties as subjects of the Crown (as their charters often claimed they could) and yet were free to alter English laws or to choose between English law and some colonial version of it? In short, who were these colonists and what role did the legal understanding of jurisdiction as homogeneous or heterogeneous play in shaping and expressing their identities?

This question was asked and answered many times over in the law courts and in the halls of Parliament throughout the late sixteenth and early seventeenth centuries, but we can look to one landmark case, decided by Sir Edward Coke, as a point of departure for most of the jurisdictional theories that followed. In *Calvin's Case* (1608) the jurisdictional issue was posed generally as a question about sovereign authority but also, more specifically, about how far beyond the immediate borders of the sovereign's authority a given territorial jurisdiction could go. *Calvin's Case* was a jumble of strange taxonomies whose immediate purpose was to grant English subject status, along with its accompanying property rights, to Scots born after the accession of James VI and to disinherit Scots born before that.[7] But if it was ostensibly confined to Scottish residents, the decision nevertheless had implications for determining the identity of people in the English colonies, and it is worth noting that while the case did not circulate in print until the 1650s, Roger Williams, whose banishment story is the focus of this chapter, would almost certainly have known about it much earlier since he had worked closely with Coke decades before.

Calvin's Case

The significance of *Calvin's Case* from the point of view of jurisdictional reform was its disarticulation of geography and subject status. For the first time it was decided that the allegiance the subject owed to the sovereign and by extension to the laws of the jurisdiction over which he ruled could not be determined by geography alone.[8] The judges in *Calvin's Case* observed that "ligeance and faith and truth, are qualities of the mind and soul of man and cannot be circumscribed within the predicament of ubi [Latin for "where"]."[9] Of course more traditional readings of the case tend to confine the implications of its holding to subjects born in Scotland after James I annexed their lands. Scholars often discuss the case as a reconsolidation of the power of the sovereign over his subjects as opposed to an extension of the liberties of the subjects.[10] In this vein the case is seen as suggesting that subjects owe their allegiance to the sovereign in his/her person or natural body and not merely to the political order he or she represents. The facts of the case also lend themselves to this more conservative reading insofar as the issue at stake for Robert Calvin, the Scottish child who was named as plaintiff, was the inheritance of a landed estate in London. In holding that Calvin was entitled to inherit the lands because he was born after England and Scotland were united, the case did not extend subject status to just anyone but rather upheld the status of the landed and reinforced their ties and indebtedness to the king. Jacqueline Stevens notes that "after conquering Scotland, jus soli gave the English king dominion over those born to Scottish parents. It also prevented potentially disloyal subjects whose parents had emigrated to France from inheriting English land."[11]

There can be little question, however, that from another point of view *Calvin's Case* was far more radical. For one thing, the language about the predicament of "ubi" points toward a more general theory about geography and subject status. The immediate consequence of the separation between *who* a person was—"the qualities of the mind and soul of man"—and *where* he was—"the predicament of ubi"—was a recognition that people all over, including the colonists of Massachusetts Bay or other English colonies, could live in diverse circumstances, according to diverse laws, and still call themselves subjects of the same king and nation. We can also assume that the case was intended to offer a new, explicitly common-law, opportunity for subjects of all social classes, living in places far beyond Scotland, to raise similar questions about birthright status, since in at least one previous instance—that of Virginia—a similar status had already been granted by legislation. Indeed as Polly Price observes, the charter given to the colonists of Virginia had been explicit in granting them "all Liberties, Franchises, and Immunities . . . *as if they had been abiding and born*, within this our Realm of England."[12] If groups such as the Virginia colonists and their Virginia-born descendants could acquire a right to be treated like Englishmen even while living three thousand miles away, then why, we might ask, did the courts bother with *Calvin's Case* at all, and why was it seen, even in its own day, as providing a new direction in the law?

The answer, I argue, lies precisely in the fact that it was issued in common-law, not legislative or statutory, terms and that as such it had particular significance in New England. Unlike the colony of Virginia, that is, which attended more to English legislation and followed it strictly, the colonies in New England were more responsive to the common law and all of its divergent legal trajectories than they were to statutory law. There are two reasons why this may have been the case. First, the English settled Virginia in 1607, Plymouth some thirteen years later, in 1620, and the Massachusetts Bay Colony ten years after that. Of course from one perspective the difference between these dates could be seen as negligible, but in terms of the common law's history, the years in between the founding of Jamestown and the Bay Colony were significant. It was during just this period, in fact, that the common law's greatest proponent, Sir Edward Coke, was handing down his most important decisions as judge and compiling his *Institutes of the Lawes of England* (the first volume of which was published in 1628), setting the stage for the ultimate predominance of the common law over statutory law in the country as a whole.

Second, the Virginia settlers, as is well known, had no particular political or legal differences with the English government and so would presumably have been comfortable with settled law in the form of England's statutes, whereas the Puritan settlers were clearly looking for certain kinds of legal flexibility that only the common law could provide. Indeed the first step in forming colonies more responsive to the common law than to statute was the acknowledgment that the legal requisites for ordering life might differ from place to place. In recognition of the differences that could be expected to arise between the colonies and England—having largely to do with climate, crop conditions, and the presence of indigenous peoples—England specified that the colonies' founders could make laws that would be suitable to the colony "as long as they were not contrary or repugnant to the laws and statutes of England."[13] As Mary Sarah Bilder explains, this language, found in almost every colonial charter, amounted to the development of a "transatlantic constitution" in which English subjects of the Crown living in the colonies might choose, depending on their circumstances and the expected outcome of their case, to be judged by the rules and regulations of colonial law or by the law as practiced and understood in England.[14] This notion was at the heart of a reconceptualization of the law that went from an insistence on the homogeneity of the law's subjects to an acceptance of their diversity, which held important consequences for how the law of banishment was applied and understood.

The Significance of Roger Williams

If the law was moving toward an acknowledgment of inevitable jurisdictional heterogeneity, religion was moving in the opposite direction. Traditionally the bounds of the parish as a designation for civil jurisdictions were coincident with those of the parish church, and that sameness among parishioners—in terms of religious faith and practice—produced its own powerful bonds. Indeed under the Act of Uniformity of 1559—so-called because its enactment was to encourage a uniformity of worship among Protestants in general—all Englishmen were required to attend church once a week in their own parishes, making the parish churches the central places of worship even for those who hewed to a different religious practice, such as the Puritans.[15]

In their own churches, moreover, including those in England and in the New World, the Puritans privileged homogeneity. As Patricia Caldwell explains, conversion in the Puritan church was less a matter of proclaiming one's faith—as it was in the Catholic Church—than of following a prescribed set of rules and narrating them in a formulaic way for public approval.[16] Indeed through conversion and prayer, Puritan church practice worked to produce homogeneous individuals—what the Puritans called a community of visible saints. Needless to say such homogeneity took on a heightened importance in New England as a result of the Puritans' relationship with England, which went from being a hostile environment under James I and Charles I, to a welcoming one under Cromwell, and back to a hostile one again following the restoration of Charles II. More to the point, the Puritans' impulse for leaving England and founding a new colony was to find a haven for just such like-minded, homogeneous individuals and link them inextricably to a certain place.[17]

In the midst of these antithetical forces—with the law moving toward jurisdictional heterogeneity and religion pushing back against it—banishment emerged as a particularly contested practice, especially in those cases in which the difference between religious and civil jurisdictions was at stake. Given that the governments in the Puritan colonies often blurred the lines between church and state, the difference between civil and religious jurisdictions was arguably at stake in every banishment order that was handed down. However, it was nowhere more visible than in the banishment of Roger Williams, who was exiled from the Massachusetts Bay Colony because of his controversial stand on the difference between the civil and the religious. Indeed the terms of Williams's banishment and the contest between church and state were played out, albeit in different ways and to differing degrees, in every banishment examined in this book, including that of Hutchinson, which, while covered in the previous chapter, occurred only after Williams's came to an end. But where Williams addressed the church/state division head-on, Hutchinson was somewhat removed from it, in part because after the Williams fiasco the Bay Colony authorities, civil and religious, were loath to let the contest emerge quite so saliently again. Hutchinson, then, is figured as a religious leader usurping religious authority when in fact she was offering a rival to the secular realm as well. Morton's banishment story also suffers from the suppression of certain aspects of the church/state divide, although in his case not because his banishment came after Williams's—it did not—but because he was not a Puritan. Thus while Morton clearly saw himself as offering a challenge to the very idea of mixing church and state in the way the Puritans did, his protest, even if it had been as explicitly concerned with the problem of jurisdictional overlap as Williams's was, would not have had a fraction of the same force.

Williams, then, in one sense is at the forefront of the banishment controversy. We might even say that the conflict between the emerging definition of legal jurisdictions as heterogeneous and the residual definition of religious jurisdiction as homogeneous was first played out in the banishment narratives written by Roger Williams and his erstwhile friend and interlocutor John Cotton over the validity of his banishment. In fact what I am calling Williams's banishment narrative is actually a series of narratives by both Williams and Cotton, with whom he engaged in a debate over his punishment that lasted for over fifteen years. They include Cotton's "The Letter of Mr. John Cotton" (1643), Williams's "Mr. Cotton's Letter Examined and Answered" (1644), Williams's *Bloody Tenent of Persecution* (1644), Williams's "Christenings Make Not Christians" (1645), "John Cotton's Answer to Roger Williams" (1647), Cotton's *Bloody Tenet Washed and Made White in the Blood of the Lamb* (1647), and Williams's *The Bloody Tenent Yet More Bloody* (1652). Not unknown to scholars of the period, these documents have nevertheless played a regrettably small role in reconstructions of the Bay Colony and of Williams's banishment, and as a result scholars have missed the fact that Williams's banishment, like so much else in early New England history, was centrally concerned not just with religious doctrine but with legal matters as well.[18]

The Dung Heap as Jurisdiction

Williams was infamous for his views on religious doctrine and caused quite a stir when he proclaimed that he could not worship in the Plymouth or Bay Colony churches because they were tainted. For the Puritan church in New England to be pure, Williams explained, it would have to separate entirely from the Anglican Church in England, and this, as it turned out, required a stricter form of practice than most of Williams's fellow Puritans were willing to accept. In a position first championed by Perry Miller, most scholars of the period have depicted Williams's position on church purity as uncompromising and have identified it as the leading factor in his banishment.[19] Scholars after Miller have quibbled about the details of Williams's stance but have largely followed him in maintaining a theological focus on the Williams/Cotton divide. Edmund Morgan links Williams's insistence on a pure church to Williams's belief that the church, in his own time, had been taken over by the Antichrist and notes that this belief led him to the "ultimate absurdity, that there could be no church at all."[20] Sacvan Bercovitch, although providing a necessary corrective to Miller's suggestion that Williams had abandoned the view of New England as the New Jerusalem, rereads Williams in the context of post-Reformation uses of religious typology.[21] For Jesper Rosenmeier, Williams's view of the separate and pure church was a result of his understanding of Christ's incarnation, while for Philip Gura, Williams's insistent separatism had less to do with doctrine than with disputes about church discipline.[22] More recently scholars have continued to weigh in on the issue of Williams's church/state separation. Teresa Toulouse, while not focused on the Cotton-Williams debate per se, stresses Williams's refusal to tolerate a visibly impure church—where saints and hypocrites would inevitably pray together—as a counterpart to the genuinely pure spiritual realm. Thus Williams, she writes, believed that "the tares and wheat should be entirely separated on this earth."[23] Viewing Williams through a similarly critical lens, Andrew Delbanco pinpoints his "overwhelming sense of sin" as the cause of his downfall, leading him to see the world as a "dung-heap" and preventing him from making the "compromise" required by the New England way.[24]

While illuminating on the question of religious purity, these assessments nevertheless make the mistake of overlooking or in some cases confusing Williams's views of the state with those of the spiritual realm. Although he did refer to the civil or secular world as a "dung-heap," Williams seems to have applied legal standards to it and embraced it in the end. Indeed his involvement with Sir Edward Coke early in his life and his interactions with the legal system later in life appear to have acquainted him with many aspects of the common law and made him not only privy to but also a major contributor in the debate on jurisdiction in his day. As an apprentice of Coke's, who admittedly never occupied an official position in the law and so probably did not acquire formal training in jurisdictional distinctions—there was a bewildering array of courts in his day that would have been difficult for anyone not professionally involved in the law to master—Williams clearly possessed an understanding of jurisdiction as a methodology for making sense of the world.[25] He would, for example, have seen Coke and his successors struggle with the complications of colonial subjects, redefine judicial boundaries, and reduce the plurality of judicial jurisdictions in order to consolidate power in the courts of the common law. In witnessing the exercise of legal jurisdiction, in other words, Williams would have learned to recognize and understand territorial as well as ideological borders and to appreciate the competing, heterogeneous ideas and identities they invoked.[26]

Never an advocate of a pure state, Williams, like his mentor Coke, believed that civil jurisdictions could no longer be coherent in the way they had been before internationalism and colonialism. The consequence of this, however, was not, as most commentators suggest, a rejection of them but rather a wholehearted embrace of them and an acknowledgment that their impurity was natural. Thus when he said that "the tares" and the "wheat" should not mix on earth, he meant only that they should not mix in earthly churches, not in the civil realm. In fact it was the separating kind of Puritans, who wanted nothing to do with the Anglican Church, who were nevertheless the first to agree that living in the world not only involved but also demanded nonseparation. In a well-known Puritan tract, *The Communion of Saincts.* printed in Amsterdam in 1607, Henry Ainsworth wrote, "but though we may have no communion with the wicked in their religion, nor any other evil action, against either table of Gods Law: yet in civill affayres we are taught of God to converse with them in space. As to eat and drink with them, buy and sell, make convenants of peace, shew kindness to them, put their estate, love them, relieve their wants, and receive from them for our own relief."[27] If the story of Williams's banishment was devoted in part to his struggle to convince the Puritans of the need to maintain a pure and homogenous church—by ridding themselves of impure congregations and when necessary praying by themselves outside of established congregations—it was equally a struggle to convince them of the need to acknowledge diverse identities in the civil sphere. If from a theological perspective his insistence on the purity of the visible church is seen as "absurd," as Morgan put it, a secular and legal perspective begins to uncover its sanity, for in holding fast to the inevitable impurity of the church in its earthly incarnation, Williams took his cue from the courts in which the impossibility of pure, that is to say homogenously populated and geographically contiguous, secular jurisdictions was being recognized.[28]

Jurisdictional Diversity

From the moment he landed in Boston in 1631, even if his more developed views about jurisdictions were not yet in evidence, Williams seemed bent on pitting one jurisdiction against another. Though he was welcomed to Boston by Governor Winthrop as a "godly minister" and soon after landing was offered the honor of serving the congregation there, Williams found himself forced to turn the job offer down because, as Winthrop noted, "[t]hey [members of the Boston church] would not make a public declaration of their repentance for having communion with the churches of English while they lived there."[29] From Boston, Williams then went to Salem, where at first he found the church's practices more conducive to his ends, although he ultimately found them disappointing and fled Salem for Plymouth. From Plymouth, where he remained for about two years, he returned, again in disappointment, to Salem, where he continued to preach but only to a small, handpicked group of "pure" Christians in a neighbor's home. With each removal in his quest for a truly "pure" and separatist church, Williams either implicitly or explicitly set in motion a rivalry between the towns that they had not experienced before (at least not in those terms) and thus caused the very sort of jurisdictional heterogeneity he so often said he found inevitable.

Similarly, with each removal, Williams also set in motion the very meddling by civil jurisdictions with sacred ones that he so deplored. In criticizing the impurity of the various congregations he was asked to serve, Williams set himself up as an unimpeachable religious authority over whom no one, including the autonomous churches he rejected as impure, had any control. The irony here is potentially infinite since in the midst of a conflict between Williams and the churches, there was literally nowhere to turn but to the civil authorities, in particular to the magistrates, who alone were seen as capable of deterring Williams from his divisive path. Thus when it was agreed that Williams would be taken on as minister at Salem after his denunciation of the Boston church, John Winthrop intervened by writing to John Endicott of Salem to "forbear to proceed till they had conferred about it."[30] Winthrop compounded the jurisdictional impropriety of this intervention when he mixed civil and sacred again by withholding land, which had been provisionally granted to Salem as a civic entitlement, to punish them further for their endorsement of Williams after the Boston church had effectively censured him.[31]

This only added fuel to Williams's fire: he was adamant that civil authorities stay away from church affairs and thus called for the total separation of church and state. It goes without saying that this was perceived by people on both sides of the divide—church and state—as threatening. Of course church authorities were given power over their own membership—largely by regulating conversion, as seen in the case of Hutchinson—and thus they were, because all church members were de facto members of the commonweal, in control of legal and political membership as well. Yet the magistrates were not to be outdone; they maintained their own supremacy by claiming control that was perhaps weaker but of a larger dominion—comprised of more than any one church or congregation but responsive to and ultimately in charge of them all. Thus when Salem the village was punished for what Salem the church did, Williams was furious. He gave voice to this fury in letters to Winthrop that expressly upbraided him for inserting civil authority where it did belong, but he nowhere more clearly stated what was at stake for him and for the civil polity than in his *Bloody Tenent of Persecution* (1644). In a passage where, as Michael Colacurcio notes, Williams drew out the facts of his own case in Salem in a more exaggerated way, Williams speculated about what would happen if civil and sacred were locked in an endless rivalry in which they vied for supremacy over each other for all time.[32] Williams wrote: "The magistrate chargeth the church to have made an unfit and unworthy choice, and, therefore . . . he suppresseth such an officer and makes void the church's choice. Upon this, the church complains against the magistrate's violation of her privileges given her by Christ Jesus, and . . . proceeds to excommunication against him. The magistrate . . . endures not such profanation of ordinances . . . and therefore . . . proceeds against such obstinate abuser's of Christ's holy ordinances in civil court of justice . . . and cuts them off by the sword."[33]

As Colacurcio suggests, the passage provides in broad outline some of the problems Williams had with the Boston magistrates when he was in Salem. Yet we take note of it here for a different reason: because it provides a telling example of how deeply consonant Williams's logic and rhetoric were with the common law. Comprised entirely of hypotheticals, the passage builds on the events of one scenario—the church complains about a magistrate—as they fold into those of another—the magistrate takes the church to court, and so on. Hypotheticals, of course, had a place in religious rhetoric as well as in the law, but the use of religious hypotheticals, I argue, usually took a typological form; the events of one scenario, from the Hebrew Bible, say, would presage the events of another, from the New Testament or from the Puritans' own day, that were virtually parallel to it. Williams's hypotheticals, however, move not from type to antitype but rather from cause to effect in a reciprocal and recursive manner, as if to reveal, through what lawyers often call the "slippery slope" approach, what could happen if the issue of the church-state rivalry were not decided once and for all.

Oddly enough, on this specific issue Williams did not take sides. Like his fellow Puritans, he believed church and state should remain separate, and he differed from them only in not giving the state, when push came to shove, the upper hand. Indeed Williams's belief about the separation of church and state was so widely shared by his fellow Puritans and so loudly trumpeted by his fellow leaders—most notably by Governor Winthrop, whose "Model of Christian Charity," written only one year before Williams arrived in the Bay Colony, made the precept foundational—that Williams was given every opportunity to rescind and recant his opinion. Indeed the events of Williams's banishment, as they unfolded on the ground, were marked by an extraordinary reluctance on the part of the authorities, civil and religious, to banish him as well as a high degree of legality, in which Williams was repeatedly called to testify before the magistrates, even though his sentence of banishment was ultimately pronounced without a trial. It is said that at the very end, just after Williams's sentence of banishment was passed by the general court, Governor Winthrop sent word to his friend to leave his house and so avoid capture by the authorities, who intended to make sure not only that he had departed the colony but also that he was shipped back to England, a fate that for the irascible Williams would surely have been worse than death.

Williams was in and out of court for roughly two years on a variety of charges before his banishment was ordered.[34] He was first called before the general court of the Massachusetts Bay Colony in December 1633 to reaffirm his allegiance to Charles I after writing a scathing attack on the colony's land practices. The next year he involved himself in two hot-button issues: he was vociferously on the side of requiring women to wear veils in church; and he was in the vanguard, along with John Endecott of Salem, in trying to ban the English flag because the cross so prominently displayed on it was deemed to be papistical. He was not called into court by the magistrates for his stand on either of these two issues, as far as is known, but his participation in them did not escape notice. The straw that broke the camel's back came only a few months later when, in April 1635, Williams began campaigning against the oath of loyalty to the governor that all male inhabitants of the colony who were older than sixteen were required to take. Williams had no problem with the oath per se, but he did not like that the oath ended with the words "so help me God," which he argued amounted to taking the Lord's name in vain if uttered by unregenerate souls. Only thinly veiled in Williams's objection to the oath, of course, was yet another attack on the ways the civil authorities had merged civil and secular realms, since the oath was intended only to bind people to the civil polity and yet impinged on their religious beliefs and, for Williams, their all-important consciences.

Williams continued to be given every opportunity to recant and revise his positions, providing us with an example of the longest prelude to banishment of those examined here. He appeared in court on July 8, 1635, and then again on October 8, 1635, and on both occasions the general thrust of the legal proceedings seemed to be aimed at giving him a chance to wiggle out of his pronouncements or getting him to change his mind. The court deployed Thomas Hooker, among others, to persuade Williams to be more moderate in all his views or at the very least to stop talking about them. But Williams characteristically refused, and the language of the banishment order that was handed down on October 9, 1635, reflects the magistrates' frustration with his refusal more than anything else. They wrote: "Whereas Mr. Roger Williams, one of the elders of the church at Salem, hath broached & divulged diverse new & dangerous opinions" and had refused to repent or retract them, "it is therefore ordered, that the said Mr. Williams shall depart out of this jurisdiction within six weeks." In the use of generalities and euphemisms such as "diverse new & dangerous opinions," the court, in this first celebrated banishment from the colony, seems to have been rather naive, making possible the inference that Williams was being punished for stating his beliefs, which was an offense that, as long as those opinions fell short of sedition, was not then or ever illegal in the Bay Colony. Despite the fact that the court quickly amended the statement to specify the charges against Williams, the impression that Williams was banished for matters of conscience has remained. Indeed as the following discussion of these more specific charges reveals, Williams's banishment, in part perhaps as a result of this early articulation of his sentence, revolves more centrally around language, rhetoric, and the license to speak and write as one chooses than any other banishment studied in these pages.

The first salvo fired in the direction of this claim was a treatise Williams wrote that directly questioned the legitimacy of the Bay Colony's boundaries. Williams's treatise on the Bay Colony's civil jurisdiction, which was written "at the request of Governor Bradford for his private satisfaction," has been lost, but the arguments he advanced in it have been preserved in a number of Bradford's other writings as well as in those of his contemporaries.[35] In brief, Williams was said to have denied the right of the Massachusetts Bay Colony to hold its lands by patent from the king.[36] For this he was charged with three violations of the law: (1) "that the king told a lie because in the patent he blessed god that was the first Christian prince that had discovered this land"; (2) "that the king had blasphemed for calling Europe Christendom or the Christian world"; and (3) "that he [Williams] said everyone who inhabits New England is under a sin of unjust usurpation on others' possession."[37]

Williams's challenge to the king's patent has been seen by most scholars as evidence of his sympathy for native rights.[38] There can be no doubt that due largely to the friendships he had developed with the Indians during his winter in Plymouth, Williams opposed the English practice of seizing ostensibly unclaimed Indian land. His *Key into the Language America* (1643), which includes an extensive Narragansett-to-English lexicon as well as his many favorable views of Indian society, is sufficient proof of that. But the challenge Williams posed to the king's patent was also part of his opposition to the mainstream Puritan view of the law of jurisdiction and should be seen in the light of Williams's participation in these jurisdictional reforms as well. The charter from James I that allowed the founders of the Massachusetts Bay Company to acquire the land that was to become the Bay Colony, for example, specified that they take only lands that were empty (which many of the Indians' lands seemed to be) and not already claimed by "another Christian power."[39] One could hardly imagine that the language of such a qualification would go unnoticed by Williams, who was well versed in the controversies surrounding sovereignty and jurisdiction of his day and felt that far from creating a legitimate civil law jurisdiction, the king had authorized the English to take New World lands by virtue of divine right and Christian universalism.[40]

Williams found the idea of Christian universalism, which included the absorption by the church of territories not previously claimed by a Christian monarch, abhorrent. For one thing it prefigured a purely Christian universe full of Christian nations, and nationalism, he believed, was not a property of the church. To this end he argued in his banishment narratives against the concept of Christendom, a subsidiary of Christian universalism, which held that wherever Christians lived was by definition a Christian place and conversely that everyone living in a Christian place was or should be a Christian. In his essay "Christenings Make Not Christians," Williams argued that Christianity was to be found in people and in the very small places—ideally the gathered churches of the Puritans—where they might congregate. "Civil alters according to the constitutions of peoples and nations," he wrote, "spiritual he hath engaged from the national in one figurative land of Canaan, to particular and congregational churches all the world over."[41] The significance of this assertion coincided with Williams's belief that nations and other legal jurisdictions not only were but also ought to be populated not by Christians alone but by diverse groups of people.

It was this belief—not about religion but about the law—that got him into trouble with John Cotton. For Williams, the law was jurisdictionally complex, a distinct and emergent category with the ability to influence his understanding of religion's place in the world. For Cotton, by contrast, law, no matter how secular, had its origins in religion and was impervious to change. For Williams, moreover, the law adapted to its subjects; for Cotton, subjects adapted to the law. From this view it followed that there could be for Cotton only one law and that if the inhabitants of a given jurisdiction were not already sufficiently homogenous, they would—and this included the Indians—soon become so, if not spiritually then temporally, as a result of abiding by the law.

Tasked with drafting a body of laws for the colony, which came to be known as *Moses His Judicials* and served as a template for the later *Body of*

Liberties, Cotton revealed the extent to which his belief in the need for a uniform and univocal law went well beyond his desire for political conformity between the churches. In drafting his code, Cotton turned to the Bible, a common place for Puritans to look for legal guidelines. But Cotton did not share his contemporaries' sense that they might "add to [the Bible] or . . . take from it, or . . . alter and change it" to fit their own needs.[42] Scriptural law, he wrote, "is of universall and perpetuall equitie, in all Nations, in all Ages."[43] The basis for Cotton's blanket adoption of scriptural law, which was so extreme that it required that the storehouses for foodstuffs in the Bay Colony be built according to the specifications for storehouses laid out in Deuteronomy, was his belief, which he shared with a number of Renaissance legal theorists, that the word of God was the intention of legislators made visible, literally.[44] The tautological quality of such a belief is best illustrated by one of Cotton's catechetical examples: "Quest: What is Sin?" he wrote. "Answer. Sin is the transgression of the Law."[45] Here the law seemingly invites not knowledge or understanding but obedience—a quality associated more commonly with one's religious as opposed to civic or legal duties.

Rhetorical Diversity

The jurisdictionally simplistic element of Cotton's theory of law emerges clearly within this paradigm, since for Cotton spiritual peace and achievement were tantamount to obedience, which in turn was tantamount to staying within the bounds. *Lex*, for Cotton, was profoundly tied to its etymological root, *ligando*, which means "binding," and was linked to his sense that the law was religious in nature and functioned not like a contractually agreed upon dictate but rather like a commandment. Thus Cotton believed that the magistrates and ministers of the Bay Colony were, simply by virtue of having been handed the mantle of power, as pure as were the judges in ancient Israel. It followed that the law that created jurisdictions, for Cotton, was not merely a part of the law but its very essence. "When God wraps us in with his Ordinances, and warms us with the life and power of them, as with wings, there is a Land of Promise," he wrote.[46]

Such a view of the law owes much not only to Cotton's faith but also to his adherence to a more generalized rhetoric of religion that taught readers to tease out meanings from texts they saw as being fixed and unalterable. The rhetorical project of the law, by contrast (and here I refer specifically to the

Anglo-American common law of the seventeenth century), taught the acquisition of meaning through the dialogical juxtaposition of texts—a method in which a given text, in the form of case law, for example, rewrote the ones that came before, if only ever so slightly. At stake in Williams's legal understanding and expression of banishment therefore was a different kind of person and a different kind of place than was specified by religious readers and inculcated in religious texts. Far from believing in a fixed and inalterable meaning, in other words, Williams believed in a shifting ground, and far from seeing New England as a divinely appointed place where inalterable meanings might prevail, he perceived it as just another human locality. After the biblical Canaan, Williams explained, God broke the mold. "Doubtless that Canaan Land was not a patterne for all lands," he wrote. "It was a none-such, unparalleled and unmatchable."[47] Having set Canaan aside for the Jews and seen it fail, as the Christians believed it had, God, according to Williams, seemed to have reconsidered not only the people he would choose to favor—this time it was to be the Christians, not the Jews—but also the model of state he had given them. Thus the land that was Israel—a unique instance of the overlay of geographical and spiritual jurisdictions—was transformed with the coming of Christ into a church without geographical coordinates. For Williams, this meant that the church, which continued to rule over the kingdom of God, had no earthly counterpart (this is why the church on earth would always be impure), and why the judges of Israel would have no earthly representatives.

For Williams, written law was not to be taken literally but only insofar as it "embodie[d] more or less directly and successfully the norms and force of the law."[48] The law, in other words, was for Williams a composite of what was written or expressed verbally and what was done or expressed nonverbally. In cultural terms we might also say that for Williams, written law was only one part of a legal nomos that included all kinds of collective customs, social patterns, and forms of human expression. The customs of Englishmen from time immemorial was the stuff on which English common law was built and what gave it its consensual basis.[49] Writing the law to account for and conform to people's customs also made the law organic and responsive to changing human needs. People in the same place might lead different lives, and people in different places might lead similar ones. In fact so central was this notion of rhetorical flexibility and practical responsiveness in the law that it became the arbiter of the law's validity. Thus, while Williams did not believe in the application of only one law for all the diverse people within a given jurisdiction, he did believe in applying the same law to everyone in the same or similar circumstances. In the course of his writings about banishment, he chastised Cotton for punishing him for doing something—namely practicing his religion as he saw fit—that he, Cotton, had done years before in England without suffering any consequence. In "persecuting of men," Williams wrote, "Cotton measures that to others, which himself when he lived in such practices, would not have had measured to himself."[50] This principle of reciprocity, in fact, not only had relevance for the art of rhetoric and persuasion but also formed the basis for a popular theory of justice in which, then as now, we are urged to make laws for others only after we imagine ourselves in their shoes.[51]

Population Diversity

Informed by this understanding of jurisdiction, Williams's writings do more than reflect his knowledge of the common law; they also engage with common-law modes of thinking and writing about social and political selves. Indeed like Coke, Williams took a historicist view of the world in which the customs of "the people"—a taxonomically mutable category that proved crucial to the common law—are considered to be the source of law and are held in higher regard than the king. Looking back to what Coke called "time immemorial," law, defined as custom or use, becomes a matter not of telling but of retelling, for in the system of precedent that Coke and other common lawyers prized, each case was a revision of the one that came before. Not even in his *Institutes*—his monumental project to modernize the system of English laws—did Coke diverge from the written record; he only rewrote the work of the medieval lawyer Thomas de Littleton. This is why even in his own day the first volume of his groundbreaking *Institutes* came to be known as *Coke on Littleton.*[52]

In terms of the debate between homogeneous and heterogeneous jurisdictions, the logic of custom at the root of the common law bears repeating: if the law was to be based on people's practices—a belief to which all the common lawyers of Williams's day adhered—and if people's practices differed, then the population of legal subjects would inevitably be diverse. For Williams, this raised serious questions about the purpose behind ridding a given jurisdiction of those who differed from the norm, the so-called undesirables. But the inevitable diversity of a given population cast doubt for Williams not only on the validity of banishing certain people—and not others—but also on those who, like Cotton, did the banishing. Cotton, Williams wrote, was "the procurer of my sorrowes," and Williams was "afflicted and persecuted by Himself."[53] If, as

Williams had argued, the banisher was no purer than the person he banished, then who was Cotton to judge? "I desire it may be seriously reviewed by all men," he wrote, "whether the Lord Jesus be well pleased that one, beloved in him, should (for no other cause than shall presently appeare) be denied the common aire to breath in, and a civil cohabitation upon the same common earth."[54] Put another way, Williams seemed to wonder whether Cotton thought he was a better judge than Jesus.

Cotton's answer to Williams's query was a rebuke of Williams and also a denial of his own agency and responsibility for the banishment that stemmed directly from his understanding of how homogeneity in a community worked. In his first letter to Williams after his banishment, he explained that he had played no part in Williams's banishment. " I indevour to shew you the sandinesse of those grounds," he wrote, "out of which you have *banished yours* from the fellowship of all the Churches in these Countries."[55] Cotton argued here that he could not have banished Williams because Williams banished himself. At the root of this claim was Cotton's belief that in insisting on the absolute separation of the churches, Williams had removed himself from community with others in prayer, making it unnecessary for anyone else to remove him.[56] But when Williams pointed out that while he (Williams) had voluntarily "withdraw[n] from the *Churches*," he had not opted to leave the *colony*—once again making the claim that religion and law were not the same—Cotton sought refuge from responsibility by claiming that in administering the punishment he was not alone. "I told him, I had not hasted forward the sentence of civill banishment: and that what was done by the Magistrates in that kinde, was neither done by my Counsell, nor consent."[57] This denial, however, which verged on self-effacement, went even further. Cotton claimed not only that he had not offered his "counsel nor consent" to aid in the banishment but also that he had interceded to prevent it, although admittedly to no avail. "Truly (said I) I pitie the man, and have already interceded for him, whilest there was any hope of doing good. . . . But now . . . you know they are generally so incensed against his course, that it is not your voyce, nor the voyces of two, or three more, that can suspend the Sentence."[58] According to Cotton, the banishment, in short, was a product of consensus, a conclusion that coincided with his view "that God's people, and godly persons are all one."[59] In the face of unanimity—a natural product of Cotton's sense of the homogenous community—a single voice of protest, such as his own, would by definition be meaningless.

If Cotton absolved himself of responsibility by hiding behind a constructed notion of a religiously inspired majority, Williams looked to the legislative history to prove that, contrary to Cotton's impression, the consensus over his banishment was not natural but forced and that not all people—certainly not even all legislators—spoke with one voice. Williams reported "[t]hat some gentlemen that did consent to his Sentence, have solemnly testified, and with teares since confessed to himselfe, that they could not in their soules have been brought to have consented to the Sentence of his Banishment, had not Mr. Cotton in private given them advice, and counsell, proving it just, and warrantable to their consciences."[60] In personal conversations with several of the magistrates, it seemed, Williams obtained all the evidence he needed to refute Cotton's assumption that a true consensus had been reached, proving once again that the population of a given jurisdiction, even a jurisdiction composed exclusively of saints, was inevitably diverse.

The jurisdiction's social diversity made banishment meaningless in other ways as well. For one thing, there was no telling how many people might require banishing. If the world, Williams wrote, was "divided into 30 parts, 25 of that 30 have never yet heard of the name of Christ."[61] The implications of this calculus were clear: to purify the earth's jurisdictions would require banishments on a scale never seen before, for if every evildoer was to be punished for his sins and those without Christ were the greatest evildoers of them all, then "how many thousands and millions of men and women in the severall Kingdomes and governments of the World must be cut off from their Lands, and destroyed from the Cities"?[62] Furthermore, with the bar for banishment set so low, how, Williams asked, could one be sure that the right people had been banished? Even the Scriptures acknowledged that errors in banishment had been made. As a case in point Williams referred Cotton to the story of Jonah and the whale, which for him embodied a lesson about how imprecise a tool banishment could be. If Jonah, who was banished from his ship by being thrown overboard, was cast out for his sins, then that alone, Williams argued, would be "sufficient ground for Magistrates . . . to throw overboard, put to death, not only hereticks, Blasphemers, and Seducers &c. but the best of Gods Prophets or Servants for neglect of their duty, Ministry &c. which was Jonah's case."[63] As Williams explained, although Jonah had neglected his duty at first, he turned out to be a great man and one of God's chosen, a career path whose significance could not have been lost on Cotton as he watched Williams, like Jonah, turn the affliction of his banishment around to create a new and thriving colony in Rhode Island.

Drawing on examples from the Bible, law, and history, Williams devoted hundreds of pages to trying to prove to Cotton and to the rest of the world that banishment—his in particular of course—was wrong and useless. His main argument was that banishment was premised on an outdated and inappropriately religious understanding of civil jurisdiction and that it tried to distinguish among people who were different on the mistaken assumption that some number of them could be gathered into a community of self-similar "saints," living together in a saintly place. To each of Williams's examples, however, Cotton offered a counterexample—also drawn from the Bible, history, and the law—and despite Williams's efforts to win him over, he remained unconvinced.

Print and Place

If scriptural reference, law, and history failed to influence Cotton, there was one tool that may in the end have served Williams better than any other: his ability to state his opinions, sustain them, and have them disseminated in print. In his narratives of banishment, Williams seems to have achieved in form what he could not achieve in substance—a kind of reinstatement in the Bay Colony. Through his use of the printed word, Williams proved that individuals were not by definition tied to their place of residence or origin but were, like texts, movable and materially unsettled. Christopher D'Addario notes in this regard that "while the delayed rhythms of [their] exchange reveal the distance at which . . . [Williams and Cotton] fought their battle, the place in which they fought it, the bookshops of Interregnum London, signals to some extent for whose minds they struggled."[64]

In addition, in his extensive retelling and recirculating of his banishment through narrative, Williams, like Coke before him, demonstrated that the law, seen by Cotton as uniform, was subject to alteration. In his discussion of the controversy over the printing of the common law—a form of law that had long "abstained from publishing," as the barrister William Hudson observed—Richard Ross notes its contrary tendencies, on the one hand, to fix debate and, on the other, to open it to variation. As a legal matter, he explains, the printing of the law "nationalized the themes and vocabulary of complaint," but "as a literary matter, [it] . . . offered a core of formulae for repetition and variation."[65] In recasting his case in printed form, Williams did nothing less than readjudicate it, moving it from one jurisdiction, the Bay Colony's courts, to another, the reading public.

The first and most obvious end to which Williams put his narrative was in making a mockery of the gag order that accompanied his banishment. Far from setting limits on the voicing of his opinions in an "arrogant and impetuous way," the seventeen-year-long correspondence between Cotton and Williams gave his ideas a new airing. To be sure, the fact that Williams used his banishment as a kind of bully pulpit to redefine his crime and his identity came as something of a surprise to Cotton, who assumed that he, like the Apostle John—banished by Emperor Domitian to the Island of Patmos for advocating Jesus' gospel—would not complain. "Where by the way," Cotton wrote, "[one] may easily discern the vast difference between the spirit of Mr. Williams, and of John the Apostle, in relating their sufferings by way of banishment: John was a beloved Disciple . . . yet he maketh no expresse mention of his Banishment, not of the howling Wildernesse, nor of frost, and snow, and such winter miseries: But (saith he) I was in the Isle of Patmos for the testimony of Jesus." Unlike the reticent John, Cotton wrote, "Mr. Williams . . . aggravateth the banishment of such an one as himself, by all the sad exaggerations, which wit and words could well paint it out withal. . . . So deeply affected the sonnes of men can be in describing their own sufferings for themselves, and their own wayes, above what the children of God be in their farre greater sufferings for the Testimony of Jesus."[66]

Cotton objected not only to the way in which Williams used banishment to engender narrative rather than to prevent it—all of which was in violation of the model offered by the Apostle John—but also to the actual publication of Cotton's opinions by Williams for which he had never given permission. Throughout the controversy between the two men, Cotton repeatedly claimed that what he had said previously to Williams either in person or in written form was intended for his ears alone. The correspondence that has come to be known as the "Letter of Mr. Cotton" was a case in point; Cotton had sent it to Williams privately after reading a copy of his *Bloody Tenent*, so when Cotton saw it in print several years later in the body of Williams's reply, retitled "Mr. Cotton's Letter Examined and Answered," he complained. "How it came to be put in print I cannot imagine," he wrote. "Sure I am it was without my privity."[67]

This ability of words to make their way into print without prior authorization is literalized in two crucial scenes of writing depicted in Williams's work, both of which suggest how words could be made to defy the homogeneity of people and boundaries implicit in banishment. The first concerns the fiction with which Williams began his *Bloody Tenent of Persecution* in which he attributed his arguments to a prisoner of Newgate who, like Williams, was punished for following the dictates of his conscience. That Williams found it necessary to attempt to obscure his own authorship of the volume is suggestive, especially since his true identity was revealed almost as soon as the book came out. But it is the story of how the prisoner's letter came to be written that captures our attention here because it shows once again how banishment, which might rid a community of the physical presence of certain people, could not prevent the dissemination of their words. "The Author of these arguments," Williams explained, "(against persecution) (as I have been informed) being committed by some then in power, close prisoner to Newgate, for the witnesse of some truths of Jesus, and having not the use of Pen and Inke, wrote these arguments in Milke, in sheets of Paper, brought to him by the Woman his keeper, from a friend in London, as the stopples of his Milk bottle."[68] As Ann Myles has pointed out, the medium of milk stands in stark contrast to the blood with which Cotton was said to write (as in the *Bloody Tenent*), but the significance of the use of milk goes much further, for ink made out of milk would have been invisible.[69] "In such Paper written with Milk," Williams continued, "nothing will appear, but the way of reading it by fire being knowne to his friend who received the papers, he transcribed and kept together the Papers, although the Author himselfe could not correct, nor view what himselfe had written."[70] Not only did the author have to conceal his text—writing on the sly, as it were—but also what he wrote was imperceptible as writing until it reached his friend, which made his letter an undeniable embodiment of the power of words to re-create themselves anew with each new reader, no matter where the writer or reader might be located.

The extraordinary scene of this writing, in which the words of the prisoner not only make it out of his prison cell to find a larger audience but also transcend the need for pen and ink, has its counterpart in the second demonstration of the extrajurisdictional quality of words: Williams's description of his own process of composition in the *Bloody Tenent Yet More Bloody*. "God is a most holy witness," he wrote, "that these meditations were fitted for publike view in change of roomes and corners, yea sometimes upon occasion of travel in the country . . . in variety of strange houses, sometimes in the fields, in the midst of travel: where he hath been forced to gather and scatter his loose thoughts and papers."[71] In this passage Williams showed not only that words can emerge from a prison—the most bounded of environments—but also that they do not need the fiction of homogeneously constituted jurisdictions to be formed or disseminated.

The detachability of words from place referenced in Williams's printed prose reflects the overturning of old assumptions about print and orality in general. No longer could it be said, for example, by the mid-seventeenth century when Williams was publishing, that oral expression, which the preacher Cotton naturally favored, was necessarily fleeting; in fact, as Cotton learned when he struggled to reconstitute his Lincolnshire parish in Boston, Massachusetts, orality catered to a specific audience rooted in a specific place. The printed word, conversely, while bound within the covers of a given text and formerly seen as immutable—like the Bible's connection to the word of God—was proving in some ways to be more mobile even than the spoken word and, by virtue of its increasingly global circulation, capable of being rendered new by readers far from its original context. That works printed in England provided the bulk of the colonists' reading matter was proof positive that texts, like people, could speak to multiple audiences at the same time. In fact, in response to an order of 1588 to search for and commit to prison the authors and printers of heretical material, presses became movable. Williams may have known this better than most, having chosen the notorious printer Gregory Dexter to print both *A Key into the Language* (1643) and *The Bloody Tenent,* for Dexter was known to use a movable press and had on several occasions only narrowly escaped arrest for his publications by fleeing quickly with his press in tow.

The printed word also proved detachable from place in ways that transcended the physical site of the book or of the printing press. Through the model of the common law put forward by Williams in his argument against banishment, there came into being a sense of writing as rewriting—that gradual accretion of meaning over time through which the common law made sense of past, present, and future experience. This system of writing, based on precedent, found its way into the rhetorical method Williams used to talk about his banishment. For Williams, the legal punishment of banishment was the occasion for a continuous retelling of the circumstances and motivations that had prompted it. Each time he told it, he appeared to find some new angle, some new articulation that redefined the crime as well as his own and his accuser's identity. In Williams's retelling, in fact, Cotton went from being the accuser to being the "defender," a designation given him by Williams that undermined the strength and popularity of Cotton's position but that Cotton nevertheless adopted in several of his own replies.

In writing by rewriting, moreover, Williams seized interpretive control of Cotton's work in much the same way Coke had done with Littleton. Formally the narratives Williams wrote and ultimately induced Cotton to write were restatements and recharacterizations of the two men's original positions. For example, Williams's lengthy "Mr. Cotton's Letter Examined and Answered," as its title suggests, reprinted Cotton's original letter in its entirety and constituted itself as new by replying to each and every point Cotton made. Cotton's "Reply to Mr. Williams His Examination" also duplicated Cotton's original letter but included a copy of Williams's response to it in addition to his own new commentary on that response, as is evident in chapter titles such as "To His Chapter 1." In addition, while Williams's *Bloody Tenent* departed from this rigid textual reciprocity in presenting itself as a dialogue between two allegorical figures, Truth and Peace, Cotton resumed the imitative structure with his *Bloody Tenent Washed*, which replicated Williams's *Bloody Tenent* chapter by chapter. Given the form of their exchange, it is not surprising that fully half of each man's narrative was devoted to a reprinting of the other man's words, albeit in a slightly different context. Although Cotton did not shrink from using this form of alternating restatement himself, the results were not always to his liking. He objected repeatedly to Williams's reiteration of his words, claiming that even though he had restated them, which would lead one to believe that they were unobjectionable, he had nevertheless misinterpreted them. Thus even as Cotton quoted Williams, who was quoting him in an apparently endless regression, he punctuated these reiterations with phrases such as "It was farre from my meaning," "my words are plaine," "suppose I had meant," "to this purpose was my speech to him," and "my words out of which he gathereth this observation are misreported."[72] Cotton even goes so far as to note the rhetorical manipulation of which Williams was capable in not merely restating but on occasion omitting several of his words. "He doth very well, and wisely to expresse the Grounds upon which I said he banished himself with an &c. for he knows that if he had related my whole sentences in my own words, he had cut himself from all opportunitie of pleading with me the cases of his Civill Banishment."[73]

Cotton's charge—that in Williams's hands his words, though undeniably his, were nevertheless distorted—only confirms the genius of Williams's rhetorical method since it proves that words, like people, are never the same. Williams, of course, was a rigid typologist in his own way, but he nevertheless seemed to appreciate that context made a difference and could make even the Bible a fluid force in history. For Williams, the preeminent example of this was the situation of the Puritans in the Bay Colony. Like-minded in their faith, or seemingly so, they nevertheless failed to constitute a homogenous community. In a final illustration of the inevitability of difference, even between Puritans,

Williams reduced his argument to a personal level, pointing to the friendship he and Cotton had nurtured over the years and that should have, despite all their theological differences, given them reason to love each other. While invoking his own fondness for Cotton and the mutual sympathy between friends, Williams chided Cotton for not being more understanding but at the same time recalled the power of reciprocity to do justice. "Had his soul been in my soul's case," Williams wrote of Cotton, "exposed to the miseries, poverties, necessities, wants, debts, hardships of sea and land, in a banished condition, he would, I presume, reach forth a more merciful cordial to the afflicted."[74]

This uncharacteristically emotional appeal, however, undid itself almost as soon as it was uttered, for the truth, as everyone would have known, was that Cotton *had* been in Williams's shoes and *had* experienced the "hardships of sea and land, in a banished condition," for had not he, like Williams, been banished from England? In fact, was not banishment a nearly universal experience for people in the Bay Colony? From a religious point of view, the answer was undeniably yes—they had all left England, willingly or not, to take up life in exile—and yet even this universality, Williams implied, was not enough to make him and Cotton or any other two or more banished Puritans sufficiently similar to create a homogenous jurisdiction out of their living space. From a legal point of view, the similarities between Puritans in New England were an illusion propped up by a religious framework that had no real world counterpart, not even the universal experience of being banished. What good was banishment, Williams seems to have asked in a final moment of irony, if after all else failed, it was incapable of providing the homogeneity of identity or place that Cotton sought?

In the end, Williams's writings on banishment issued a general challenge to the Puritan community to define the basis on which they claimed to be homogeneous and then, on the basis of that homogeneity, claimed jurisdictional legitimacy. Initially the authorities had pointed to a religious self-similarity, but if this had served the ends of church formation, it failed as a basis for civil jurisdiction under the pressure of Williams's attacks. While Anne Hutchinson raised the possibility that religious uniformity was an illusion (and did so, notably, just a few months after Williams's banishment), Williams preempted her by asking whether religion, uniform or not, was an appropriate or even desirable goal for civil jurisdictions. In the face of such a claim, the Puritan authorities had to reassess their recourse to banishment, for ridding the community of any visible religious difference would not address the question

Williams raised, which was how to deal with difference in an inevitably diverse civil sphere.

This left the Puritans looking for strictly legal grounds for asserting their homogeneity. If the Puritans were not religiously homogeneous and could no longer legitimate their civic or legal community on the basis of a religious homogeneity, as Williams argued, then what about other, more secular criteria? Might they constitute a homogeneous jurisdiction based solely on their legal beliefs or ties? Their efforts to find such common ground left them arguing that they were colonial subjects who had all crossed the Atlantic to start their own community. But once they invoked these criteria—of a shared colonialism and transatlanticism—they became vulnerable to others who, like the Quakers, could claim similarity in this arena but maintain difference in all others. The story of how the Quakers' response to their banishment made room in the Puritans' conception of community for a certain degree of political and legal diversity as well as a religious one is taken up in the next chapter.

CHAPTER 3

"To Test Their Bloody Laws"

I dare take upon me . . . to proclaim to the World, in the name of
our Colony, that all Familists, Antinomians, Anabaptists, and other
Enthusiasts shall have free Liberty to keep away from us.
—Nathaniel Ward, "The Simple Cobbler of Agawam"

THE QUAKERS' RESPONSE to the use of banishment as a punishment in Puritan New England was, more than that of any other individual or group who came before or after them, calculated to achieve certain legal and political ends. With an almost military precision that entailed planning the place and time of their border crossings, the Quakers came into the Bay Colony with a consciousness of how their presence within the jurisdiction would challenge the existing legal order. In fact the Puritans referred to the Quakers' entry into and presence within New England during those early years of settlement, from 1656 to 1661, as an "invasion"—a term that was reappropriated by the Quakers as a badge of honor even as they dismissed it as prejudicial and extreme.

From one perspective the idea that the Quakers were invading New England seemed improbable: how could a small number—a trickle really—of newly minted Quakers constitute an "invasion" of any kind?[1] After all, aside from a few who reportedly ran naked through the streets, they were law-abiding and prayerful, and like the Puritans, they wanted only to live according to the dictates of their consciences. The Puritans, however, who had been deluged with anti-Quaker information before their arrival, were led to believe that the Quakers would behave raucously and destructively, like the Anabaptists and other so-called enthusiasts, who had stormed the German city of

Munster more than a century before and are named in Nathaniel Ward's litany in the epigraph above.[2]

That the banishment of the Quakers was the most violent of the banishments studied here, and that its violence ultimately turned the tide of popular opinion against banishment as a punishment, only suggests how powerful a subtext the Anabaptist takeover of Munster remained throughout the Quaker "invasion" of the Bay Colony. If the Puritans assumed that the Quakers were like the Anabaptists, in other words, they had good reason to fear them, for the Anabaptists had ushered in a reign of terror in Munster that utterly transformed that city and lasted for nearly a year and a half, from January 1534 to June 1535. In two waves, the first under the leadership of Jan Matthys and the second under John Leiden, the Anabaptists took the town by force and deposed the magistrates in order to introduce the practice of adult baptism and communal theocracy. In April 1534, after only four months in charge, Jan Matthys was deposed, again by means of military force, by his rival, Leiden, after whose installation as "king" things took a turn for the worse. By Leiden's order Matthys's head was displayed on a pole and his genitals on the city's gates. Under Leiden, moreover, polygamy was allowed (Leiden had sixteen wives, one of whom was supposedly beheaded in the marketplace). Needless to say, the Munster massacre (also known as the Munster uprising or rebellion) did not end well for the residents of Munster or for the Anabaptists. After the town was retaken by the ousted Catholic bishop, the Anabaptists were killed and their bodies stored in cages that hung from the steeple of St. Lambert's Church.

If the shadow of the Anabaptists hung over the Quakers as they entered the Bay Colony, the reality of their entering was quite different. Not only did the Quakers lack the numbers the Anabaptists had, but they also lacked the type of radical religious agenda that impelled the Anabaptists to cause the kind of damage they did. There was more legitimacy to the analogy made between the Hutchinsonians and the Anabaptists of Munster by the Puritan authorities some twenty years earlier, since at least those two groups of so-called heretics shared a more clearly radical, and to the Puritans politically unsettling, belief in revelation. Indeed it was Hutchinson's admission of her own revelation that led Governor Winthrop to conclude "that the Court did clearly discerne, where the fountain was of all our distempers, and the Tragedy of Munster (to such as had read it) gave just occasion to feare the danger we were in."[3] In addition, though the Quakers came, as their leader George Fox urged, to spread "the sound of Truth . . . abroad," this first wave of Quakers did not, like their descendants who settled in New Jersey and Pennsylvania a century later, draw vast numbers of people to their faith or threaten to shake the Puritan grounds of government.[4] In fact the few converts they made tended to reside in the former Dutch colonies on Long Island or in Williams's religiously tolerant Rhode Island, with only a small number in Plymouth and the Bay Colony. Yet, as has been the case with so many other banished individuals or groups, it has generally been maintained by literary and social historians that the Quakers came to the Bay Colony to challenge Puritan religious beliefs, expressed themselves through a primarily religious rhetoric, and were seen as religious rivals by the Puritans.[5] This emphasis on the Quakers' religion has persuaded even legal historians to see the Quakers' criminal presence through a religion lens, making "these Quaker cases," as the historian William Nelson wrote, "unsurprising."[6]

However, the Quaker cases—in which the Quakers were banished or, more precisely, were tried for entering and later for refusing to leave the colony—*were* surprising. Examining the narratives they and others wrote about their stay in New England, including George Bishop's *New England Judged by the Spirit of the Lord* (1703), Francis Howgill's *Popish Inquisition* (1659), Humphrey Norton's *New England's Ensigne* (1659), and John Norton's *New England Rent* (1660), reveals where those surprises lie. Specifically it can be argued that even given their concern with minute differences over notions of grace, the practice of the Quakers' faith was far less important to the Quakers than their alternative view of community formation and of legal membership, which in contrast to that of the Puritan authorities, insisted on the inclusion of political resistance and dissent.

The threatening potential of this insistence is easy to appreciate in any context—no legal or political community sets out to embrace its detractors or dissenters, not even democratic ones—but it was especially threatening to the Puritans of the 1650s, who were experiencing disruptions to their government, both good and bad, of an unprecedented nature. Indeed while it may at first seem odd to view this decade through the lens of the Quaker banishments, to do so in the end proves a new and remarkably coherent strategy for understanding how these upheavals in religion and the law might have been read by contemporaries on both sides of the Atlantic.

From a religious perspective, which unquestionably informed the legal one, the Quakers came at a bad time for the Puritans, as seen in the analogy made to the Munster uprising. The point needs to be stressed because despite the Puritans' fear that the Quakers would do to their colony what the Anabaptists did to Munster, the reason for the ferocity of the Puritan response to the Quakers was not obvious; not only were the Quakers not as fearsome as they were made out to be, in other words, but the 1650s were times of religious triumph for the Puritans in many respects. The beheading of Charles I and the installation of Oliver Cromwell as lord protector were welcomed by the Puritans as a dream come true. The Reformation of the Anglican Church, of which they were the instigators, had come to pass, and as Francis Bremer has written, "[t]he example of their 'city on a hill' was being followed."[7]

Nevertheless at the end of the civil wars in England there was no consolidation of Puritan power as such. As many scholars have noted, the opening provided by the king's death for the rise of the reformed religion had ended in a free-for-all by the multiple and varied reformist sects, in which the Presbyterians came out on top. The Presbyterians offered an alternative that many partial to if not outright members of the reform church preferred to that of the Puritans, against whom resentment and resistance had been building throughout the 1640s. Starting at the end of the 1630s and continuing throughout the 1640s, a number of reformers or reformist sympathizers had made trips to the New England colonies to witness the success of reformed religion but had returned to England disappointed by what they saw. Lord Saye and Sele, for example, was shocked to discover the extent to which Puritan congregations controlled the membership of the Puritan commonwealth; instead of allowing churches the power to determine membership in the civil polity, he believed that legal membership should follow the rules of aristocratic and hereditary right, not religious purity.[8] Similar complaints were leveled by other "friends of the Colony," including Hugh Peter and Thomas Weld, ambassadors whom the colony had sent to England, and Governor Winthrop's son Stephen, who was a colonel in the parliamentary army and one of Cromwell's closest advisers. Most vocal of these critics, however, were the Presbyterians, who found the Puritans' practice of restricting the franchise to church members and even then not to all church members but only to those who qualified as "visible saints," as they were called, to be in violation of the civil liberties guaranteed to all Englishmen.

One reason the Puritans may have reacted at such a fever pitch to the Quakers was that, like the Presbyterians, the Quakers positioned themselves as defenders of the civil liberties of Englishmen. Unlike the Presbyterians, however, the Quakers were on the scene in New England, and their presence may have reminded the Puritans that though few in number, they were not alone. The reminder that the Puritans had enemies back home in England may also have come as more of a shock than it might have at another time, since the

1650s, under Cromwell's rule, were proving to be relatively peaceful for them. Cromwell, of course, was sympathetic to their needs as Congregationalists, and they felt for the first time since the colony had been founded that they had some influence in the highest ranks of the English government. They also benefited from an unofficial policy of benign neglect during these years. With so many in England preoccupied with the regicide and new government, few bothered to worry about the autonomy of the colonies or threaten the legitimacy of their charter, as had been the case during the banishments of Morton, Hutchinson, and Williams in the previous decades. One of the biggest threats posed by the Quakers, then, was increased communication between the colonies and the English government. With the Quakers in their midst, unwelcome news about the colonists' hierarchical practices was getting back to England more quickly than the Puritans would have liked, and while Cromwell was a friend, he was also critical of extreme sectarianism, having already come down hard on Fifth Monarchy men and Unitarians for that reason.

A final piece of the puzzle that may help us understand the Puritan response to the Quakers can be found in the Bay Colony's relationship with its Dutch neighbors during these years. Tensions with the Dutch in New York ran high throughout the 1640s, and though the Bay Colony was less immediately threatened than were the Bible commonwealths of New Haven and Connecticut, the Bay Colony was nevertheless involved militarily and financially. If the Dutch continued to encroach on their Puritan allies in the colonies to the south of them, the Bay colonists would continue to be called on to provide money and soldiers, all of which they could little afford with mounting Indian troubles of their own. Fortunately, Cromwell, who had proved relatively unconcerned when it came to the Puritans' forms of government and church practices, had been a staunch defender of their borders against the Dutch and had provided military aid. But as the 1650s wore on and Cromwell's hold on the government weakened, less aid was available, and when Oliver Cromwell was succeeded by his son Richard in 1658, it virtually came to an end. The Dutch, of course, would have remained a threat unrelated to that of the Quakers had the Quakers, who found the Dutch far more accommodating than the Puritans, not begun to move to some of the Dutch-held outposts on Long Island, from which they continued to travel north to Massachusetts Bay.

For these and other complicated reasons, the Quakers, who arrived on the shores of Massachusetts Bay in admittedly small numbers, were met from the start with a high degree of alarm and an unprecedented effort to mobilize the law against them. Indeed the story of the Quaker presence in the Massachusetts Bay Colony is largely of Puritan lawmaking and of the Quakers' legal protest against it, all of which emanated from the many efforts that were made to banish them. Thus when Ann Austin and Mary Fisher, the first two Quakers to enter the Bay Colony, arrived on board the *Swallow* in the Boston harbor in July 1656, their first concern was to resist the application of the law, which if it did not yet call for their removal, had immediate and harsh consequences for them. On the strength of no more than á suspicion, Austin and Fisher were confined on board ship while their boxes were searched for heretical books and papers. Once found, these books were burned and the women committed to prison for five weeks until the *Swallow* was ordered to return them to Barbados—the Quaker outpost in the West Indies. Knowing little about the Quakers but fearing much, the Puritans felt these harsh measures were authorized by the colony's general laws against heretics, which prescribed the death penalty for those worshipping "any other God but the Lord God" or for "reproaching the holy religion of God" and prescribed banishment for those who should try "to subvert and destroy the Christian Faith and Religion, by broaching and maintaining any damnable Heresies."[9] As it turned out, not one of these activities was sufficiently in evidence to support the Puritans in their campaign against the Quakers, and the heresy prosecutions against Austin, Fisher, and others soon proved ineffectual. Worth noting too is that any initial enthusiasm the Puritans may have had for pursuing the Quakers as heretics under the terms of the heresy law may have been tempered by the memory of Anne Hutchinson's trial, in which the prosecution for heresy provided her—from the Puritan point of view—with a regrettable chance to speak her mind and counter the Puritans' legal arguments with legal arguments of her own. Failing to find evidence of any specific heresy, the Puritans made an effort to identify the Quakers as witches, but the search for tokens on their bodies proved fruitless time after time.

Had Austin and Fisher been the only Quakers to enter the Bay Colony, the Quaker "invasion" would almost certainly have fizzled. But in the absence of any legal remedy against them, more Quakers arrived in the Bay Colony, and more questionable punishments against them were meted out. Two days after Austin and Fisher left the colony, eight more Quakers, among them Christopher Holder and John Copeland, arrived and were imprisoned for eleven weeks. At this point not only did the religious agenda of these strangers remain uncertain, but also their correspondence from within prison with Samuel Gorton, a heretic who had previously been banished from the

Bay Colony for the vaguest of reasons, served to muddle further their religious identity.[10] It is little wonder, then, that while these individuals were still in prison, the Puritans conspicuously shifted their attention away from trying to discern the nature of their religious beliefs and focused on the making of a law specifically against them, a law that, like the one against the Jesuits and the Anabaptists, targeted them by name. The law passed in 1656 began with the words "Whereas there is a cursed sect of heretics lately risen up in the world which are commonly called Quakers."[11]

This effort to target the Quakers with a separate law soon backfired largely because the Quakers were difficult to identify, aside from those men who kept their hats on during religious services and others who let slip a tell-tale "thee" or "thou." So the Puritans set about making new and better laws in an increasingly urgent effort to rid the colony of them. On October 14, 1657, for example, a law was passed targeting anyone who "knowingly brought a Quaker into the jurisdiction," by requiring the forfeiture of one hundred pounds and a fine of forty shillings for every hour a Bay Colony resident entertained a Quaker. This law also provided that on the first offense a Quaker "have one of his ears cut off . . . and for the second offense shall have his other ear cut off . . . and every woman Quaker . . . shall be severely whipped, and so also for her coming again she shall be alike used . . . and for every Quaker, he or she, that shall a third time herein again offend, they shall have their tongues bored through with a hot iron." On May 19, 1658, yet another anti-Quaker law proscribed the holding of Quaker meetings, and on October 19, 1658, a fourth and final law was enacted threatening Quakers in the colony with hanging and was accompanied, most importantly, by an order that banished them "on pain of death."[12]

Making the Quakers' presence within the colony a capital crime was obviously a desperate move. Banishing them on pain of death not only leveled the harshest possible penalty on the Quakers but also violated one of the Puritans' proudest legal achievements, which was to reform English common law by reducing the number of crimes that warranted capital punishment. England had a long list of capital crimes, while the Bay Colony had few. In light of this reform, then, we can begin to see how the pain-of-death provision against the Quakers exposed the law's rhetorical function more than its material one. The law banishing the Quakers on "pain of death," that is, was intended not to kill the Quakers—we can only assume that the magistrates never dreamed it would lead to that—but rather to silence them and keep them from engaging the Puritans in further legal debate. The fact that the new law threatened the Quakers with death, however, did not deter the Quakers, who took it as another provocation to debate. On hearing of the pain-of-death provision, the Quakers, who had previously been slipping into the colony at night or undercover by day, now made no secret of their efforts to cross over into the Bay Colony's jurisdiction. In 1658, just after the law was passed, for example, Marmaduke Stevenson entered the colony from Barbados, and others, among them William Robinson, Mary Dyer, and William Leddra, soon followed; all four were hanged in the end.[13]

That there was something central to community formation and to membership identity at stake in the order to banish on pain of death, however, becomes evident only in the Quakers' response to it, for in entering the colony openly, they were engaging in what sociologists call "rational rule-breaking," the kind of rule breaking that is accompanied by attempts not to evade authority but to defy it.[14] A law that the Puritans passed in order to end debate, in other words, was reinterpreted by the Quakers as yet another point of entry for it and so served as a testament to the essentially rhetorical, community-making nature of the law. For Marmaduke Stevenson, for example, the publication of the new order was the very reason he made the trip from Barbados, for his purpose was not to spread the gospel but, as he said, "to test their bloody laws." Similarly for Mary Dyer, who first gained notoriety as an antinomian and friend to Anne Hutchinson but subsequently took up Quakerism with a vengeance, it was the law, not religion, that impelled her to enter the colony. Indeed Dyer, who was scheduled to hang with Stevenson and Robinson but was reprieved at the last moment by a personal appeal made to the governor by her husband and son, found herself having to defy the banishment law not once or twice but three times in order to trigger the pain-of-death provision. Official records of her death report that on "being asked [on the gallows] what she had to say why the sentence should not be executed, she gave no other answer but that she denied our lawe, came to bere witness against it, & could not choose but to come & doe as formerly."[15]

In Dyer's and Stevenson's statements we have the perfect example of how a law designed to exclude people from a territory could be diverted from that purpose and made to serve the opposite purpose by existing in a rhetorical sphere in which it served to prompt rather than shut down conversation. In particular, as the arguments of those Quakers who did not fall victim to the law suggest, it was the law's narrowly circumscribed vision of community— and of the possibilities for inclusion in or exclusion from it—that compelled the four Quakers to defy it in the first place. Specifically, in making defiance of the law their primary concern, the Quakers confronted the Puritans with a subject bent on expressing that defiance from within the jurisdiction as opposed to outside it.[16] In the narratives, including the many pamphlets, letters, and diaries about their treatment written by the Quakers and the Puritans, the nature of this defiance takes shape, and we come to see not only how directed and deliberate the Quaker critique of the Puritans' use of the common law was but also how important the Quaker-Puritan dialogue about the law became to the colony's ever-evolving identity.

Making Law

The most devastating feature of the Quakers' critique of the Puritans' law was their attack not on any specific law but on the Puritans' lawmaking in general. The Quakers reminded the Puritans that in making laws against them, the Puritans had strayed far from the origins of the common law and its concept of governance, which, as it developed through the writings of legal theorists such as Glanville, Bracton, Hooker, St. German, Grotius, and Pufendorf, put the law on a par with the king and thus made it a potential rival. At the hands of its greatest champion, Sir Edward Coke, the common law superseded the king in authority, but in addition judicial holdings—the mainstay of the common law—were arguably considered more binding than legislation. For Coke, new law, in the form of legislation, was made only when absolutely necessary and even then was considered a matter of mere discovery, a "process and result of revelation," not of change.

Because the common law was thought to have preceded any "made" law or positive law, as it was often called, the activity of making law was especially fraught as far as common lawyers were concerned. While modern and postmodern societies acknowledge lawmaking to be a central purpose of government, the same was not necessarily true in early modern societies, especially in early modern England. As J. P. Sommerville has noted, under James I virtually no new laws were made from 1610 to 1624, and under Charles I there was no legislation between 1628 and 1640.[17] When new laws were made, moreover, common lawyers were quick to recast them as mere codifications of what was already "customary" in the law, warning, as Coke often did, that "it was most dangerous to alter any fundamental point of the ancient common laws and customs of the realm."[18]

If legislators in England, however, could refrain from lawmaking for a time without suffering adverse consequences—they lived, after all, in a world where all laws were by common consent always already there—the Puritans in New England could not. Unfamiliar material conditions, among other things, compelled the formation of new agricultural habits for which new laws had to be made. We recall that the Bay Company was authorized to make what laws they needed on the condition that those laws were not already addressed by preexisting English laws and were not "contrary and repugnant to the laws of England."[19] It was with this caveat in mind that the Bay Colony authorities set out to draft a series of new laws, which culminated in the *Body of Liberties* in 1641. The product of many years of work and of much argument (as well as a source of conflict for other banished individuals, such as Roger Williams), the *Body of Liberties* was hailed by most settlers as a comprehensive and exhaustive code. However, it was this argument that the Quakers turned back on the Puritans when they declared that having published all the new laws they would need, the Puritans were now—post-1641—in a position in which their lawmaking, like that of their English counterparts, had to be restrained.

According to the Quakers, in other words, things not thought of at the time of the drafting of the *Body of Liberties* were not to be legislated against, for there could be only two kinds of law: new legislation specified in the legal code of the colony or of England; and the "ancient" common law. With the support of most common lawyers, the Quakers argued that all other laws were illegal. Imagine, then, the Quakers' surprise when after their arrival the Puritans started the lawmaking frenzy against them. In a summary of these new laws, Edward Rawson, first secretary of the Massachusetts Bay Colony, described how urgent and unusual these new laws must have seemed, even to the Puritans.

> [A]nd accordingly a law was made and published prohibiting all masters of ships to bring any Quakers into this jurisdiction, and themselves from coming in, on penalty of the house of correction till they could be sent away: notwithstanding which, by a back dore, they found entrance, and the penalty inflicted on themselves proving insufficient to restraine their impudent and insolent obstructions, was increased by the loss of the ears of those what offended the second time, which also being too weak a defense against their impetuous frantick fury, necessitated us to endeavour our security, and upon serious consideration, after the former experiments by their incessant assaults, a law was made that such persons should be

banished, on pain of death, according to the example of England in
their provision against Jesuits, which being regularly pronounced
etc.[20]

The first thing to note in this description is the sheer variety and multiplicity of the anti-Quaker laws, which suggest that far from understanding the
common law as imposing a restraint on the making of new laws, the Puritans
seemed to see it as a license for proliferating them. The second thing to note,
however, is that even within the context of this proliferation, caution was
exercised in stepping up the severity of the law by degrees—a caution suggesting that the Puritans were aware that what they were doing was in some
way unwarranted. As Rawson explained, the Puritans first tried to prevent
the Quakers from coming in by making a law against the shipmasters, which
would have sufficed if the Quakers had not found a "back dore" way of entering the colony. This contingency compelled a new law authorizing the crop-
ping of ears, which was also found to be insufficient and thus required a new
law, and so forth. Indeed in their lawmaking against the Quakers, the Puritans
represented themselves as doing all they could to avoid making new laws and
doing so only when forced.

The Quakers, however, who were ready to see even minor Puritan legal
reforms as illicit, read these and other, similar descriptions of lawmaking as
indicating the appearance of restraint but not its reality. By likening the Puritans' anti-Quaker laws to those of the Spanish Inquisition, the Quaker Francis
Howgill went so far as to suggest that the gradualism of the Puritans' law was
an index not of their leniency but of their desire to inflict an even greater
degree of pain. He wrote, "And is not this your Judgement also that the Magistrate ought to proceed gradually? That is, to inflict punishment by degrees
with lingering torture, like their Inquisitions: And where in doth thy doctrine
differ from theirs in this?"[21] Speaking of another deterrent to the Quakers'
presence, James Cudworth noted in a 1658 letter to a fellow Quaker that the
Puritans tried to "make a law serviceable to them" by altering existing legislation that prohibited people from "neglecting the Worship of God *and* setting
up a Worship contrary to God, *and* the Allowance of this Government [my
emphasis]." The alteration, as Cudworth explained, consisted of "putting out
the Word and putting in the Word which is a disjunctive and makes every
branch to become a law."[22] Observing a similar underhandedness in the laws
leading directly to their banishment, the Quakers suggested that in regulating
the behavior of the shipmasters, the Puritans effectively imposed a form of

banishment on the Quakers that looked like the common law but was tantamount to new law or new legislation. Thus the Quakers referred the Puritans
back to the "ancient law" that already addressed the conduct of shipmasters
and that to their minds should have been sufficient for them as it was for
other Englishmen. "And did ye not compel Robert Lock, a master of one of
the ships," wrote the famous Quaker apologist George Bishop, "to carry them
back on his own charge . . . and bind him in bond so to do, and to land them
nowhere but in England?—a strange usurpation over other countries, and
your own, and the master and them."[23]

The language that Bishop used here—of usurpation—is of particular interest in our effort to understand the Quakers' legal strategies to defend their
entry into the colony and their corresponding notions of community and
jurisdictional boundaries. While the term "usurpation" was often used to critique the ascription of sovereign power to someone other than the king, it was
here used to critique the writing or, to put it more succinctly, the rewriting of
the common law. The usurpation in question, that is, is not of the king's law
but of a country's laws—others and their own—and of the individuals, such as
shipmasters, who claimed certain customary liberties under them, in this case
the ability to resist coercive bonds and to take their passengers wherever they
chose. Here the Quakers directly targeted the particular combination of territory, authority, and rights that the Puritans imposed. Implicit in this reference
to the laws of the "country" was a terminological distinction that was made
as early as the *Magna Carta* between positive law (or the kind of law made
by kings and legislatures) and the "law of the land," or the common law.[24]
Commentaries on the law in the mid-seventeenth century, such as William
Ball's 1646 "Constitutio Liberi Populi or the Rule of a Free-born People," were
replete with the language of the people's liberties.

A Place of Due Process

Adding the "usurpation" of the common law to their arsenal of complaints
against the Puritans, the Quakers also compared the colonial community, and
in particular the colonial notion of imprisonment, to the community and
policy on imprisonment in England. "And, during the long seasons of their
imprisonment aforesaid," continued Bishop, "did ye take care for the maintenance as ye ought to have done?"[25] The Quakers devoted much space and time
to cataloging and complaining about a wide variety of their punishments, all

of which tied into their overall critique of the law. To be sure, scholars have long noted the nature of these complaints, drawing parallels between them and the general discourse of suffering that was so prominent in the English Quaker writings. In England suffering was a major focus of the Quaker platform; the English Quakers went so far as to establish meetings exclusively for the purpose of discussing their sufferings, and many scholars agree that much of the Quakers' energy in this regard was devoted, following George Fox, to establishing a basis for religious martyrdom.[26]

But if religious suffering was a central element of the English version of these complaints, it was arguably diminished if not absent in the colonial versions in which the discourse of suffering took a far more legal turn and focused on what membership might mean in a community in which people were deprived of their liberties without due process. By contrast with their English counterparts, the colonial Quaker accounts of their mistreatment at the hands of the Puritans provide fewer details of bodily injury and dwell less on mental deprivation, while spending far more time on the legal inequity of their condition. The moral imperative—the "ought" in Bishop's statement above—does not appear to rest on religious principles at all. There is a conspicuous absence of religious language in Bishop's more than four-hundred-page-long account of Puritan abuse, which is based rather on the Quakers' profound and extensive knowledge of the "ought" of the law and in particular on the elements of due process surrounding imprisonment.

To this day due process provides the basis for many of the law's normative claims, but it would appear that the seventeenth-century Quakers were the first to make good use of it. Thus it was with due process in mind that the Quakers complained about the excessive nature, variety, and timing of the Puritans' punishments against them. A letter signed by three members of the Southwick family, for example, as well as by the Quakers Samuel Shattock and Joshua Buffum complained that the law under which they were initially imprisoned differed from the law that continued to keep them behind bars: "[N]ow that which we do expect is . . . not to put us in upon the account of law, and execute another law upon us, of which, according to your own manner, we were never convicted as the law expresses."[27] The problem with this practice, as George Bishop observed, is that "they suffered not for a law already broken, but for one that was intended to be made."[28] Here Bishop tied the Puritans' illegal lawmaking with their failure to meet the due-process standards. Bishop went on to note, moreover, that in the case of Christopher Holder, John Copeland, and John Rous, three other Quakers held for lengthy periods in Puritan prisons, the complaint against the Puritans had to do with their unfairly multiplying offenses. "To have suffered your law once before," Bishop observed, "should have cleared them from further suffering, for by the law of England, a man having suffered the penalty is clear, as if he had not transgressed the law."[29]

With respect to the actual punishments meted out against them, the Quakers referred the Puritans back to the sentencing guidelines that were required by due process and that the courts in England typically used. Although they were never officially written into the rules, sentencing guidelines were dictated by the nature of the crime and by the socioeconomic status of the defendant—with corporal punishments reserved for the lower classes and fines for members of the upper classes who could afford to pay them. Under this regime, the Quakers argued, they should not have been subject to corporal punishment at all. Francis Howgill confirmed this sense of legal inequity when he wrote, "but is not putting off the Hat too ones Equal, or not joining or coming to your Congregation, that they deserve punishment suitable to Thieves, Fornicators and Fellons, but Persecutors and blood-thirsty men were neer blind."[30] Of course some of the confusion in the Quakers' case may have arisen from the fact that they refused on principle to pay fines, but there were so many other instances in which a punishment outside the sentencing guidelines ended up being applied to them that the Puritans' policy on fines could hardly account for them all.

If a general appeal to due process provided the Quakers with a basis for arguing against their punishments, however, the specific due-process requirement that the law obey itself underwrote their more targeted attack on the Puritans' notion of community. To this end the Quakers called upon the provision in the *Magna Carta* stating that "No free man shall be taken or imprisoned or disseised of his Freehold, or Liberties, or free Customs, or be outlawed, or exiled, or any other wise destroyed, nor will we go upon him nor send upon him, except by the lawful judgment of his peers or by the law of the land."[31] Though it was arguably authorized by the Puritans' charter, even the banishment law had to be enforced according to the principles of due process, which, as Coke confirmed, were a central feature of the common law.

The major element of the Quakers' due-process argument against the banishment law was that it was made ex post facto to respond to behavior that had not previously been criminalized. "Reader, take notice," Howgill wrote in *The Popish Inquisition*, "they had no Law at all when the Quakers came into New England till they consulted with the Prince of Darkness to make one."[32]

As the Quakers were wont to point out, even the *Body of Liberties*, which included laws banishing Jesuits and Anabaptists by name, was silent on the matter of the Quakers. Needless to say, ex post facto laws violated the general due-process requirement that one's behavior be evaluated according to the law of the land (where laws of the land meant the law of custom or the common law). But in this critique the Quakers were not limited to general due-process principles since the *Body of Liberties*, in an almost precise echo of the *Magna Carta*, specified "that no man's life shall be taken away; . . . no man's person shall be arrested, restrained, banished, dismembered nor any wayes punished . . . unless it be by . . . *some expresse law of the Country . . . & sufficiently published.*"[33] Reminding the Puritans of their own insistence that their laws be "expresse" and "published," the Quakers made frequent requests to "see" the banishment laws, which the Puritans consistently refused. Referring to one such request—made to Governor Endicott—Bishop wrote: "And did he not further manifest it when he told them 'They should not have a copy of those laws,'—a tyrannical reply,—when they desired it, that they might know on what ground they went, to the grieving of the people then present, who said opening in the Court, 'How shall they know then, when they transgress?'"[34]

Taking up the language of the common law for their own ends, the Puritans were not silent on this issue. To the charge that they were making laws ex post facto, they offered a counterlanguage of gradualism, also suggested by the precepts of due process. "We acknowledge it to be pious wisdom of the magistrate," John Norton wrote, "to proceed gradually, and where gentler means may rationally be looked at as effectual there to abstain from the use of any severer remedy."[35] In pointing to a gradualism in their infliction of criminal penalties, the Puritans not only engaged the Quakers on their own ground but also demonstrated a due-process restraint that was far greater than that of England. Seemingly in conflict with the "always already there" aspect of the common law, reforms directed at the criminal law, which had ballooned out of control in England and included punishments that were widely seen as too severe, proved an exception and were even endorsed by Coke, for whom most legal reform was anathema. In accordance with Coke's beliefs, the Puritans took it upon themselves to make English criminal law less chaotic and less arbitrary when they settled in the New World. To this end they set about reducing the number of capital crimes and encouraging more lenient penalties, of which banishment, ironically, was one. (Nor did they see their frenzied lawmaking against the Quakers as violating this aspect of their agenda, since it too fell short of making their presence in the colony a capital crime until the very end.) What the Puritans failed to see, however, in their never-ending struggle with the Quakers over the terms of the common law was that where they saw their reforms as fulfilling the dictates of due process by reducing the number of criminal prohibitions, the Quakers, together with most mid-century Englishmen, saw them as tampering with the civil liberties with which they were, as Englishmen, naturally and historically endowed.

Liberties versus Prohibitions

The banishment narratives affirm the difference between prohibitions and liberties as being central to the split in the visions of the Puritans and the Quakers related to the common law and in particular to their approach to the formation of a society based on common law. Court records describing the case of William Leddra suggest that had the Puritans' wish for the Quakers to leave their colony been couched in terms of a liberty as opposed to a mandate in the form of a prohibition, the Quaker crisis might have been averted. "Att this Court," the record reads, "William Ledra and Peter Peirson, two of those called Quakers . . . apeered and were demanded severally whether they would depart the gou'ment in some competent time, viz., two or three dayes, in case wheather and strength were suitable . . . ; they answered they could not engage to any certaine time to depart the gou'ment." When asked again at another court appearance a few months later, Leddra elaborated, "only sayeying 'Its like if I were att libertie out of prison I might depart in the will of God ere long'"; but he would not reverse the situation and "resolve to depart by such a time" in order to secure "his libertie."[36]

For the Quakers, in other words, liberty was not a by-product of legal negotiation but the paramount goal of the common law. As proof they could point to one of the century's most important common-law efforts: the passage of the Petition of Right championed by Coke in 1628. The Petition of Right put a limit on the king's ability to imprison people without Parliament's consent or to call for the forced quartering of troops and was, according to Coke's mid-century heirs, the crowning achievement of Coke's career.[37] It seemed to have ushered in a period of expanded liberties and inspired later bills ensuring the right to a jury trial and the right to appeal, both of which figure centrally in the Quakers' repeated demands of the Puritans. Bishop, for example, reported that "they appealed to England to be tried there, which they did once and again, . . . but neither would ye yield to this, but slighted and disregarded their such appeal; your governor and deputy-governor with one voice saying, 'No appeal to England! No appeal to England!'"[38]

If the common law supported the Quakers' investment in legal liberties, it provided a basis for the Puritans' prohibition-oriented version of civil sovereignty as well. We note, for instance, the centrality of prohibition to the works of Hugo Grotius, in particular to his *De jure belli ac pacis*, published in 1625. In this volume, commonly translated as *On the Law of War and Peace*, Grotius outlined a theory of law that made prohibition and protection the centerpiece of the social contract. For Grotius, who wrote at the height of the century's religious wars, the reason people gathered into social units in the first place was to be able to prohibit others from invading. Thus much of his treatise is taken up with what constitutes just means of prevention and prohibition, such as those favored by the Puritans. "Sovereign powers," he wrote, "have a right not only to avert, but to punish wrongs. From whence we are authorized [*sic*] to prevent a remote as well as an immediate aggression."[39] This defense-oriented version of the common law comported with the Puritans' reading of the Hebrew Bible. In *The Heart of New-England Rent at the Blasphemies of the Present Generation,* for example, the Puritan John Norton urged the Puritan magistrates to consider the Quakers' presence in the Bay Colony as an attack against which they, like the Israelites, could justifiably defend themselves. "As God hath armed the Magistrate with Civil power," Norton wrote, "for . . . defence . . . so hath he animated him unto the regular and seasonable exercise thereof," which includes "the putting away of evil from Israel," "the preventing of infection," and "the preventing of the wrath of God."[40]

Jurisdiction and Defense

The Quaker incursion or "invasion," as it was called at the time, mobilized a Puritan rhetoric of defense: hence the use of the language of what amounted to a kind of "national" security in Rawson's summary of the anti-Quaker laws. It was the Quakers' "frantick fury," he noted, that "necessitated us to endeavour our security." To be sure, this sense of jurisdictional vulnerability on the part of the colonists predated the so-called Quaker invasion, but never before, not even with respect to the Indians from whom they feared constant assaults, had the Puritans perceived a threat greater than that of the Quakers, who shook not only the physical but also the intellectual foundation of their borders. The assault by the Quakers was commonly cast as a life or death situation for the Puritans. In his history of the Quaker presence, the Quaker Burroughs reported about the Puritans that "[t]he[y] . . . say, The Quakers dyed not, because of their other Crimes, how capital soever, but upon their Super-added Presumptions, and incorrigible Contempt of Authority, braking in upon us, notwithstanding the sentence of Banishment; had they not been restrained, there was too much cause to fear that we our selves should quickly have dyed, or worse: and they would not be restrained but by death."[41] The Puritan John Norton spoke with a similar sense of urgency about keeping the distinction between insiders and outsiders clear when he suggested that the Quakers' impulse to attack was primal and predatory. "The Wolfe," he wrote, "which ventured over the wide Sea, out of a ravening desire to prey upon the sheep . . . hath no cause to complain, though for the security of the Flock, he be penned up."[42]

The Quakers by contrast had a far more porous, more transient, and more inclusive sense of borders and jurisdiction. In an inversion of Norton's analogy, they often referred to themselves as sheep or more precisely as lambs, whose relationship with God compelled them to seek out new venues where their gospel could be heard.[43] So seriously did they take the commandment to travel, in fact, that they commented on how strange it was for a people, such as the Puritans, to congregate in one place as opposed to circulating through many. "Like the priests of old," Bishop wrote, "they [the Quakers] went from one place to another, from city to city, and from country to country," while the Puritans "lived in one town for many years together, as these priests do now."[44] Thus even at this early stage of their development—the first Society of Friends appeared in England in the late 1640s—the Quakers had traveled to many parts of the globe. As Frederick Tolles has observed, "If one had an animated map of the Atlantic world, it would show Quaker beachheads being established in rapid succession in every one of the British provinces between 1655 and 1660."[45] Of these places Tolles named Surinam, Newfoundland, Barbados, the Leeward Islands, Jamaica, the Bahamas, and of course the Massachusetts Bay.

Still it would be a mistake to gather from their travel that the Quakers had no sense of borders or of a permanent population. Their travel or "visiting," as they called it, seemed to have instilled in them a heightened awareness of countrywide boundaries, which according to Henry Cadbury spurred them on to maintain even stronger ties with England.[46] In contrast to the Puritans, they thought of the jurisdictions in which they lived as places they might depart from but also return to at will. As the Quaker John Rous wrote, "I was not driven from my Fathers house, but in obedience to the Lord I left it, and when the Lord shall have cleared me of this Land, I shall return to it again."[47]

In or Around

If the Quakers' sense of jurisdiction was inflected by their frequent travels, it was also profoundly informed by the common law, and in particular by the legacy of *Calvin's Case,* decided by Sir Edward Coke in 1608. As discussed in Chapter 2, *Calvin's Case* expanded the possibilities for claiming a shared affiliation, among other things, and it was this new, somewhat dislocated affiliation that the Quakers pointed to when they claimed a right to enter the Bay Colony. To this end they reminded the Puritans that as Englishmen they were as entitled to come and go in the Bay Colony as they were in England: "But why not [are the Quakers admitted] into this, your jurisdiction? Are you entailed thereunto, you and your heirs forever? How came ye so to be and by what right? Is it because ye came out of Old England? So did these. Is it because you are Englishmen? So are they."[48] At the heart of this reminder about shared ancestry is a not-so-subtle hint that the jurisdiction established by the colonists belonged not to them as individuals but to the government of England and to the people as a whole. Bishop asked the Puritan magistrates, "Are ye Lord's Propriotors [*sic*] of the *Creation*? May not the *Lord* of Heaven and Earth send *His* messengers among *ye,* without your leave? May not an *English* Man come into an *English* Jurisdiction? What insolency is this?"[49] After all, the Bay Colony was public land, not private property—which was not coincidentally the only kind of property that could be entailed— and as public property it was devoted not to the ends of any one individual but to the commonweal. To make this point Bishop wrote: "I pray, how came you into New England, and by what right and title do ye claim privilege to sojourn there, and to rule as lords? Is it not by right of nature, with which the law investedth you, as natural Englishmen, into its natural habitations?" The law of nature that Bishop invoked here is not a general law pertaining to all men as a species but rather that version of the natural law that informed the English common law and that belonged to Englishmen as a group. "Can that which is natural, or general, or common to all," he continued, "as much to one man as another, be changed into particular? Can it be broken with a force to nature? Or, is it not broken when it is made particular? And is it not made particular when some are excluded from the common benefit?"[50]

The line Bishop drew here between the private and the public or the particular and the general gets at the major difference between the Puritan and Quaker visions of legal jurisdiction and reminds us of their differing accounts of how spiritual communities were formed as well. For the Quakers, the spirit of the Lord was like the common law—something that was general, in the air, and not to be sought after but rather tapped into by its members. For the Puritans, by contrast, the spirit, also like the law, at least as they understood it, was particular—the end result of an investigative process by which certain people discovered grace and others failed to do so. Put another way, for the Quakers, what was common—in law or spirit—was not *in* but *around* them, rendering them its temporary apparition. What was common for the Puritans by contrast was not atmospheric but rather a property and product of the individual, and on this account the law, like the spirit, could be altered by the inclusion or exclusion of certain people.

In terms of jurisdiction, it followed that for the Puritans, the Bay Colony was not the first of many English outposts but the result of a uniquely successful instantiation of *Calvin's Case*, a kind of legal conversion. For them the law that sanctioned England's expanding borders was given force by its application to and embodiment by certain individuals who had a responsibility to reinforce the effectiveness of the law by making their borders defensible against others in turn. The logic here will be familiar to many as the logic of private property, and so it is not surprising that when the Puritans next responded to the Quakers' view of jurisdiction, they drew on the metaphor of a house—the ultimate sign of property ownership:

> Again, on the seventh day of the seventh Month, we three were sent for (from the prison) [and John Endicott asked us] Why we came hither? We answered, That the Lord (whose Law is just) required it of us to come, in obedience to him we came. Then one called Major Denison, asked us, Whether every man is not Master of his own house? . . . Then Major Denison said, If a man should forewarn another man from coming into his house, and should stand with Ike (or a Sword) at his door, and yet for all this, the other should attempt to come into his house, and should be slain, Would not this man's blood be on his own head.[51]

The metaphor of the house is telling in two respects: it is a foreshadowing of the premium the Puritans placed on those who had already qualified for legal membership by being allowed to buy land in the colony and build on it; and it further justifies their defensive posture with respect to their jurisdiction.

Resistance

The particularity of the Puritans' notion of jurisdiction was of a piece with the Puritan sense of the law as focused on prohibition and defense, for the law that speaks in terms of prohibition produces social cohesion through its effect on the individual; this law, in other words, works only if the individual subject responds to it by doing or, for that matter, not doing what the law demands. This is what Foucault, in another context, has called the sovereign-subject model of government in which the sovereign's command—whether the sovereign is understood as a person or as the law—is directed at the individual. This relationship to the law is most visible in the area of property ownership, in which the individualist contours are extreme, but in addition it includes most criminal prohibitions, which, in taking the form of the biblical injunction "thou shalt not," offer only two possible responses: affirmation or denial. "If we restrict ourselves to the sovereign-subject relationship," Foucault explained, "the limit of the law is the subject's disobedience."[52] But where Foucault's account differs from that of the Puritans is in admitting the possibility of disobedience at all. In the Puritan commonwealth, while certain criminal violators were punished and then reabsorbed into the community, there were many, such as the Quakers, who were not reabsorbed and for whom this mode of being in relation to the law—of being incorporated by the law while maintaining a resistance to it—was inconceivable.

Pushing this boundary produced a new and lasting legal and social relation in the Puritan world. In a community such as that envisioned by the Quakers, conceived, that is, as something other than the sum of its parts, disobedience was not only allowable but also essential. The ability to respond to the sovereign through the kind of denial Foucault described was at the very heart of the Quakers' complaints about the banishment law. More specifically, they were intent on demonstrating that the denial itself—even after the individual had been punished for his offense by being banished or killed or otherwise disappeared—could not rob the individual of membership. The space bounded by the jurisdictional borders, in other words, was not, as some theories of territory would suggest, "socially emptiable" but made permanent members even of those it evicted.[53] However, the Quakers seemed to have more than simple denial in mind. In defying the law, in refusing to obey it by returning "on pain of death," the Quakers hoped to show how resistance to Puritan forms of legality could become an acceptable form of legal response. In this, to borrow Foucault's terminology, their view of community was premised not on individuals or a simple subject-sovereign relation but on a "population" with its own developing properties. "The government of populations," Foucault wrote, "is completely different from the exercise of sovereignty over the fine grain of individual behaviors."[54]

Some light can be shed on the Quakers' interest in populationwide responses to the sovereign by recalling Jürgen Habermas's further elaboration of it. For Habermas, an insistence, such as that of the Puritans, on obedience from all members fails to acknowledge how important the law is in the formation of communal identities. Citizens, he explained, find fulfillment in all aspects of political and legal life, including or even especially those that set them apart from each other.[55] While the Quakers were not yet citizens in Habermas's sense, it is clear from their writings that they were moving toward something like his sense of legal action and inclusion. Even as their religious differences from the Puritans escaped clear classification, the nature of the Quakers' social and legal order, which welcomed the common man and regarded ordination and the sacraments as unnecessary, pointed to the very kind of inclusiveness the Puritans abhorred. In defying the law of the Puritans, the Quakers embodied a subject position that had not until that time been contemplated by the social or legal order—a subject position that was not clearly criminal, or at least not criminal in the usual way—but that demanded inclusion in and respect by the public sphere.

Far from representing themselves as breaking and entering into Puritan houses, therefore, the Quakers raised the possibility that by entering the Puritans' jurisdiction against the Puritans' wishes, they were recommitting themselves to the colonial government as a whole. "We are no Enemies unto Government it self," Burroughs explained in his petition to the king after witnessing the treatment of the Quakers in the Bay Colony, "as these our Accusers do charge us, but it is our Principle, and hath ever been, and is our Practice to be subject to whatsoever Government is set up over us, either by doing or suffering."[56] With the phrase "doing or suffering," moreover, the Quakers indicated that they were not contesting the right of the colonial government to define criminality; on the contrary, as they had shown for years in England, where their legal activities revolved around their perpetual and prolonged imprisonments, they were willing to accept the authority that designated them as criminals as long as they were able to contest its validity from within its precincts. In "suffering" the designation, in other words, they still counted as members of the community, whereas in New England, where they were sent outside without a chance to demonstrate an allegiance that was nevertheless mixed with displeasure, they were denied this opportunity entirely.

Inhabitant or Foreigner

The nature of the Quaker claims about their behavior and their complex and ultimately untenable position as members of a "criminal" population can further be illustrated by reference back to the *Body of Liberties* and its division of the law's subjects into two—and only two—categories: inhabitant and foreigner. There were, admittedly, provisions in the law for so-called "strangers"—they could not stay in the colony for more than three weeks, and they could not buy land during their stay—but in the vast majority of cases, the law acknowledged a distinction only between "inhabitants" and "foreigners."[57] While the provisions addressed to inhabitants and foreigners typically called for their equal treatment under law—as in the entry specifying that "everie man whether Inhabitant or Forreiner, Free or not Free shall have libertie to come to any publick Court"—this "equality" nevertheless appears quite limited when juxtaposed to the wide range of liberties available to individuals who qualified as foreigners in England. Among other things, in England, under a common law inspired by *Calvin's Case*, a host of possible subject positions for the "foreigner" was unfolding within a taxonomy that included "native born subjects," "naturalized subjects," "aliens," and within the category of alien divisions among "friendly aliens," "enemy aliens," and "perpetual aliens."[58]

Perhaps it goes without saying that in distinguishing only between inhabitant and foreigner, the Puritans were merely giving voice to the Manichean worldview that colored their approach to everything. But the distinction seems to imply something more, for in designating people either as inhabitants or foreigners, the Puritans reinforced the primacy of their understanding of civil jurisdiction and social exclusion. What was most important to them about legal subjects, in other words, was where they stood with respect to the colony's borders—in or out. In this regard the Quakers found themselves in a double bind, since they came into the colony not only from a place outside the jurisdiction, which made them foreign in one sense, but also in the face of prohibitions that criminalized their conduct, which made them foreign in another sense as well, for as Foucault observed, the criminal once designated as such becomes a stranger in his own land.[59]

The stark division between foreigner and inhabitant also translates easily into another distinction that underscored Puritan and Quaker views of the law: the distinction between friend and enemy. We can begin to understand the depth of this division as an element of the inhabitant-foreigner distinction if we look to Carl Schmitt's work on the political, for it was in Schmittian terms that the Puritans seemed to understand their conflict with the Quakers. For the Puritans, as for Schmitt, the political was always antagonistic: "Each participant [in the conflict of politics]," Schmitt explained, "is in a position to judge whether the adversary intends to negate his opponent's way of life and therefore must be repulsed or fought in order to preserve one's own form of existence."[60] That the Quakers figured for the Puritans as enemies is yet another indication of how their view of the common law borrowed from their faith, for the concept of a religious enemy who might appear in the form of a devil was widespread. When used in a secular, legal context, however, the term "enemy" had a different connotation and usually referred, as Meredith Weddle has pointed out, to an enemy of the king.[61] For example, according to Grotius, an enemy of the king—what he called *hostis*—had to appear in the form of a body or collectivity similar to the collectivity to which he was opposed; barring that, he was merely *inimicus*, a private enemy or foe.[62]

One of the reasons that the distinction between *hostis* and *inimicus* was important was because it was tied at the time to arguments over the legitimation of violence. As Richard Tuck and others have shown, the humanist tradition of the sixteenth and seventeenth centuries with which the common law was allied justified violence on the part of the state in order to protect the state's interests and borders.[63] This meant that if the Bay Colony could successfully present itself as a state with coherent jurisdictional boundaries and its own claim to sovereignty, the colony would be justified, if attacked, in inflicting violence on the attackers—justified even in *banishing* them on pain of death and then *putting* them to death, if it came to that. Thus it was that the Puritans seemed to treat the Quakers—discursively at least—as *hostis*, even though there were scarcely enough Quakers to constitute a threat of war. "You are greater enemies to us," Humphrey Norton quoted the Puritans as saying, "then [sic] those that come openly, while you come under pretence of peace, to poison the people."[64] From the Quakers' perspective, however, such a claim was absurd, not only because there were so few of them but also because to figure the Quakers as enemies of the state, or of the king, flew directly in the face of their shared place of origin. How could the Quakers be enemies of the Puritan state when they were already in effect a central part of it?[65]

Neighbors

Even if one assumed the Puritans' position that the Quakers were foreigners who could plausibly be understood as occupying a place outside the jurisdiction, then what, the Quakers asked, did the Puritans make of the colony's growing number of inhabitant Quakers, a new and seemingly impossible category of persons? This question turned the argument about the membership status of the Quakers from a theoretical one into a practical one. In the face of severe anti-Quaker laws, instances of local sympathy with the Quakers were few, but they did not go unnoticed. To protest the harsh treatment of the first two female Quakers in prison, for example, Nicholas Upshall, a Boston tavern keeper, brought them food and water even though he was fined heavily for doing so; and there were several people in Salem who demonstrated openness to the Quakers by inviting them into their homes, holding meetings with them, and in a few cases openly converting.

Not surprisingly, given the sharp distinction they drew between inhabitant and foreigner, the Puritans crafted an entirely separate series of punishments to deal with the slowly swelling number of local, nonforeign Quakers. These punishments did not include banishment on pain of death, but they did include the levying of stiff fines, occasional whippings, and imprisonment. Instead of pointing to the disparity between their punishments and those of the inhabitants as a means of reducing the severity of their own treatment, however, the so-called foreign Quakers simply noted that the local punishments were equally, if not more, unjust. "And now they come to their own Inhabitants," Howgill wrote, "and thou shalt hear their judgement concerning them, and thou shalt see how they love their Neighbours."[66] By calling attention to the harsh treatment of their own inhabitants, of course, Howgill was attempting to make a mockery of the Puritans' distinction between inhabitants and foreigners in the first place. But by invoking the concept of the neighbor, he was reminding the Puritans of a category of subject position and social arrangement that they had overlooked and yet were bound, by religious precepts if not legal ones, to honor. Indeed the Quakers' indirect reference to the commandment to "love your neighbor" found in "Leviticus" as well as in the New Testament, became a mainstay of the Quakers' extended common-law critique of the Puritans' community.

Like their sense of boundaries in general, the Quakers' concept of the neighbor had roots in their religious practice. In contrast to the Puritans, the Quakers believed in a conversion that turned on the communication of a general religious methodology rather than on a particular religious content. The Quakers' notion of conversion was less a radical turning around, as the etymology of the term would suggest, than a silent transmission that occurred partly as a result of the physical proximity of parishioners, who usually prayed standing next to each other in a small, spare room. They were not "evangelizing with the purpose of converting others," Weddle wrote, "but rather were traveling in search of like-minded souls who would discover their convincements within themselves."[67] Carla Pestana too has confirmed this sense of the Quaker community at worship: "That the light within might shine forth from anyone tended to break down boundaries between individuals, highlighting that which was shared. Friends made decisions collectively, arriving 'at the sense of the meeting' through repeated discussion, and if necessary, the postponement of any matter upon which the group was unable to agree."[68]

If the Quakers' sense of the importance of the neighbor stemmed from biblical injunction and their own religious practice, it was not a strictly theological concept for them. Their thinking about the neighborhood—the place where neighbors lived—was almost certainly rooted in their experience with the law in England, where communities, towns, and parishes were far more diverse than has generally been assumed. In fact the English-born Quakers, who were welcomed in some parts of England but were the object of mob violence in others, would have had firsthand knowledge of this diversity, in both negative and positive ways. In suggesting proximity without necessarily expressing homogeneity, the figure of the neighbor, as opposed to the stranger, foreigner, or friend, had already begun to signal a general cultural uneasiness that the Puritans were eager to avoid.

Yet the Puritans had neighbors in this more diverse sense too. Though far more homogenous than communities in England, towns and parishes in New England, as Roger Williams so often pointed out, were growing more varied every year as a result of religious sectarianism as well as the influx of people after the Great Migration who came to the colonies for economic more than religious reasons. It was over the question of how to deal with the Quakers that the Puritans would have experienced an additional element of the tension and uncertainty inherent in the concept of neighbor as they attempted to convince the colonies around them to adopt stringent anti-Quaker policies like theirs. As the Quakers wrote: "it's like to be a bloody time amongst us; for they [the Puritans] have not onely combined to kill and banish amongst themselves in the Massachusetts, but (as we hear) have by all means used to hedge up all wayes of succor to us in the Neighbour-Collonyes which some of them had more tenderness, then themselves."[69]

If the Quakers thought that the colonies surrounding the Bay Colony might conspire against them in the service of the Puritans' more restrictive sense of neighbor and neighborhood, however, they had little to fear. Under considerable pressure from the Bay Colony, some colonies did refuse admission to the Quakers, but no single colony agreed to banish them on pain of death; the Quakers were considered a menace in the Dutch colony of New Netherlands, but the response there, though not entirely effective, remained banishment without the threat of death. In the common-law colony of Connecticut, more significantly, Governor John Winthrop Jr. openly resisted the Bay Colony's pressure in saying that he would "go on his knees before the magistrates to arrest their [the Quakers'] execution," and in this way the potential diversity inherent in a neighborhood—in this case that of the United Colonies—was brought home to the Puritans.[70] From this division within the colonies, moreover, we can extrapolate to the imperial context as a whole. The concept of the neighbor, that is, not only served to tie individuals together within England or within the colonies but also joined England to New England, one colony to another within New England, and New England and England to the colonies in the West Indies and beyond. In putting forward different views of the neighbor, then, the Puritans and the Quakers were debating the contours of the empire, with the Quakers once again proposing a more inclusive sense of empire that might include Barbados—their preferred outpost—while the Puritans looked to New England alone.

As a central emblem of social diversity, the neighborhood that has emerged in recent theory as a new, nonviolent way of thinking about social, legal, and political space could be said to have stemmed from the Quakers' version of it. For theorists from Jacques Lacan to Slavoj Žižek, the neighborhood suggests the possibility of harmonious social relations between people who are simultaneously familiar and strange, loved and loathed. The theory of most interest here, however—because it speaks directly to the issue of jurisdiction and jurisdictional identities—is that of Alan Badiou, for whom the idea of belonging, whether it be to the state, the nation, or the neighborhood, is an inappropriate and inaccurate way to describe people's relationships with places. This theory of Badiou's derives from his more general ontology, which is deeply indebted to set theory and is most readily understood in the terms in which his many commentators have explicated it. For Peter Hallward, for example, "Badiou's ontology recognizes no constraints (social, cultural, psychological, biological, or other) as to how people are grouped together";[71] while for Kenneth Reinhard, "Badiou's notion of the neighborhood as a set where no boundary separates the set and its members and no limit is drawn between inside and outside, can contribute to the elaboration of a political theology of the neighbor."[72]

This feature of the neighborhood—the elision of inside and outside—seems to have been at the heart of the Quaker challenge to the Puritans' banishment law. Indeed one of the Quakers' main objects was to show that in banishing them, the Puritans were making laws that necessarily went beyond the limits of their own jurisdiction or, to revert to the more technical definition, the space over which they were authorized to rule. The Puritans, in other words, were making laws that addressed people outside their boundaries and were thus engaging in a paradox that, though seemingly abstract, could not have been unknown to them. It was after all for this reason that Grotius specified that a state had no power over those it banished.[73] In adding the provision "on pain of death" to their banishment law, moreover, the Puritans seemed to involve themselves, from the Quakers' perspective, in yet another jurisdictional contradiction in that only those who were already outside the jurisdiction could be banished on pain of death since their ability to exist inside the jurisdiction was the very thing that was proscribed. To make such a paradox visible, the Quakers complained that the Puritans preferred their "deaths present" to their "lives absent," a rhetorical chiasmus that demonstrated not only that the Puritans' law had crossed over into another jurisdiction but that the individuals against whom it was directed were forced to cross over too.

In drawing here on Badiou and theories of jurisdiction that have more to do with twentieth-century politics than seventeenth-century law, my hope is not to portray the Quakers as harbingers of things to come but rather to suggest how in the midst of an always changing common law, two groups—in this case the Quakers and the Puritans—imagined and reimagined the communities and member identities afforded by the law and further how those imaginings ultimately communicated with and influenced each other. One can, for example, see how the Puritan version of the common law—their tendency to think of jurisdiction strictly in terms of defensible property or of communities as aggregates of individuals—pushed the common law toward constitutionalist ends. But we can also see how that constitutionalism—as it was articulated in the later part of the seventeenth century and the beginning of the eighteenth century—took on a more inclusionary shape as a result of the Quaker challenge. Seen in the context of the Puritans' approach to the Quakers, England's harsh but selectively enforced set of laws that admittedly left hundreds of Quakers in prison to die begins to look like a form of tolerance, or at least a form of England's unwillingness to sign on to the Puritans' vision of a community that was so exclusionary that it rid itself of dissenters altogether.

Even in the Bay Colony the Quaker banishment controversy had an immediate legacy. For one thing, it was surely with the Quaker admonition about neighbors in mind that some magistrates, such as Judge Hathorne of Salem, chose to overlook many of the meetings between inhabitant Quakers and foreign Quakers and to levy much smaller fines on the inhabitant Quakers than the law allowed. More significantly, we can draw a direct line between the Quaker banishment narratives and the suspension of the laws against them in 1661 by order of the king.[74] We might also, albeit less directly, see a shift in the Puritans' strategy toward resistance just a year after the Quaker banishments came to a bloody end, when in 1662 the synod of churches passed what has come to be known as the Half-Way Covenant. By this order the recalcitrant, if not explicitly resistant, members of the second and third generations of Puritans were granted church membership without having to recite conversion narratives; the new rule allowed that if their parents had been baptized, they could be baptized and so maintain the semblance, if not the reality, of their faith. Whether or not the Half-Way Covenant was an indication of a weakening sense of faith on the part of the second and third generations—a question about which there has been much scholarly debate—it is safe to say that the Half-Way Covenant represented a resolution of conflict that moved toward incorporation of resistance or dissent as opposed to its expulsion—a lesson the Puritans may have learned from their experience with the Quakers.[75] In addition we can look to the circumstances of the Indians, their banishment to Deer Island in the Boston harbor and their ultimate incorporation as agents under the common law—the subject of the next chapter—as possible consequences of the space opened up by the Quakers for resistance within the borders of the Puritan community.

CHAPTER 4

Deer Island and the Banishment
of the Indians

Oh, come, let us go down to Deer Island, and kill all the praying
Indians.
—Report by Daniel Gookin of what some Englishmen said after the
burning of Medfield, in *Historical Account of the Doings and
Sufferings of the Christian Indians in New England in the Years
1675–1677*

TO INCLUDE A chapter about the Indians in a book about banishment
in early America would seem almost to go without saying. After all, as
many historians of Native American culture have shown, the story of the Indians' relations with the white English settlers was from the start about the loss
of territory and social exclusion. But if the loss of territory accurately char-
acterizes the drift of Native American history after European contact, it does
not necessarily encompass the phenomenon of banishment as we have come
to understand it. The history of the Native Americans' loss of land is about re-
movals, reservations, and relocations that suggest not banishment but rather,
as Jean O'Brien so aptly puts it, a "dispossession by degrees."[1] Banishment, by
contrast, is not about a gradual deprivation of space or confinement within a
given space, but about a sudden and catastrophic separation of person from
one place to a spot beyond the bounds of a given jurisdiction.

To say that the course of Indian dispossession differed from the course of
banishment is not to minimize the hardship of Indian relocations but rather
to recognize that the instrument the Puritans used repeatedly to rid their

communities of other undesirables was not generally applied to the Indians. In fact when it came to the Indians, banishment was nearly impossible. Unlike Hutchinson, Morton, Williams, or even the Quakers, the Indians could not be effectively banished to a place outside the colonial jurisdiction because (1) this would have made a shambles of the jurisdictional integrity of the Bay Colony, which owed its existence to the expansion of its borders through the acquisition of Indian lands that lay by definition outside of the colony, and (2) if the Indians were in an important sense already outside the colonial jurisdiction, where, if banished, would they go? As Stuart Banner and others have shown, the Indians were, contrary to popular opinion, the acknowledged owners of the land, and most if not all colonial acquisitions of land through lawful purchase reinforced the notion that what was not within the colonial jurisdiction belonged to the Indians outside it.[2] If those lands that had not been purchased or commandeered by the white settlers belonged to the Indians and were subject to their governance, then how could they be banished to them?

The answer becomes visible in the story of the only Indian banishment in their early postcontact history and entails the separation of the Indians from the land—any land—altogether. The retelling of this singular event provides an unusual window into the role the Indians played in reshaping the Puritan notion of community and of community membership. In late October 1675, after the Indians had won a number of strategic battles in King Philip's War, an order came down from the colonial authorities that the vast majority of the praying Indians—amounting to roughly five hundred—then living in five praying towns scattered across the Massachusetts Bay Colony were to "be forwith sent for, & disposed of to Deare Island as the place appointed for their present aboade."[3] In this removal to Deer Island, a bleak and barren rock in the Boston harbor that, as I argue, rose to the level of a banishment, we witness not only one of the war's greatest atrocities but also the grounds for a previously unnoticed change in the way the Indians came to be represented under English law, which differed from the representations entailed in removal, relocation, and reservation. Specifically it was in part as a result of their banishment to Deer Island that the Indians of the Plymouth and Massachusetts Bay Colonies moved from a legal status dependent almost exclusively on territorial affiliations—which kept them outside the dominant subject positions made available by English common law—to one dependent on their actions and thus constitutive of membership in the sense of common law.

During their nearly eight-month stay on Deer Island the Indians were for the first time in the history of their contact with the English fully deter-ritorialized.[4] Far from being yet another hardship in a long line of territorial hardships that began with European conquest and ended with the system of Indian reservations, Deer Island represents a radical departure from the his-tory of the gradual dwindling of the Indians' territorial possessions and sover-eignty. In sending the Indians to a place *within* the Puritan jurisdiction instead of outside it and in holding out no promise of ownership of or long-term habitation within it, the Puritans effected a banishment that was unlike any other.[5] Previously defined in a legal sense by their geographical coordinates and their attributes as property owners, the Indians, now robbed of their usual connections to the land reinforced variously by tradition, ritual, agriculture, and most significant of all, legal title, suffered the loss of a primary identifica-tion with the land that altered the categories by which they knew themselves, by which they were known to the English, and perhaps most importantly, by which the Puritan community made members legal.[6]

The Indian banishment to Deer Island, moreover, and the subsequent emergence of the Indians into the common law as fully recognized actors must be read, like all the preceding stories of banishment, against the particu-lar events of the day. Perhaps even more than the other banishments related here, the Indian banishment seemed determined by the nexus of political and religious conflicts on the minds of the Puritans at the time—by the push and pull of post-Restoration politics and by the internal divisions of post–Half-Way Covenant congregations. Needless to say, once Charles II ascended to the throne in 1660, the Puritans' hopes for securing an audience sympathetic to their agenda in the inner circles of English government were dashed, as were the occasional grants in aid they had received under Cromwell. However, this alone would not necessarily have created any particular urgency for them; rather it was the increased scrutiny by the king of their internal affairs that upset them, and most pertinent, the ratcheting up of this scrutiny along with the start of King Philip's War.

With the war came increased expenses; the Puritans needed soldiers, and the soldiers needed arms and food. These expenses were covered in part by the United Colonies, a confederation, originally, of the Massachusetts Bay Colony, Plymouth, New Haven, and Connecticut (which by the time of King Philip's War had absorbed New Haven), but the United Colonies were forced to appeal repeatedly to the king, who found the whole affair distasteful. Most significant was the king's skepticism about how the war came about: the Puri-tans claimed that they were the victims of Indian aggression, but the king had reason to believe that it was the other way around—that the Indians were, like the king himself, duped by the Puritans' overreaching. As Stephen Saunders Webb observes, "That . . . the puritans [*sic*] admitted, even boasted of their abuse of both native proprietors and royal right only re-emphasized the opinion of nearly every commentator in England that the Bostoners had arrogantly begun the war."[7] Copies of these pamphlets would not have been hard to come by even in the colonies, and so it could not have escaped the Puritans' notice that in the ultimate battle to maintain their borders as colonies against their greatest enemy, the Indians, they were in some sense also fighting their king.

In the midst of a decades-long effort by the Puritans to establish clear boundaries around their communities through the exercise of banishment, as opposed to war, in other words, war obviously added another complication. Other than the Pequot War of 1637 and the occasional Indian skirmish, war had played a relatively minor part in the line-drawing enterprise of the Puritans. But King Philip's War introduced even greater complexity to the enterprise since it could no longer be clear in the political context of post-Restoration England whether the boundaries that were at stake in the war were, as the Puritans believed them to be, between them and the Indians alone. In the earlier years problems with the Indians had by and large been internal, colonial affairs. Charles I and Cromwell were concerned but happy to let the Puritans solve these problems on their own. By the 1660s, however, the king saw the Indians as allies in a growing struggle with the colonists, and so by maintaining their borders against the enemy Indians, the colonists may have believed that they were also maintaining their borders against encroachment by the king. But the king's belief that both he and the Indians were being similarly victimized by the colonists may also have put pressure on the Puritans to make good use of those Indians who were or claimed to be on their side. Indeed the mistakes made early on in the war in failing to distinguish between enemy and friend among the Indians may have brought to the fore the idea of keeping the friendly Indians together and yet within their borders, and so the strange solution of banishing them to an island in the Boston harbor was born. It may also have become apparent after a decade of serious incursions by various sectarian groups, such as the Quakers, that the friendly Indians were the lesser of two (or more) evils and worth incorporating as the Puritans' own, even if that meant pushing them aside for a time.

If the boundaries between the enemy Indians and the Puritans were made more complex by the king's attitude and interference in the war, the boundaries between the friendly or Christianized Indians and the Puritans were under an unprecedented pressure of their own. Since the establishment of the first native towns, of course, and arguably before, the so-called Christian Indians were in a kind of limbo. As many scholars have noted, the "praying" Indians were unfairly confined to the boundaries of these artificially constructed towns, where because they were often established in the worst locations, they could do little to make their own way, ironically, but pray. But few if any studies have noted the strange convergence of these praying towns, which were yet another effort by the Puritans to impose an isomorphic relationship between religious community and geographical space, with the crumbling of just such a relationship between their own churches and legally defined communities. If the Half-Way Covenant fixed the problem of declining church membership, it brought on another crisis of its own, as people who moved from place to place maintained their memberships in their original congregations instead of transferring them, creating what Stephen Foster calls ecclesiastical "resident aliens."[8] By the terms of New England's congregational policy—the so-called New England Way of consociation and separation that was set forth in John Cotton's sermon, "The Way of the Churches of Christ in New England," members of a legally defined community were supposed to be members of the church in and of that place, not members of another church.[9] Yet many lived in one place and, as Foster puts it, worshiped in another. There were recorded instances of this phenomenon long before 1662, of course, but the numbers seem to have increased in the years following the Half-Way Covenant, producing a relatively unnoticed rift between legal communities and religious communities.[10]

English Only Actors

It is in this context, then, that we must read the banishment of the praying Indians to Deer Island, for the experiment in banishment represented in this move was in some sense doomed not only by the extremity of the material conditions on the island but also by the confusion surrounding legal and religious borders in a variety of areas and by the primacy that legal personhood seemed to be enjoying over religious personhood at the time. Indeed through their banishment to Deer Island the Indians gained recognition for the first time as persons within the terms of the English common law. Unlike other forms of law, the common law derived from, even as it addressed itself to, the actions of the people, which made seventeenth-century conceptions of legal persons different from those that preceded or followed them. Based on common custom, the common law understood persons, subjects, and later citizens in terms of their actions, staying away from the regulation of emotions or states of mind. As Richard White explains, while seventeenth-century legal persons were still subjects and not yet citizens, they might nevertheless best be seen not as subjects in the medieval sense but rather as "centers of personal agency" whose relationship to the law was reciprocal.[11] Based on the common law's understanding of custom as the actions that, though unwritten, passed directly into law by virtue of the universality of their practice, such reciprocal agency meant that performance according to the common law was less about legal ritual or specific declarations of authority than it was about the apparently transparent way people's everyday actions—as opposed to their aspirations, assumptions, or beliefs—helped to make the law.[12]

However, the common law also privileged action in a way that went beyond its intended sphere of influence. It used people's actions as material for its own development, adding new actions to its rhetorical registers and absorbing them as new precedent as it evolved, making new communities, new members, and new lawmakers over time. But the agency at the heart of the common law was not, conveniently, open to all, for as the common lawyers insisted, only the English could make English law.[13] "The Englishman, who saw his realm as a fabric of custom," Pocock has explained, "saw proprietor, litigant, judge, counselor, and prince as engaged in a constant activity, one of preserving, refining, and transmitting the usages and customs that made him and England what they were."[14] This prohibition against the incorporation of any actions but English actions into the common law served as an impediment to the recognition of Indian agency under the law and may have had some bearing on the Indians' efforts to gain a recognizable status through conversion, the area that has been the focus of most scholarly attention to this matter.[15] But the acts of the Indians during their conversions, as reported by John Eliot and others, have recently been given a new meaning by scholars working in the field of performance theory. The use of performance theory to understand the praying Indians has gained numerous adherents in recent years, no doubt because many aspects of their dual identities—part Christian, part Indian— were so obviously staged.[16] Once seen as forms of cultural accommodation that led, in the words of one commentator, to "cultural suicide," these kinds of performances, which included religious speeches and involved the adoption of many English customs, are now seen in a far more positive light.[17] As an approach that sees an increasing number of culturally inspired acts as the staging and carrying out of certain kinds of expression, performance theory allows us to view the Indians as no more authentic or inauthentic in their performances than anyone else. Alice Nash, for example, argues that Indian performances were often dismissed by the English as "antic" not because the Indians were disorganized or uncivilized, as the English liked to say, but "because they mixed up categories kept distinct by English sensibilities."[18]

Performance theory also helps us see that performances on the part of both the Indians and the English were far more complex than they might otherwise appear. Joshua David Bellin and Sarah Rivett, for example, have found in the conversion narratives of the Indians evidence not of capitulation to Puritan forms of expression but of newly dynamic forms of religious expression all their own. Other scholars, such as James Ronda, Jenny Hale Pulsipher, and Daniel Mandell, have enabled us to see the newly mixed identities of the Indians as a way of maintaining their autonomy in a range of Anglo-Indian practices, from farming to governance to trade.[19] Matt Cohen has recently uncovered another attribute of performance by extending the category to include all forms of native communication, including healing practices, speech, and writing, which worked to create what he calls a "networked" community.[20]

If these studies of performance contribute to and pave the way for other studies, they do not yet encompass the area of performance that is of concern to us here, namely legal performance, or what lawmakers think of as legal agency. To be sure, since Ann Marie Plane observed that "even the best analyses of early American law have failed to mention the fate of indigenous legal systems," much has been done to uncover what legal performance might have meant in Native American terms.[21] But as useful as such work on indigenous legal autonomy and sovereignty has been, it fails to address how the Indians "performed" within the terms of law familiar to the Puritans: the legal system known to the English as the common law. Nor have the few scholars who currently work on legal performance found a way to incorporate common-law agency into the idea of performance. As Julie Peters explains, current uses of the concept of legal performance tend to fall into one of two categories: the law as theatrical ritual—for example the trial, the scene of arrest, the scene of execution; and the law as discursive enactment—for example the jury verdict, the judicial opinion, and linguistic declarations such as "I do" that bring legally recognized relationships into being.[22] But performance in the common-law sense is not necessarily staged or conducted in what performance theorists have called a "performative context." With legal performance we are not concerned with what Pocahontas may or may not have intended when she allegedly lunged to cover John Smith's body with her own as her fellow Powhatan Indians raised their tomahawks against him.[23] Rather legal performance in the common-law sense is typically mundane and includes the most fundamental manifestations of human agency, such as crossing the road, planting crops, or raising children.

Needless to say, these kinds of acts, though performed differently by different people at different times, are universal, the very quality that threatened the English and kept them from recognizing the Indians as actors in this sense. But it is important to understand how difficult it was to keep the Indians at bay in this regard, how hard the Puritans struggled to disregard their contributions as actors, and how they eventually gave way to admitting the Indians as actors in the aftermath of King Philip's War. Indeed it was in their roles as soldiers for the English that the banished Indians were eventually able to assert themselves as actors under the common law. This was in part because their military actions were so conspicuously agential that they could not be ignored and in part because the military—in the form of the militia—served the colony as a peripheral social system whose regulations differed from but ultimately filtered back into the larger social sphere as a whole.[24]

The emergence of this new common-law identity for the Indians can be traced in some of the literature from the period immediately before, during, and after the Deer Island banishment, including records of religiously inspired acts by John Eliot of Indian conversions; acts of Indians as aides and interpreters in King Philip's War as described by Benjamin Church, William Hubbard, and Daniel Gookin; and acts that were officially regarded as legal in the certificates and petitions filed after the war by the Indians and by the English on their behalf. In these legal and quasi-legal records, I argue, the relatively static vision of the Indians' legal identities that has emerged from a scholarship largely confined to the limited archive of cases and legislation typically looked to in this area gives way to a picture of the Indians as common-law actors. These documents show a gradual positioning of the Indians in terms of legal agency from an aspirational status that appears in the optative modality, a phase associated with the conversion literature about the Christian Indians; through the subjunctive or conditional, a phase associated with the histories of the Deer Island Indians; to the declarative, a phase in which Indian acts are presented as statements of fact and are expressed in the indicative mood. Through a brief discussion of the aberrant nature of the Deer Island situation as a banishment as well as the dominant use of territorial status as legal markers for the Indians in the period before Deer Island, each of these rhetorical identities can be treated in turn.

Landowners, Nonactors

To appreciate the enormity of the shift brought about in Indian identities as a result of their banishment to Deer Island, a brief review of the overwhelming and exclusive identification of the Indians with territory is in order. From the moment of first contact, territorial descriptions of the Indians prevailed in Puritan accounts. The undeniable evidence of Indian settlements throughout New England made territorial markers the most sensible option for understanding the Indians from the start. Thus in *New England's Prospect* (1634), one of the earliest descriptions of the New England Indians, William Wood set the stage for the use of such terms. "The Indians," he wrote, "to the east and northeast, bear . . . the name of Churchers and Tarrenteens; these in the southern parts be called Pequots and Narragansetts; those who are seated westward be called Connecticuts and Mohawks."[25] Within a given colony the Indians were often identified in more specific ways—as in "the Cape Indians" or the "Indians of Mount Hope"—but they remained tied to land-based designations. Even the Indians in the praying towns continued to be identified in terms of their place of residence, as in "the Indians of Natick" or the "Indians of Punkapoag."

As legal historians of the period have explained, the Puritans recognized the Indians as the rightful owners of the land on which their settlements were established.[26] It followed, then, that the vast majority of cases in which the Indians came into direct contact with the English were over the purchase and sale of land—a fact that the case law from the period makes indisputable. In addition such territorial designations comport with the English emphasis on the importance of property within the law, and thus at least initially the land-based view of the Indian was not out of keeping with many of the designations the common law used to describe English subjects. For John Fortescue, for example, and other early theorists of the common law, the maintenance of private property was the most important task of the law and one of the ways in which English law, which upheld the sanctity of private property, could be distinguished from French law, at least until the time of the French Revolution. It was also the subject of Sir Edward Coke's first common-law masterpiece, *Coke on Littleton*. As Donald Kelley has written, it was "on the basis of the law of private property . . . that the professional monopoly and national mythology of common law were established."[27]

That the common law was based on and stemmed from the law of property, however, did not mean that the Indians were accepted as common-law agents. This point bears repeating. If most Anglo-Indian legal cases in the seventeenth century concerned property relations and fell under the rubric of property law, it was a type of property law and practice that was set apart from its counterpart in England. In England property law was instituted to protect property rights, effectively carving out a zone in which others could not interfere. More significantly, perhaps, a number of other, personal liberties followed from property ownership, including the ability to apply for church membership, sit on juries, and vote, which taken together created a class of people who were recognized by the common law as subjects of the law and lawmakers all at once. Needless to say, the Indians, though recognized as property owners, were denied these liberties and refused membership in this class.

There were a variety of reasons for this refusal. The first concerned a peculiarity of the Indians' legal position in the eyes of the English who regarded them as sovereign nations—a status that becomes visible not in case law as much as in treaties.[28] Individual Indians were considered not only as owners of individual parcels of land but also as residents of their own politically bounded jurisdictions, and in this too they were distinguished from English landowners. By definition treaty law—reserved for negotiations between autonomous polities—accorded to the Indians the status of separate but sovereign "friend" nations and extended mutual obligations to both the Indian and English sides.[29] The history of treaty law between the Indians and the English, even more than that of case law, reveals the rootedness of certain tribal governments in certain areas of land. So entrenched was the notion of Indian sovereignty over certain areas that even when tensions escalated between the Indians and the English and the treaties between them began to reflect not equality between the two nations but the subservience of the Indian nation to the English one, the English proved reluctant to infringe on the Indians' territorially bounded autonomy. When, for example, Miantonomi, sachem of the Narragansetts, and Uncas, sachem of the Mohegans, agreed under the terms of the Hartford Treaty of 1641 to swear allegiance to the English king and to present all intertribal conflicts to the English, the English refused to enforce the terms, surrendering Miantonomi after a particular bloody intertribal struggle to Uncas to wreak his own revenge in a place—the court's language here is notable—"outside the bounds of the English jurisdiction."[30]

Another part of the explanation for this reluctance on the part of the English can be found in the volatile political atmosphere between the English and the Indians and in a general preference on the part of the Puritan authorities not to interfere, despite their insistence on supremacy in the treaty. But the prominence of the use of territorial identities for the Indians and the autonomy they implied may also be accounted for by the Indians' own highly evolved legal system, which may have signaled to the Puritans a more specific potential for conflict in this sphere. More to the point, while it did not depend greatly on territorial concepts and thus offered little to compete with the English imposition of them, the Indians' legal system abounded in nonterritorial notions of the individual, based on kinship and, like English common law, on agency. As Katherine Hermes has reminded us, "the Indians' traditional view of jurisdiction as primarily personal [that is, not based on territorial affiliation] became a sublimated source of legal misunderstanding as Anglo-Europeans imposed territorial jurisdiction as the dominant form of governance."[31] Yasuhide Kawashima and others have postulated that it was a direct violation of Philip's personal jurisdiction over the Indians rather than the continuing barrage of territorial encroachments that served as a catalyst to the hostilities that began King Philip's War.[32]

The recognition of Indian tribal sovereignty also precluded recognition under common law for another reason: it affirmed the status of the Indians as non-Englishmen. Rooted in and reflective of custom, the common law was presented as an impregnable, never-ending feedback loop at the center of which was a vision of the law as a social and national constant. The acts of persons in the same place in the past, in other words, were binding on and yet subject to alteration by people in the present. "The act of a public society of men done five hundred years since," the political philosopher Richard Hooker wrote, "standeth as theirs who presently are of the same societies, because corporations are immortal; we were then alive in our predecessors, and they in their successors do live."[33] That this action-oriented historicism was asserted in the face of all kinds of contradictory evidence—including diverse populations with diverse customs and the effects on English law of the Norman invasion, which added continental law to the equation—mattered little to those who, like Hooker, Coke, and Selden, made the assertion in the first place. A law that was based on the customs of people from "time immemorial" was by definition derived from and applied to people with a shared birthplace and ancestry. This was a factor used by many individuals and groups who were banished—Morton and the Quakers preeminent among them—to wheedle their way back into the fold.

In the case of the Indians, however, it was futile. Going so far as to liken
the Indians to the Jews, the Puritans never made the mistake of confusing the
Indians with the English. Not coincidentally the earliest protoethnographic
accounts from the Puritans about the Indians dwell on the exotic nature of
their customs—their habits of eating, greeting, hunting, and farming—that
set them apart from their English neighbors. Such accounts, written in large
part to satisfy a morbid curiosity on the part of the English reading audience
about the "savages," had the added effect of confirming that Indian customs,
unlike those of the Irish or the Welsh, who were slowly being assimilated into
common-law status at the same time, were so far removed from English customs as to be completely outside the law. It goes without saying that within
such an understanding of the common law, the Indian could not hope to find
purchase. Thus legal pronouncements made reference in mysterious terms to
ostensibly natural proclivities among the Indians that would prevent them
from filing their own suits under the common law or for that matter being
sued by the Puritans as a way of entering into the English legal system as
peers. A typical law of this sort proclaimed that "noe Indians hereafter shalbe
trusted before hand for anything by any English on penalty of being barred
the recovery of any debts by action or plaint."[34] If the law was premised on
the assertion "that there was nothing in English law and government that was
not customary and autochthonous," Pocock noted, then it followed "that the
English possessed a historical and immediate sovereignty over themselves."[35]
To this the Indian, differently sovereign, was clearly not entitled.

The common law reinforced this exclusionary logic in its procedural reliance on English actors in English precedents, which meant that any case
that involved Indian customs and Indian actors would by definition be non–
precedent setting. Inasmuch as precedent served as a link not only between action and law but also, through the force of myth, between past, present, and
future, within this paradigm the Indians were denied a legal future as agents
under the common law. The recognition that Indian customs were not English
customs also meant that in addition to being excluded from judgment under
the common law, the Indians were excluded from judging. That the law derived
from the people meant that only the people, in theory at least, were adequate
arbiters *of* it, and thus the common law stressed the importance of a jury of
one's peers. More significantly the calculus that juries were instructed to use
for assessing the facts pertinent to a defendant's case was based on probability
and directed toward discovering whether the actions in the case at bar were
in probable accord with the actions and customs of English people. Needless

to say, only those familiar with English customs were considered capable of deploying this measure, and thus only juries composed of Englishmen were considered to be fair in English cases. The peer makeup of juries was such a central concern that the Puritans felt the need to meet at least the appearance of fairness by putting Indians on juries in criminal cases in which Indians stood accused. However, these cases were not considered part of the common law.[36]

Denied an identity based on individual actions that would have put them on a par with their English counterparts, the Indians were also barred from occupying positions as subordinates within the common-law system, whose agency was questionably limited but present nonetheless. Unlike the Irish or West Indians, the Indians typically did not register in the law as having a personal status of this kind, even though they sometimes lived with English families as servants.[37] However, the Indians did surface in other subject positions, typically as criminals and traders, but the legal assessment of them in these roles was limited. As criminals or deviants, as Kai Erikson has suggested, they did not contribute to the body of affirmative acts that stood at the center of the common law, and even as traders they remained on the law's margins, addressed through a parallel legal system that included setting aside special days for conducting Indian business in the English courts.[38]

Praying Actors

How, then, did the Indians begin to figure as common-law actors? In a word the answer is, poorly. They began to be recognized legally as actors through their participation in conversion ceremonies in which they were offered legal identities that did not replace but served rather to supplement their identities as owners of and inhabitants of territory. As such these Indians were referred to alternately as Christian, praying, or poor. Laura Stevens notes that "the term poor invoked no legal privileges in English, only emotion," but I would argue here that it did more to move the Indians along the spectrum of legal agency than it did to enhance their status as authentic converts, for in adopting Christianity the praying Indians were adopting a quasi-legal identity that was formed at the point where legal and religious discourses intersected.[39] This intersection is evident not only in the description of Indian subjects in Eliot's reports but also in the divided structure of those reports, written as they were not only for the Society for the Propagation of the Gospel, a religious body that facilitated conversion by disbursing funds for missionary purposes, but also for Parliament, a legal body that helped determine who among those not born in England might still be counted as English. While conventional accounts of the praying Indians tend to focus only on their religious audience, the focus here is on the legal audience in order to reveal the extent to which the Indians occupied an ambiguous place between two discourses—the legal and the religious—from which they emerged as protoagents yearning for the English God but never quite ready to receive him.

The ambiguity of the Indians' status as aspirants to conversion, as Indians still engaged wholly by prayer, has traditionally been read by scholars as evidence of the Puritans' unwillingness to admit them to church membership, while the degree to which this ambiguity contributed to their gradual entrance into a membership within the civil sphere has been largely overlooked.[40] An example of the legal meaning of this ambiguity can be found in Eliot's *Tears of Repentance* (1653) and in his *Late and Further Manifestation of the Progress of the Gospel amongst the Indians in New England* (1655), in which the Indians often cast themselves as sinning and repenting in rapid succession, which if seen from a religious point of view suggests a certain fickleness on their part but from a legal point of view gives them a stage for making their small actions count.[41] One of the most dizzying of such confessions is Monequassun's in *Tears of Repentance*: "When I first heard instruction, I believed not, but laughed at it, and scorned praying to God; afterward. . . . I still hated praying, and I did think of running away . . . but after that I thought I would pray rightly to God, and cast away my sins; then I saw my hypocrisy, because I did ask some questions, but did not do that which I knew. . . . Then again a little my heart was turned after God . . . [and] then I thought that as yet, I do not repent, and believe in Christ; . . . and then I prayed to God . . . [and] after that again, I did a little break the Word of Christ."[42] More circuitous than most, the "one step forward, two steps back" movement represented in this passage was characteristic of a general trend in which the Indians' agency was constructed as aspirational or preparative, which carried with it an infantilizing connotation.

In his preface to *Tears of Repentance*, for example, Richard Mather wrote that "since the Word of God hath been taught and preached among them, the Spirit of the Lord hath been working thereby in the hearts of many of them such Illumination, such Conviction, & c. as may justly be looked at (*if not as a full and through* [sic] *Conversion, yet*) as an hopeful beginning and preparation thereto."[43] Intending to praise the Indians' progress toward conversion,

Mather nevertheless drew our attention to their status as novices in that regard by distinguishing between the "full and through [*sic*] conversion" that was not yet theirs and "an [*sic*] hopeful beginning." But if we view this progress in legal terms, we can shift our attention away from the rigid meaning of preparation for religious conversion to note the way the Indians' status as aspirants put them in a common-law protocol in which aspiration was par for the course. In other words, people who appeared before judges in common-law courtrooms, as every common-law agent would have known, were sometimes successful and sometimes not, and aside from losing their case at the time, the losers or failed aspirants, to use the more religious terms, were not stigmatized with regard to any action they might bring in the future.

The Indians' special relationship to and affinity for prayer, above all other forms of religious instruction or practice, seem also to have contributed to their characterization by Mather and others as perpetual aspirants toward conversion and yet never in possession of it. "Their frequent phrase," Eliot wrote, "of Praying to God, is not to be understood of that Ordinance and Duty of Prayer only, but of all Religion, and comprehendeth the same meaning, with them, as the word [Religion] doth with us."[44] Much has been written on what prayer might have meant to the Indians—Robert James Naeher has speculated, for example, that the Indians made it the cornerstone of their Christianity because "it met, in a meaningful and emotionally satisfying way, deep human needs"—but there can be little doubt that while prized by the Puritans, prayer was not viewed by them as sufficient for conversion.[45] In particular, learning how to read and to restate the lessons of the Bible correctly by listening to lengthy sermons on Bible passages was also central, but there is little evidence that the Indians excelled in this. The Indians' apparent inability to articulate the wisdom they had gleaned from prayer—even though it would have been insufficient in itself—was almost certainly, from the Puritan point of view, an additional stumbling block in their progress toward conversion. While Eliot's efforts to record their confessions suggest that he, perhaps alone, had confidence in their ability to express themselves, he also revealed the limits of that confidence by asking them to restate their conversion experiences over and over again. One subject heading in Eliot's *Tears* is representative of this syndrome: "The next," he wrote, "are the Confessions of Nishohkou; who twice made preparitory [*sic*] Confessions."[46] But if this process devalued their narratives from a religious point of view—and how authentic could their conversions be if they needed to restate them—from a legal point of view these repetitions served rather to incorporate them into the common-law system of

precedent. Within the law the effort to repeat, clarify, or amend their statements looked more like persuasion and thus escaped the taint of inauthentic-
ity such repetition took on in the religious sphere.

In the final analysis, however, the praying Indian remained an aspirant
even in legal terms, but the same could not be said of the praying-Indian-
turned-soldier—the shooting Indian, as it were. From their perch on Deer
Island, praying Indians were released individually or in small groups to serve
as spies, scouts, guides, and soldiers and thus exercised their agency on the
Englishman's behalf in a central and highly visible manner.[47] Admittedly this
was not the first time the English had turned to Indians in time of war; the
Mohegans had joined forces with Connecticut to defeat the Pequots in 1637,
and the use of Indians as guides in battle was not unknown. In these cases,
however, the Indians were seen not as legal agents but as military allies who
were judged, as they were in a number of land dealings, according to the law of
sovereign nations and not according to the common law. During King Philip's
War, by contrast, the Indians figured as actors of individual actions, which
while not exactly mundane—they involved shooting, spying, and interpret-
ing, among others—could be broken down into individual components of the
kind the English recognized as legally constitutive.

Would-Be Actors

The absence of a territorial affiliation, which came about as a result of the Indians' banishment to Deer Island, together with the opportunity the English
offered some to leave Deer Island in order to help in the Englishmen's war
effort, gave rise to some Puritans' representations of the Indians' actions as
having the potential of acquiring recognition under the common law. The
Indians, in short, were no longer aspirants to action but surrogates for it, a
rhetorical shift that moved them one step closer to common-law action. Indeed so consequential were the actions of the Indians in their roles as soldiers,
scouts, or spies that they could be found in numerous histories of the war
written by contemporary Puritans. That they were remarked upon within the
pages of histories was an achievement insofar as history, while not the law, was
the next best thing to the law, a legally proximate form of the written word. A
record of fact and of physical evidence prized by the law in general, historical
narrative was especially privileged within the common law because history—
the story of ancient customs—was, as Coke and many other common lawyers

conceived it, the foundation for the law. Even more to the point, the common law embodied the very logic of history in its procedural reliance on precedent: the adjudication of the facts of a case in the present based on a comparison with those of a case in the past.

That said, in most histories of the war in which the Deer Island Indians are discussed, the Indians tend, as with Richard Mather's comment about the praying Indians, to be diminished even as they are singled out for praise. Nathaniel Saltonstall's *The Present State of New-England with Respect to the Indian War* (1675) and Increase Mather's *A Brief History of the Warr with the Indians in New-England* (1677) fall into this category. Others, such as William Hubbard's *Narrative of the Indian Wars in New England* (1677) and Benjamin Church's *Diary of King Philip's War, 1675–1676* (written some years after the war and first published in 1716), mentioned the Indians and attributed greatness to them but always in the shadow of their English counterparts. In Hubbard's work the actions of the English soldiers were described as heroic; on one occasion the English offered to the enemy "a resolute and valiant repulse," and on another "a stout resistance." The Indians, by contrast, were typically described as "faithful"—a trait taken for granted among the English troops.[48] That Hubbard chose faithfulness as a measure of the Indians' military service reinforces the sense that, while significant, the actions of the Indians were not of the history-making kind. Even when he occasionally detailed the movements of the more noteworthy Indians, he did so in a way that emphasized their native sagacity over their physical prowess: the Indians were depicted as engaged in "politic stratagems," including hiding behind trees, wearing moccasins instead of noisy boots, and blacking their faces to look more like the enemy, all of which lend the appearance not of "courage"—the word used to describe the English—but of cleverness, or what Hubbard in a phrase that damns with faint praise called their "subtle service."[49]

Church followed Hubbard's lead in representing the Indians by recording their presence while devaluing their service when compared to that of the English soldiers. The English had pursued Philip on their own for months, only to lose more men in ambushes than ever before. It was only when they engaged Church, a captain of the forces of the United Colonies, and allowed him to put together a mixed company of Indians and Englishmen that they began to make real progress. But while Church's military strategy suggests his high opinion of the Indians as soldiers, his narrative proves a tribute more to his own genius in deploying them than to the Indians' military skills. He began his description of their service by dwelling at length on the controversy caused by his suggestion to use the Indians in the first place. "As for sending out Indians," he reported, "they thought it no ways advisable and, in short, none of his [Church's] advice practicable." Not long afterward, however, he noted that he was given power "to commission a company of 200 where the English do not exceed the number of 60."[50] Subsequent descriptions occasionally mentioned Indian military actions, but so fixed was Church on congratulating himself that he reduced the Indians under his command to mere products of his leadership. Indeed Church appears by his own reckoning to have been such a magnetic leader that unlike Hubbard, he attributed no particular ingenuity or subtlety to the Indians but praised them solely for doing his bidding.

In the central role it accorded the praying Indians in the war, the history written by Daniel Gookin stood alone and, if only for its focus on the Indians as opposed to the English, signaled that its treatment of the Indians' place in history would be more generous and capacious. Gookin wrote: "Forasmuch as sundry persons have taken pains to write and publish historical narratives of the war, between the English and Indians in New England, but very little hath been hitherto declared (that I have seen) concerning the Christian Indians, who, in reality, may be judged to have no small share in the effects and consequences of this war."[51] The key phrase in this passage is "effects and consequences," for it suggests that Gookin, in stark contrast to his peers, intended not only to catalog and document the heroic feats performed by the Indians but also to consider those feats as precedent setting. Gookin, who served as a Bay Colony magistrate from 1652 to 1676 and as superintendent of the Indians from 1661 to 1687—an official and legally recognized post—wrote of the Indians with a heightened appreciation for the legal ramifications of their "doings," as he dubbed their actions during the war. In his emphasis on the precedential nature of the Indians' actions, Gookin often turned his attention to their outcome, stressing the specific ways in which their "doings" altered events. On one occasion he told the story of how he secured the temporary release of two praying Indians from Deer Island to "gain intelligence of the state of the enemy." "The two spies," he explained, not only "acquitted themselves in the service prudently" but also provided vital information to the English: "the enemy purposed, within three weeks, to fall upon Lancaster . . . as this man declared."[52]

If Gookin displayed a keen awareness of what it might have meant to acknowledge Indian soldiers as common-law actors—"do-ers," in his phrase—and to give them an appropriate reward for their actions, the fact that he told a story in which colonial prejudice against Indians still loomed large dictated that his legal witness would remain a preliminary one. Giving voice to his frustration with the constraints imposed on the Indian soldiers, Gookin effected a substantive and stylistic shift roughly halfway through his history, substituting for a detailed inventory of the actions the Indians *actually* undertook a description of how much their actions *could have* meant had they been given a wider scope, hence the surrogacy noted earlier. On the general subject, for example, of keeping the praying Indians in their own towns and using them as a kind of front line for the English, Gookin wrote: "And *had* the suggestions and importunate solicitations of some persons, who had knowledge and experience of the fidelity and integrity of the praying Indians *been attended and practiced* in the beginning of the war, many and great mischiefs *might have been* according to reason prevented."[53] Gookin adopted the same subjunctive formulation in more specific circumstances as well. Speaking of the initial plan to keep the Indians in the field instead of disbanding them, he wrote: "and *had their counsel been practised*, as I was credibly informed by some upon the place, he [King Philip] *had probably been taken*, and his distressed company at that time." On yet another occasion he observed, "so that if the counsel of our Christian Indians *had been put in practice*, according to rational probability they had taken or slain Philip, and so retarded his motion that the rest *might have come up* with him and destroyed his party."[54]

Replete with these and similar expressions, the second half of Gookin's work reads like an extended exercise in the hypothetical, a fantasy of what would have happened had the circumstances of the war played out otherwise. In this sense the second half of this history affirms the injustice of English actions documented in the first half, not by continuing to attribute blame for them to the English but by imagining the outcome of the war's various moments differently. Indeed the hypothetical posture of the second half of *Historical Account of the Doings and Sufferings* extends beyond Gookin's reflections on the precise circumstances of the war to his musings on the "what ifs" of the Christian Indians' treatment by the English in general. His greatest preoccupation in this regard becomes visible in his repeated references to the defensive "walls" the Indians' villages *might have* provided for the colony against the enemy Indians *had* their English neighbors allowed them to live there in peace. "It was also a weakening to the English in removing these frontier Indian plantations and forts," he wrote in a typical passage, "which would have been as walls under God to us, as the sequel proved."[55] But the hypothetical, contingent mood marks his many other thoughts as well. In reflecting, for example, on the prejudice of countless Englishmen toward those few who defended the praying Indians as loyal subjects of the English, Gookin offered this syntactically fraught and drawn-out formulation:

> It might rationally have been considered that those two persons above named [Eliot and Gookin himself], who had . . . been acquainted with, and conversant among those Christian Indians, should have more knowledge and experience of them than others had, and consequently should be able to speak more particularly concerning such of those Indians whom they knew . . . to be honest and pious persons. And if, at such a time, they should have been wholly silent and remiss in giving a modest testimony concerning them when called thereunto, God might justly have charged it upon them, as a sin and neglect of their duty, had they for fear declined to witness the truth for Christ, and for these his poor distressed servants, some of the Christian Indians.[56]

In this passage the idea of how the English *might have* responded to his and Eliot's defense of the Indians *had* they taken their greater knowledge of the Indians into account is offered as a corrective to the actual unfolding of events during which Gookin and Eliot were defamed and excoriated and for which, Gookin went on to say, "(God knows) there was no ground." It also serves in Gookin's alternative history as the prelude to yet another contingency: what it would have been like if Gookin and Eliot "at such time, should have been wholly silent" and said nothing in support of the Indians at all. The possibility for imagining other outcomes here seems almost endless.

In constructing a hypothetical, alternative history, moreover, Gookin paralleled the common law's logic insofar as he looked back to history but altered it just enough to reinsert acts that were in the past unfairly excluded from it. In adopting the subjunctive mode to tell his story, Gookin also provided a model that would later be adopted by the common law in addressing the kinds of wrongs—such as race-based wrongs—that demanded a look back not to the actual past, which was riddled with error, but to a hypothetical past that was a more perfect representation of what the future should be. "The principle of rectification [for past wrongs]," the political philosopher Robert Nozick has explained, "will make use of its best estimate of subjunctive information about what would have occurred . . . if the injustice had not taken place."[57] In the absence of such a hypothetical reconstruction of the past, of course, the centuries of wrongs against the Indians, slaves, and other ill-served groups could never have been overturned within the law.

Still, if through his use of the subjunctive Gookin opened up a rhetorical space for talking about the Indians as if they were or at least could have been history-making agents in King Philip's War, Gookin, like his fellow historians, could not fully bring about the translation of that rhetoric into a common-law context. Like the cases that finally overturned unjust precedents in the area of racial-based jurisprudence, that achievement would have to wait to be recorded in the legal documents, in particular the certificates Gookin appended to his text, which move beyond the paralegal writing of history to legal rhetoric. Unlike his subjunctive history, these legal documents shift into the indicative mode not only to prove the Indians' bravery but also to serve as passports to a widening sphere of agency for the Indians within the law.

Common-Law Indian Actors

The subjunctive mode that Gookin used to assess the Indians' actions and to evaluate the potential consequences of those actions turned seamlessly into the indicative mode that prevailed in the narratives that began to proliferate in the postwar period about the Indians and to serve as an expression of compensation for their actions in the war. Presented in the form of affidavits of their good conduct, these certificates were issued to Indian soldiers for the purpose of allowing them to continue to act in the future without being apprehended or disturbed. Ironically, while these certificates enlarged the sphere of action for these Indians, they became necessary only because in the aftermath of the war further restrictions were placed on those Indians who had survived. Prohibitions on the Indians' leaving their praying towns without an escort were immediately put into effect after the war, but far harsher restrictions were contemplated, including legislation to prohibit Indians from entering English towns without permission of town committees of militia and to reinstate the death penalty for any Indians presenting arms against any person or running away when ordered to stop.[58] Fortunately these harsher laws were not passed, but the general requirement for those Indians moving beyond the borders of their towns to have certificates of good conduct remained.[59]

These certificates, the best examples of which are appended to Gookin's history, appear at first glance to be identical in form, but the actual differences that emerge under a closer analysis tell the story of a rhetorical shift toward common-law recognition. In fact in the certificates appended to Gookin's text as well as in a number of others in the legal and genealogical records of the Indians, three classifications emerge, revealing a range of common-law commitment to Indian agency.[60] The first type makes the weakest and most general claim on the Indians' behalf: that they were of good character and proved courageous and loyal in the war. An example can be found in the certificate by Major Thomas Savage:

> These do certify that I, Thomas Savage, of Boston, being commander of the English forces at Mount Hope, in the beginning of the war between the English and Indians, about July 1675, and afterward in March, 1676, at Menumesse and Hadley. In both which expeditions, some of the Christian Indians belonging to Natick, &c., were in the army; as at Mount Hope, were about forty men, and at Menumesse six men. I do testify, on their behalf, that they carried themselves well, and approved themselves courageous soldiers, and faithful to the English interest.
>
> Dated at Boston, the 20th day of December, 1677.[61]

The generality of Savage's language is evident in his reference to the Indians as groups: "about forty men, and at Menumesse six men." Yet even here we note important signs of the kinds of agential individuation on which the common law relied. In contrast to the histories or conversion narratives, for example, the groups formed by the Indians appear to have been small and selective; they were placed at the scene of specific battles, and they were considered part of the "army," a measure of their acceptance by the English never before seen.

The individuation that begins to emerge in Savage's certificate grows more prominent in the second type of certificate, which ascribes to the Indians an even more visible agency. "Captain Samuel Hunting's Certificate about the Christian Indian Solider" exemplifies this type of certificate:

> These are to certify, that I, Samuel Hunting, of Charlestown, in New England being, by authority of the Governor and Council, appointed commander of the praying Indians living in the Massachusetts colony, in New England, in the war against the barbarous Indians. . . . The said company, with myself, served the country, in several expeditions, for about one year's time. In all which service, the said Indians behaved themselves courageously and faithfully to

the English interest; and I conceive that the said company did kill and take prisoners above two hundred of the enemy, and lost but one man of ours; besides about one hundred persons they killed and took prisoners at other times, when I was not with them, and they went out volunteers. And, in testimony of the truth hereof, I have hereunto set my hand, this 13th day of December, 1677.[62]

Several features of Hunting's certificate are noteworthy. He referred to the Indians not only as being in the army but also as constituting a company of soldiers unto themselves, and he ascribed to them certain memorable feats, including the taking of prisoners. He also noted that, unlike the English soldiers who were paid for their military service, the Indians served as volunteers, which underscored the need to compensate them after the war. In addition Hunting remarked that the Indians acted on their own; though he commanded them, at times, he noted, they acted "when I was not with them."

The third type of certificate is perhaps the most important in that it acknowledges the transition of the praying Indians from banished Indians to Anglo-Indian soldiers, offering direct evidence that during the war and in the postwar period the Indians assumed a new legal identity. "Captain Daniel Henchman's Certificate concerning the Praying Indian Soldiers" is of this type:

These may certify, that I, Daniel Henchman, of Boston, being appointed and authorized by the Governor and Council of Massachusetts, not only to look unto and order the praying Indians, for some part of the time that they were confined to Deer Island; but, likewise, to have the command of several of them as soldiers, both at Mount Hope, in the beginning of the war, 1675; and also in another expedition, May and June, 1676, when I had the command of the English forces at Weshakum, Mendon, and Hadley; in all which time I had experience of the sobriety, courage, and fidelity of the generality of those Indians. And this I do testify, under my hand, and could say much more on their behalf, if time and opportunity permitted. Dated at Boston, this 29th of November, 1677.[63]

Here Henchman indicated that he had two different relationships with the Indians. In the first, before their release from Deer Island, they appear to have been little different from children under his supervision, but in the second under his command they transformed into soldiers capable of performing new acts and, in the process, taking on new agential roles. By including both types of relationships, Henchman at once signaled and certified the emergence of the Indians' new legal identity.

Although each of these three types of certificates suggests a slightly different and still tentative approach to the Indians' entrance into the common law, together they represent a tendency to turn the Indians' actions during the war into a basis for legal compensation, the ultimate sign of incorporation by the common law. When carried by the Indians outside their towns, these certificates guaranteed the "life and liberty" that had previously been promised to the praying Indians but rarely realized. There were, of course, still instances in which the certificates were ignored by English authorities, but for the most part they were honored. More significantly these certificates paved the way for the praying Indians to assert a legal voice of their own: emboldened by these English-authored documents, the Indians commenced a petition-writing campaign to request leniency for relatives still being held as prisoners by enemy Indians.[64] Worth noting too is that in these Indian-authored petitions the Indian veterans did not *beg* for mercy, as they had previously been wont to do, but rather asked that the precedent for recognizing and rewarding military service set by the common law be followed in their case as it was in the case of their English counterparts.[65] Here again we see the importance of the pairing of the Indians' banishment with their military roles in facilitating their transition to common-law status.

Perhaps most significantly, both Indian- and English-authored certificates changed the Indians' status within English common law by enabling them to participate in the judicial system in ways that embraced issues beyond those of personal liberty and that extended beyond the immediate postwar period. Jean O'Brien makes the point that many Indians who had served the English as soldiers were able to parlay their military service into protection against fraudulent land deals. "Having approved our selves faithfull to ye English interest," reads one such petition, "In ye Late Warr, and joined them most of us As Souldiers . . . we Doe hereby Declare to the hond Court yt wee or pdeceser had & have a Naturall Right to Most of the Lands Lying in the Nipmuck Country . . . for which we Desire the Country & Genll Court will give us a Compensation."[66] For years after King Philip's War—through King William's War and Queen Anne's War—Indians were frequently employed as soldiers and were recognized legally for that service by means of monetary payments, titles to land, job opportunities, or greater freedoms.

Daniel Mandell notes that the Indians emerged from the war in the Massa-chusetts Bay Colony confident of the future.[67] Traditionally a refuge for the rootless, the military had proved once again to be a fertile place for identity transformation.

If the Indians emerged from Deer Island with a new identity, however, they did not emerge with the full range of liberties and responsibilities ac-corded to most English people under the common law. The observation of a shift in the Indians' legal identity, then, should not be taken to imply that they achieved any sort of lasting legal equality as a result of their banishment to Deer Island. The legal records of more than three centuries of Anglo-American and Indian colonial relations show all too well that the Indians were never put on a legal par with members of the dominant white population. In fact legal historians have typically observed a marked deterioration in these relations toward the end of the seventeenth century. Jenny Hale Pulsipher, Yasuhide Kawashima, and James Ronda, for example, all note that King Philip's War marked a turning away from a more equitable treatment of Indians within the English legal system. According to Pulsipher, "by the beginning of the eighteenth century, popular animus against the Indians was finally matched by legislation that codified divisions between English and Indians along race lines."[68]

If the common-law designation of Indian acts and identities became pos-sible only in the absence of earlier designations based on territory and sov-ereignty, however, it may be the case that racial designations for the Indians became possible only in the presence of the common-law categories, for now the authorities were forced to search for yet another way of making the Indian a performing "other" again. As the Deer Island banishment and its rhetori-cal instantiations show, though, in the period leading up to and immediately following King Philip's War—a period before the law had carved out a racial-ized place for the Indian—the question was not whether whites were play-ing Indian, as Philip Deloria puts the issue, but whether the Indians were playing—or players—at all.[69] The question, in short, was the far more basic one of whether Indian acts, like English acts, could be seen as customary and thus accord the Indians membership within the Puritan communities, not by way of the quasi-legal optative or subjunctive moods but in the indicative of a shared Indian and English reality. By examining the changes associated with the site of the Deer Island banishment, then, we can begin to answer the call issued by recent scholars of Native American history to focus not on the Indians' vanishing—a common theme of Native Americans studies after

King Philip's War—but on their persistence in those years when they served as traders, builders, sailors, carpenters, and domestic workers and in those roles "interacted with municipal, county, and state entities" that altered the kinds of communities and community memberships the Puritans and their heirs created.[70]

Conclusion
_____

The Ends of Banishment: From the Puritan Colonies to the Borderlands

Whether as a penalty or as a political measure, exile is either prohibited or not practised in most countries.

—*Study of the Right of Everyone to Be Free from Arbitrary Arrest, Detention, and Exile* (United Nations Commission on Human Rights, 1964)

IN THE WORDS of a Supreme Court case from 1958, banishment is a "fate universally decried by civilized people."[1] In that case, *Trop v. Dulles*, a former U.S. army private who had been convicted of desertion from the army in 1944 was denied a passport and effectively "de-nationalized" more than eight years after his crime was committed and his time had been served. However, Chief Justice Earl Warren overturned the decision because, in his words, banishment was "a punishment more primitive than torture."[2] In spite of its status in Warren's mind, as well as in the popular imagination, as primitive and archaic, banishment, as *Trop* suggests, had not disappeared. In the more than three centuries between the time the Puritans' authority to banish was revoked and the decision in *Trop*, banishment continued to insert itself, even if under a different name, into social, political, and legal orders all over the world as a means of ridding communities of undesirables. In the eighteenth century banishment was carried on in England in the form of transportation: the practice of sending criminals to the colonies; and in the nineteenth century banishment became deportation: a means of practicing immigration policy that remains at the heart of government policy today. Indeed even though more than half a century has passed since *Trop*, banishment survives, one might even say thrives, despite Chief Justice Warren's condemnation of it.

What, if anything, can we make of the history of the common law of banishment after its official end more than four hundred years ago? Despite the profound differences between the early modern period and subsequent centuries, between their material, social, and intellectual conditions, the parallels between the uses of banishment over time remain intriguing. Moreover when examined in the right light, these parallels ultimately provide the grounds for a deeper understanding of how social exclusion works and why sending someone outside ostensibly fixed territorial boundaries has remained such an enduring form of punishment, in spite of its being thought by most to be "primitive and archaic." Still, one objective here is not to offer any answers about why banishment endures but rather to reopen a conversation about banishment that has in many ways been prematurely shut down by rigid, modern assumptions about how communities and the concept of membership within them operate. If we return to the contours of banishment in the period of its most frenzied use, the seventeenth century, perhaps we can return to its essential messiness as well, a messiness enabled and facilitated by the common law, by which interpretations of two terms fundamental to banishment, "space" and "sovereignty," were fundamentally ambiguous. By means of the debate over those ambiguities, banishment became in seventeenth-century America a primary means of thinking through how communities might reconceptualize the very notions of space and sovereignty. Since then banishment has moved into more formal and more legislative incarnations and has become more regulated, more streamlined, more of a fixture than something to be reckoned with. Even in today's more international, arguably global order, where traditional notions of space and sovereignty have been challenged and in many cases dropped away, the conversations about banishment and the challenges to it, rooted more in constitutional rather than common-law terms, have narrowed.

Revisiting the terms of banishment in seventeenth-century New England can highlight the strains of continuity and discontinuity between banishments now and then. *Banished* began with a simple, if paradoxical assertion: that there can be no inside without an outside and that communities depend on the distinction between inside and outside to make and keep members. After examining the world of the early Puritans in New England, however, in which these assertions were arguably more vigorously applied and repeatedly tested than in any other, *Banished* ends by retreating from them. In the stories of those who were banished from Plymouth and from the Massachusetts Bay Colonies, for example, we note not only the complexities of maintaining a distinction between what was inside and out but also the constant re-formation of those communities in which the specific configuration of inside and out that precipitated the exercise of banishment was either superseded by another configuration or found for other reasons to be untenable. The specific arguments leveled for and against banishment by all of the major figures studied here show a multiplication of differences—between a community's members as well as the spaces they occupy—that in each case made the dichotomy on which banishment relied less viable than it first appeared.

Indeed *Banished* suggests that far from representing a fixed sense of inside and out of the sort presupposed by the exercise of banishment, communities in early America exemplified a sense of shifting terrain in which inside and out were always being renegotiated. The stories of Anne Hutchinson and Thomas Morton, for example, reveal the possibilities for thinking about inside and out by offering a different set of spatial coordinates than those that marked the boundaries of the colony and to which social, political, and legal differences had once seemed inextricably tied. In their emphasis on hospitality Morton and Hutchinson shifted the boundaries of inside and out to the home, creating new social and legal orders that competed with those of the colony and shifted the center of the circles by which their communities were defined. The story of Roger Williams confirms a similar shift in coordinates, in his case from the distinction between the inside and outside of the Puritans' community on earth to the inside and outside of their soon-to-be-realized kingdom in heaven.

In each case studied here, moreover, once the lines within and around the communities began to shift, it was no longer clear who was inside one or outside the other because it was no longer clear which lines had primacy. If we think about communities not as groups of isolated individuals, for example, but as collections of homes—as places like the communities of early modern England and New England that extended special privileges to those who situated themselves within homes as opposed to those who predominantly existed outside them—then the people inside Hutchinson's home or gathered around Morton's Maypole had as much if not more of a claim to membership in the community than many others did. Shifting coordinates also account for the claim to membership of the Christian Indians examined in Chapter 4, who proved to be never more inside the Puritan community than when they were sufficiently outside all competing jurisdictions, and who became members of the Puritan community only when it became clear that in being beyond the boundaries of the Indian lands that were themselves outside the Puritan ones, they were rendered insiders by definition.

In addition to noting the differing perspectives on space that led to a shift in the kinds of coordinates that mattered for determining what was inside and out, however, in *Banished* one can observe a shift in the concept of membership itself that, like its more physical, geographical counterpart, contributed to the Puritans' confusion about who was inside and who was out. This shift revealed itself in the form of an abstract and at times contradictory sense of what it meant to have met the criteria for membership within the community. This confusion about inside and out can be tied directly to the law, for it was the common law's position on membership that made banishment controversial in the first place. As explained in *Banished*, the law's position on membership has largely escaped scholarly notice precisely because it is so difficult to pin down, appearing especially difficult in this regard when juxtaposed to the clarity offered by the religion on the basis of which the Puritans were said traditionally to have made all of their membership decisions. Of course religious membership, as the Puritans understood it at least, had a kind of absoluteness that lent itself more readily than the law to the dichotomous nature of inside and out. In order to gain admission to a Puritan congregation, for example, one had to conform actively to a master narrative—of conversion—and in this act of (and active) conformity one achieved a status that was similar to that of everyone else. This reinforced the notion that membership meant being part of a homogenous population, and while this did not prevent disputes about whether certain membership criteria had been met, it tended to prevent disputes about the validity of the membership criteria themselves.

The "Half-Way Contract"

Legal membership in the Puritan colonies, perhaps because it was a more capacious category than religious membership or perhaps because it required no particular affirmation, was, however, not as cut and dried. There were, for example, no legal conversion narratives to which members had to adhere; nor were there obvious admission requirements, other than financial self-sufficiency. Other than casting the occasional vote for the General Court or governor and applying for property ownership, there was little opportunity for the Puritans to express their sense of legal affiliation except, paradoxically, through banishment. In turning people out, the Puritans gave themselves and others a rare if not unique opportunity to state their beliefs about membership and to air the many different ways in which they believed membership should and could take shape. But what turns up in the examination of banishment laws and banishment narratives is far from monolithic. In addition to providing scanty evidence of membership affiliation, the laws of banishment, which attempted to identify who counted as a member by specifying who did not, were both structurally and circumstantially vague: structurally because the law was by definition in the business of making communities and thus always providing competing notions of what it meant to be inside or outside the community at any given time; and circumstantially because material changes, including increased mobility and imperial expansion, put unprecedented pressure on drawing the very boundaries that made the recognition of what it meant to be inside and outside possible.

It is suggested in *Banished,* then, that the ambiguity about membership in seventeenth-century New England was endemic to the operation of the law and to the context in which the Puritans found themselves operating legally. Taken together, these two factors made the little that was set down in the law about membership uncertain. From a circumstantial point of view, perhaps the most vexed criterion by which legal membership was assessed was shared ancestry, also known as birthright or jus solis. Originally thought to be a rather easy matter to settle—one was either born in England or one was not—by the time of the white settlement of New England, one could be born outside the traditional boundaries of England, say in Scotland or in the colonies, and still claim English ancestry by law. But if one could be born in the colonies and claim membership as an Englishman by one day taking up residency in England, then the converse also had to be true: that one could be born in England and claim membership in the colonies. Logically sound, this conclusion was nevertheless found to be unacceptable by the Puritans, for they had no intention of letting Englishmen who were English only by virtue of their birth into their hard-won settlements.[3] In fact an insistence that English ancestry was not enough to gain membership in the colonies lay behind their exclusion of the Quakers, who raised the issue of whether small associations of Englishmen, with interests or commonalties that went far beyond their ancestry, could exclude other associations of Englishmen or whether the quality of simply being English might trump them all.

In addition to the struggle over what kinds of membership inhered in one's birthright and by extension in the quality of being English, there was

the issue of what it meant to be physically present in a place. A condition
that was by definition shared by all who were to be banished from the Puritan colonies, being present was not a guarantee of membership, especially at
a time when people were more likely than ever to travel, but it did compli-
cate the meaning of membership. For one thing, being present in the colonies, as opposed to being present in England, was as close to an affirmation
of belonging as one was likely to get at the time; the voyage was arduous,
and the people who made it, at least in the early years, had a good idea of
what to expect in terms of building a community. For another thing, even
as English law veered away from requiring physical presence in England as
a prerequisite for membership in the incipient English nation, the law of
the Massachusetts Bay Colony drew toward it, restricting membership in
the colony to those who came there expressly to live and to pray. Moreover,
if there was a legal or quasi-legal argument to be made that being *in* a place
meant that one was *of* the place, then the difference between being inside
and being outside in the law was plainly different from that in religion,
where one could be physically present—in a church or congregation—and
yet be seen as merely aspiring to or learning about what membership might
mean, as was long the case with the Christian Indians. Compounded by
the extent to which colonial banishment—that is, banishment from the
colonies—was often premised on uncertain or ill-defined criminal violations, mere expulsion from the community failed to rebut the Puritans' presumption about what it meant to have come among them in the first place.
This presumption about presence, which considered life in the colonies as
something altogether different and arguably of a higher order than life in
England, was also at stake in the case of the Quakers, who took the promise
of membership implied by physical presence to a new height by arguing that
even after their death—because it occurred at the hands of the colony—they
remained irrevocably members of that place.

Implicit in the Quakers' claim about the relationship between physical
presence, even in death, and membership is another prominent claim about
membership that was made by all of the figures whose stories are retold here.
This claim relates not to the passive mode of gaining membership through
birthright or presence but to the active mode of achieving membership
through human agency. It scarcely needs repeating that at the heart of every
case of banishment was a claim that the banished was not acting the way a
community member ought to act—in short, that the person was a bad actor
who had violated some code of conduct or law that made his or her behavior

unacceptable. Nor do we need to dwell on the fact that in each case the banished denied these claims. What has gone unnoticed until now, however, is the nature of that denial, which took as its target not the question of whether the act had occurred but rather whether the act was outside the bounds of good behavior. For Morton and Hutchinson, for example, denial took the form of an insistence that far from making perpetual guests of the inhabitants, who as guests would then be conspicuously subject to expulsion, membership in the colony conferred on residents a capacity, even a mandate, to be hospitable to others, a status that strongly implied their own sovereignty, while for Williams, denial took the form of an insistence that only the heavenly kingdom as opposed to the earthly one could be homogenous. For the Quakers and the Indians, denial took the form of an argument about agency: that prohibiting action on the part of certain actors was simply not enough to make their actions bad; and further, that defiance of such prohibitions could prove to be examples of good, not bad, membership.

These re-formations of membership brought about as a result of the narratives that banishment provoked had two major consequences for our understanding of early American communities: they undercut the fantasy of homogeneity that the Puritans' religious membership criteria ostensibly served; and they opened up the concept of membership to differing levels of participation as opposed to the all or nothing demanded by the dichotomy between inside and out. Indeed we might think of banishment as ushering in a "Half-Way Contract," a legal counterpart to the Half-Way Covenant, the controversial measure passed by the synod of Puritan churches in 1662 that allowed for the inclusion of members, in particular members of second- and third-generation Puritans, who for whatever reason refused to attest publicly to their conversions. Just as the Half-Way Covenant brought about a loosening of membership requirements in the church, as Robert Pope and others have argued, the debate over banishment brought about a loosening of requirements for membership in the civic polity.[4] Through the arguments made by the banished, membership in the Massachusetts Bay and Plymouth Colonies was reconceptualized in order to include diverse people, as well as forms of partial participation among them. Nor did these alterations derive solely from the arguments made against banishment by the banished. In exercising their privilege to banish, the Puritan civil authorities issued the first challenge to the terms by which inclusion and exclusion were understood and enforced in England—that is to say, as no longer available on the level of the parish or neighborhood but given over entirely to the nation, and as no longer in the

hands of the sovereign or monarch but in the hands of Parliament in consultation with the king. By their assumption of a right to banish (banishment was
exercised in a manner that directly conflicted with the English exercise and so
arguably violated the right to banish in the Bay Colony's charter), the banish-
ers positioned themselves as sovereign in a way that rivaled the sovereignty
of the king and so raised the question of how space and sovereignty could be
coupled and decoupled to remake the legal understanding of membership in
ever more creative ways.

Many of these couplings and decouplings are worth bearing in mind as
we think through the past in order to further our conversation about the uses
of banishment in the present. The most significant perhaps is the decoupling
of person from place in the early modern period, a result largely of increased
mobility on the part of a formerly fixed population as well as shifting labor
needs and economic advantages. As people began to identify themselves in
terms of more than one place—born in one town but living and working in
another—perceptions of space began to shift, reinforcing some of the ambiguities in the law's understanding of what being inside one place and outside
another could mean. Indeed once the sovereignty of England was officially
extended to its colonial possessions, the legal understanding of how space and
sovereignty combined to render a given space jurisdictional became even more
complex and ambiguous than it had been before. For the first time jurisdictions became not only bigger as a result of the expansion of geographical coordinates but also smaller as a result of the contest within jurisdictions over
where the new center and periphery lay. Could the part—the colonies, for
example—stand in for the whole jurisdictionally? If so, what might this suggest about the relationship between sovereignty and jurisdictionally defined
space? The conflicts between the Massachusetts Bay Colony and the kings of
England between 1630 and 1684 over who had the authority to make decisions about social inclusion and exclusion begin to suggest the kinds of tensions that were provoked in this regard and demonstrate how changeable the
links between space and sovereignty were in this period. However, concepts
of space were affected not only by changes in space but also by changes in the
technologies for self-expression, most significantly by changes in print technology, which gave many people who were banished from territories bounded
by certain geographical coordinates the chance to speak as if they were still
inside them. The prominence of banished voices speaking across jurisdictional
divides in the early American context was instrumental in changing people's
perceptions about the fixity of space as well as the possibilities for governing

it, since the common law gave a privileged place to those who continued to be in a dialogue with one another.

Rhetorically Speaking

These and other instances of the coupling and decoupling of space and sovereignty within the seventeenth-century controversy over banishment law underpin the story this book has worked to tell. But statements about *how* the law links space and sovereignty through its exercise of rhetoric form one of the most important argumentative strains of that story. Indeed the argument in *Banished* is that in part the peculiarity of the common law—in particular its insistence that those who were subject to the law were also its creators—made membership in and banishment from the community such a perplexing and yet revealing issue. If to be English, for example, was to make English law and to make English law was to be a member of the legal community, then in the debate over who could be in and who had to be out of the community, the Puritans were arguing not only about how their community should look but also about how the law should work. Among other things this understanding of the law alters our view of what it meant for the Puritans to take English common law with them to the New World. The controversy over banishment, in other words, was not simply a matter of importing English law wholesale, as many scholars have implied, or even of altering it to suit their own needs.[5] The cases of banishment studied here even escape the otherwise capacious parameters for thinking about colonial law provided by Mary Sarah Bilder's notion of a transatlantic constitution, in which people in the colonies and in England depended on each other to make sense of English law.[6] Rather in providing a forum for talking about community membership, banishment engaged the Puritans not in establishing legal reforms (evident in their often-cited attempts to cut down on the number of capital crimes specified by English statutes) but in re-forming the law whose very purpose—to make communities—was newly at stake.

One of the more significant ways in which the banishment controversy invoked the common law as a source for community formation came in the use of the common law's many origins, from the mythical to the empirical, by some of the banished. That the common law, for example, derived in part from the law of nations, as Hugo Grotius dubbed it, was made most visible in the debate over hospitality in the banishments of Hutchinson and Morton.

Hospitality, as noted in Chapter 1, was a custom that permeated the common law but had its roots in the welcome offered, or in some cases mandated, by people in one nation to those of another. We can now add to this interesting reconfiguration of the common law through banishment an awareness on the part of the early Americans of a connection between English common law and the international order. This awareness fundamentally changes our perception of the Puritans, who, as it turns out, were not nearly as insular as we have been led to believe. The law that the Puritans discovered and deployed in the course of the debate over banishment in large part transcended the very boundaries they sought to establish; it was a law that gave voice to English nationalism, as Coke and others conceived it, but at the same time acknowledged a wider world from which the English descended and to which they were accountable. The common law thus was confined to England, and yet by a certain birthright of its own, it was indebted to the international legal order.

This fluidity of legal origins suggests a multiplicity of uses of the law that was matched only by the multiplicity of legal speakers made possible by the debate over banishment. In reinforcing the question of inclusion and exclusion, of inside and out, in the form of debate and disagreement, the narratives of and about banishment reinforce the idea that legal communities are made through the constant repositioning of an "us" versus a "them"—that in any debate or disagreement, indeed in any form of interlocution, there is an initial divide between speakers that paradoxically produces a community that gets reshaped (although not necessarily unified) by the end. This process of coming together as a community by means of a shared form of communication—regardless of the content—and the coming apart of that same community in the divide required for community formation in the first place is the process of interlocution or rhetoric, a process that, as Jacques Rancière explains, both includes and excludes speakers at the same time. The process, according to Rancière, "doubly includes in the argument situation he who rejects its existence—and who is justified in the existing order of things in rejecting its existence. It includes him initially in the supposition that he is indeed included in the situation, that he is capable of understanding the argument. . . . It includes him in it as the second person implicitly in a dialogue. And it includes him a second time in the demonstration of the fact that he is trying to escape from the situation, trying not to understand the argument and perform the nominations and descriptions adequate to a situation of discussion between speaking beings."[7] For Rancière, that is, rhetoric is as much about the destruction of a shared world as it is about its reconstruction; rhetoric in the form of argument and communication does not simply exist within the world but shifts what he calls "the partitions of the perceptible."[8]

To the extent that the law and in particular the law of banishment operated rhetorically—by being constituted as a means of persuasion and manifested as a form of interlocution between people on opposite sides of a physical and metaphysical divide—it not only made and unmade communities but also produced community members by having them speak the law. In this way the law could be said to recapitulate rhetoric. To use English law was to make English law, and to make English law was to acknowledge one's place within the social order. To speak through the law, which invoked an English audience, was also to renounce certain other criteria for membership within that audience, including those that separated people from each other across territorial divides that were incommensurate with rhetorical ones. In other words, if banishment was intended to separate those who were outside the law (and its jurisdiction) from those who were not, it failed in part by causing the number of speakers capable of using the law to proliferate. In terms of the banishment debate, the banished, now physically outside the jurisdiction, continued to speak to and with those who were still inside it and in their use of the law made the law more expansive. Put another way, the mere fact that there were speakers on either side of the boundary undid what the law of banishment, as wielded by the Puritan authorities, seemingly hoped to accomplish in setting up those boundaries in the first place.

Banishment Redux

If the stories of banishment told here suggest that the lines people draw around themselves and others can multiply to the point of untenability, these lines do not disappear entirely. *Banished* therefore concludes not by heralding the collapse of the inside/outside distinction but by noting that the aggressive pursuit of these distinctions is a constitutive part of community making, not just in colonial America but also in communities across the globe and over time. The question then becomes not whether we can do without these distinctions but rather how we handle them, what kind of value we place on them, and to what degree we use the law to reinforce them.

Officially the practice of banishment among the Puritans came to an end when the colonial authority to banish was revoked along with the Bay Colony's charter in 1684. Indeed between 1684 and the early to mid-1690s, when royal rule was solidified, the Puritans seemed to turn their attention away from the problem of how to rid their communities of people and toward how to keep them from moving away. Frederick Jackson Turner points to this period as the beginning of the American frontier. "[I]n 1690," he writes, "a committee of the General Court of Massachusetts recommended the Court to order what shall be the frontier and to maintain a committee to settle garrisons on the frontier with forty soldiers."[9] Notions of the frontier had surfaced before, of course, from the time of the first white settlements and then increasingly as those settlements pushed further into Indian land. However, it was during this period that the "frontier" as such first emerged as a topic worthy of focused legislation. More significant is the fact that the frontier emerged at this time as a physical border or edge, a militarily defensible line by which the community was defined or, conversely, threatened. Turner notes that based on how the concept of the frontier developed in this period, "[i]n American thought and speech the term 'frontier' has come to mean the edge of settlement, rather than, as in Europe, the political boundary."[10] Of course no direct link can be drawn from the period of frenzied banishments to the emergence of the frontier as the "edge of settlement." Even so, one cannot help but wonder about the effect of the banishment controversy on the development of this concept, for in the wake of all those banishment narratives, the association between the "frontier" and a political or legal boundary would have been hard to maintain.

Even if banishment in the form of the infliction of exile on individual offenders came to an end with the transfer of colonial power back to the Crown, the practice of ridding a place of undesirables continued not only to thrive but to become more efficient. While the colonies abandoned the practice of banishment, England, where it had fallen out of favor long before, revived it in a different form, calling it "transportation." Transportation, as its name suggests, entailed the shipping of convicted felons, usually en masse, outside of England, but unlike banishment, its purpose was not to expel them from the domain as a whole; indeed most felons were transported to English colonial possessions. Like banishment, transportation was a product of custom and was imposed as a punishment by judges of the common law. However, it quickly found its way into legislation, the Transportation Act of 1718, which helped change it from one of a host of common-law punishments to a routine punishment that led Sir William Blackstone to remark somewhat erroneously, "exile and transportation are punishments at present unknown to the common law; and, whenever the latter is now inflicted, it is either by the choice of the criminal himself to escape a capital punishment, or else by the express direction of some modern act of Parliament."[11] Since courts all over England were still imposing transportation as a sentence, Blackstone's observation is less accurate than it is indicative of how nearly invisible and widely accepted transportation had become as a way of dealing with undesirables.

Ridding England of criminals by means of transportation transformed the practice of expulsion from one that aimed to reduce the population permanently into one that simply redistributed it, keeping the undesirables out of certain privileged areas but maintaining the population by putting them to a better use.[12] This was a major step in the modification of the banishment policy and arguably a direct, if partial result of the banishment debates in New England. Of course material circumstances also invited such a policy. Increasingly throughout the seventeenth century and certainly by the time of the 1718 act, labor shortages in many of the empire's outposts were severe. "Profit, not penal policy," according to Roger Ekirch, "set the fate of British exiles" in this period.[13] But it was the penal policy that set forth a term of years for most transported convicts—typically seven—and allowed them to return to England with full pardons for their crimes.[14] In this way transportation worked to reinforce the criminal's usefulness to the nation and to increase the value of the nation to the criminal.[15] Aside from this shift in policy, however, perhaps the biggest difference between banishment and transportation was that transportation was imposed largely without discussion or contestation.[16] Certainly by 1718 transportation had become a systematic way to empty English prisons, and the practice came to an end only with the American Revolution and the disappearance of a convenient place to send the prisoners.[17]

Still, the drive to deal with undesirables by expelling them from fixed territorial boundaries did not dissipate, and for many, transportation remained a reasonable way to ease the overcrowding in England's prisons. Thus when the thirteen American colonies were no longer available sites for transported prisoners, the English looked to Australia. Almost as soon as transportations to Australia were begun in 1786, however, there was widespread protest against them. Convict colonies, it was argued, were dangerous by definition and were made even more so by the scarce resources with which the convicts were supplied. In a letter urging the abolition of transportation, the attorney general of New South Wales explained that it was "the impossibility of establishing free and honest colonial government where convicts are, that is quite as much to be considered as their bad conduct; and few will doubt the impossibility who reflect, that a free government there must be formed either of the masters and their convict servants, which nobody proposes, or of the masters without their convict servants, in which case the latter will infallibly be treated like unprotected slaves."[18] The other source of protest was economic. Many in England argued that the cost of maintaining what was essentially a jail in Australia, some twelve thousand miles from home, was exorbitant. Whether or not these arguments were valid, the popular conception of the cost of transportation was felt by most people to be too high.[19]

Just as banishment gave way to transportation, transportation gave way to deportation, which has arguably brought about the most significant changes in the category of policies and laws authorizing expulsion to date. Deportation, unlike banishment or transportation, effectively decoupled expulsion from criminality, at least the kind of criminality traditionally held to make the target of expulsion undesirable. Rooted largely in late eighteenth-century theories about race, imperialism, and sovereignty, deportation is said to have begun in America with the Alien and Sedition Acts of 1798. Passed by the Fifth Congress of the United States and signed into law by President John Adams, these acts—actually a set of four bills—were triggered by a contemporary naval war with France but spoke to many Americans' preoccupation with so-called enemy aliens in general. The two provisions that are most relevant for our purposes were the Act Concerning Aliens, which gave the president the power to deport any resident alien considered "dangerous to the peace and safety of the United States," and the Act Respecting Alien Enemies, which gave the president the power to arrest and deport resident aliens if their countries of origin were at war with the United States. Although the Alien and Sedition Acts were controversial in their day, they did not issue in a single deportation order, and their significance for us resides in their initial attempts to tie aliens—that is to say, people of different nationalities—to criminal activity or, to use the language of the law, activities that might prove "dangerous to the peace and safety of the United States." It was, in other words, only because their countries were at war with the United States and not because they themselves had violated any law that the aliens subject to the Act Respecting Alien Enemies were deportable. Using the law to deport people because of their status as opposed to their behavior was widely recognized as risky—especially in the context of the Japanese-American internments during World War II—but remarkably the act remains valid today.[20]

The effort begun in the Alien and Sedition Acts to collapse the distinction between the immigrant and the criminal had a more lasting and insidious iteration roughly one hundred years later with the passage of the Chinese Exclusion Act of 1882. This law, which barred the entry of Chinese laborers into the United States for a period initially of twenty years, later reduced to ten years, did not even bother to make a connection between the immigrant and "danger" or to justify the expulsion on criminal grounds.[21] Rather the Chinese Exclusion Act was aimed expressly at the influx of Chinese immigrants who were recruited to build the railroads but chose unexpectedly, and much to the government's chagrin, to stay in the country after they were built. The act barred the entry of any Chinese wishing to come to the United States, but more controversially it ordered any Chinese found to be unlawfully residing within the country to be removed "to the country from whence he came." To be sure, the trigger for deportation was "unlawful" residence, but what made the residence unlawful was difficult to determine. More significantly, adding the clause about unlawful residence to the Chinese Exclusion Act deliberately bypassed the channels offered by the nation's naturalization laws, which were normally used for such determinations.[22]

The novelty of the Chinese Exclusion Act lay in the ease with which it moved from social exclusion to removal.[23] Some of the signs of this move were visible in the case of the Quakers, who were removed or threatened with removal from the Massachusetts Bay Colony merely because they had entered it. Yet even in the Quakers' case, as evidenced by the frenzy of Puritan lawmaking described in Chapter 3, the alleged criminal activity of the accused remained a touchstone of the law. Leaving to one side the question of the legitimacy of the Quaker exclusion law, which was highly questionable, we can nevertheless follow the logic by which the Puritans considered their entry into the colony evidence of their criminality. Not so in the case of the Chinese. The Chinese had in the large majority of cases been invited into the United States earlier in the century and were deported some years later only because their presence was no longer desirable. This mixture—what Allegra McLeod calls a convergence—of the criminal law with what is more accurately seen as a membership matter is at the heart of the problem with deportation, as it was practiced then and continues to be practiced today. As McLeod observes, "Relying upon the criminal law for informational advantage (as an immigration regulatory proxy) presumes that criminal law contact adequately captures features of unbelonging or undesirability. . . . Justificatory frameworks grounded in a conception of trespass, or contract violation, or political expediency likewise fail with regard to many of the noncitizens targeted by criminal immigration enforcement."[24]

A microcosmic version of this unjustified mixing of criminal law with membership decisions can be seen on the level not of extranational deportation but of intranational banishment, which according to many recent scholars has also been on the rise. Many states have outlawed banishment, and yet many, including some that do not necessarily sanction it, still exercise it as an option.[25] In particular the state of Georgia appears to be committed to using banishment laws to keep people in their place.[26] Interestingly, many Indian tribes have also resorted to banishment recently, with many touting its restorative effects, although only when used properly. "Where banishment is implemented as a pragmatic tool to police reservations," one commentator has noted, "it provides Indian tribes with a mechanism to keep tribal members safe from the ills of criminal behavior that too often go unaddressed by the criminal justice system."[27] Of course, as this statement suggests, Indian tribes have their own, very different legal systems, giving them recourse to punishments unavailable to the states. Yet critics of the Indian system have leveled similar attacks on it, warning against the potential for selective enforcement and the possibility for mixing civil and criminal controls.[28]

Scholars who have noted a resurgence of banishment cases involving criminal populations, including drug and sex offenders, also note the frequency with which such charges are now applied to the homeless. As Katherine Beckett and Steve Herbert suggest, banishment is back in the form of exclusion or "no go zones" from which the deviant or homeless are barred: "Increasing swaths of urban space are delimited as zones of exclusion from which the undesirable are banned."[29] Among these "no go" spaces, Beckett and Herbert include local parks, streets, parade grounds, and boardwalks. Because these spaces are small, moreover, the power to ban people from them resides with the police, not with government officials, and this, Beckett and Herbert argue, further complicates the already fine line between civil punishment and criminal punishment. Although a single disgruntled property owner might provide the impetus behind a given banishment order and thus make the order look like a mere trespass complaint, the potential for expanding the area of exclusion from a street to a park to a neighborhood brings it closer to a state action without providing the banished with the legally requisite opportunity to protest or complain along state action lines.

The potential for abuse of power in rendering banishment decisions that blur the lines between civil and criminal control of the population is exacerbated when the banishments in question bar people from the nation as a whole. The question of who has the authority to banish—a major factor in seventeenth-century New England—remains central to the policy on social exclusion, albeit in an altered way. If in the seventeenth century one of the central questions was whether the Puritans could legitimately banish others at a time when the right to banish had been relegated to the king and Parliament, the question today is whether the more firmly established sovereign power to banish or deport can be exercised without the necessary criminal findings or, to put it another way, whether the sovereign's power to control the borders around his or her nation is the same as the power to control the population within it. In expelling people found to be within the territory unlawfully (as opposed to people who have violated the terms of their grants to reside within the territory or alternatively are caught stealing into the country), deportation turns from a principle of border control to what Daniel Kanstroom calls "post entry social control."[30] That there is a fine line between these two is particularly troubling to scholars of the current deportation regime, which has in the last decade or so been enforced more aggressively and with more disruptive consequences for immigrants and asylum seekers than arguably at any other time. Certainly the numbers of deportees have never been greater. Kanstroom notes, for example, that since 1925 more than 44 million people have been deported from the United States, 720,000 of them in the years from 2001 to 2004.[31]

Massive deportations also invite us to think about the extent to which social exclusion has been written into the rules of membership in the nation.[32] Aggressive deportation of individuals who have been in the country for long periods of time has changed the quality of membership for these people in troubling ways. As it stands now, between the time people enter the United States and the time they are eligible to apply for legal residency or citizenship, they are subject to a vigorously enforced regime in which they can never be sure of their rights or status. This has led to constitutional challenges to deportation by those claiming that it violates the liberty of people inside the United States to travel (a liberty protected by the Fourteenth Amendment) and to freely associate (a liberty protected by the First Amendment).[33] That these liberties are protected by a written document, as opposed to the unwritten law that dominated banishment discussions in the seventeenth century, might seem at first glance to provide more of a buffer for those struggling against exclusion. Yet in the end it has only made it more difficult for them, for even as the Constitution affirms the rights of the groups of people subject to it, it serves as a limit on them, protecting only those rights enumerated in the document and only those people deemed worthy of holding them.[34] As a consequence, the expansive conversation found within the banishment narratives of early America—a conversation about how membership within the community might be reconceived in the first place—has in many ways narrowed to become a conversation about rights, leaving intact the fundamental notion of membership already inscribed in the founding document. This in turn has led to a tiered system in which certain people within the borders of the nation are designated as full citizens while others occupy a subordinate and partial status. Thus if arguing in favor of something less than full participation was for the Quakers a new way of acknowledging diverse but no less equal membership patterns, it has today become a way of creating caste systems among inhabitants, ranging from full-fledged citizens, to legal residents, to guest workers, among others.

Still, if the conversation about banishment and deportation has contracted on the level of the nation, it has regained some of its original breadth in the international arena. For one thing, the international or global arena lacks a single constitution, and so the question of membership remains a multiply determined one subject to cultural, legal, and political attitudes not only about rights but also about space, sovereignty, and language. New configurations of space and sovereignty abound in this context, from the European Union, to multiple treaty organizations, to the United Nations, to The Hague; these organizations not only cross national boundaries but also begin to imagine an international, even global, space all their own. Indeed a growing awareness of globalism has shifted the terms of the banishment debate in many ways, offering us a final context for examining the dichotomy of inside and outside on which banishment depends.

The World Wide (Banishment) Web

What does it mean to be a member of an international or global order, and how does such belonging interact with laws about exclusion? Many scholars are hard at work on this question, but one prominent answer points us toward the concept of cosmopolitanism, a form of membership or identity often described as allowing for a combination or coexistence of affiliations. To be a member of an international order suggests not just a loosening of boundaries between nations but the absence of boundaries altogether, leading to a condition of mixed membership and a sense of multiple belonging. As Kwame Anthony Appiah puts it, cosmopolitanism "deserves serious attention as a habitable middle ground between liberalism and relativism."[35] However, making such a claim for cosmopolitanism skirts the issue of what underwrites a sense of multiple belonging, and for this we look to the idea of universalism. As Yasemin Soysal has observed: "A new and more universal concept of citizenship has unfolded in the postwar era, one whose organizing and legitimating principles are based on universal personhood rather than national belonging."[36] Reminiscent in many ways of the claims for membership put forward by Roger Williams and examined in Chapter 2, universalism or universal personhood tends to rely on one of two conceptions of space: a space that is truly boundless, which for Williams, was realizable only in God's kingdom in heaven; or one that is grounded in the territorially divided space now inhabited and yet joined together by notions of universalism. Indeed this is the vision that Seyla Benhabib and her coauthors promote when they recognize that "cosmopolitanism does not exist in a vacuum but stems rather from a process of mediation or integration in which so-called universal norms are mixed in with more local forms of government and produce over time a more international world."[37]

There are several drawbacks to this vision, however. One lies with the idea of universal norms; in order to imagine a universal order, one has to identify what universalism is, and few, if any nation-states could be said to agree on this. Even Benhabib and her coauthors' understanding of a type of universalism that is mediated by individual nations or territories seems to depend on a shared sense of how this mediation would work—a sense that bears a striking resemblance to democracy. Is universalism, then, a euphemism for what is democratic, as it appears to be for Benhabib and her coauthors, and if so, what are the possibilities for government outside these parameters?

Other scholars who have deliberately moved away from the space of the nation to other more flexible substitutes have addressed some of the drawbacks entailed in theories of universalism and universal personhood. One such theory concerns the rise of the concept of borderlands, which are spaces established precisely where nations meet, where they form an edge, as Edward Casey has written.[38] The cultures that arise at these places, such as La Frontera, which stretches along the United States–Mexico border, are often constructed with the border prominently in view and are therefore acts of spatial, cultural, and legal resistance, like those we ascribed to the Quakers in Chapter 3.[39] These borderlands are sometimes places of cultural harmony, but they are just as often quite the opposite; an example of the latter is the space encompassed by the drug trade that passes across the U.S.–Mexican border at all times. Thus this collapse of borders or thinning out of them is not in itself an inherent good and suggests the limitations of the cross-border place.

Indeed aspirations for a global, cross-border, or even borderless world have not yet materialized despite the official conclusions reached by the

United Nations (noted in the epigraph to this chapter) that banishment and deportation had come to an end in most places by 1964. As with many such conclusions, the news—in this case of of banishment's demise--was greatly exaggerated. As Nicholas de Genova and Nathalie Peutz point out, deportation has instead become a kind of global order in which states assert control over social interactions by actively kicking out undesirables.[40] Global deportations, moreover, are a particular problem for people who cannot stay in their own countries for reasons that are beyond their control, as in the case of a brutal dictatorship, and yet are barred from entering others, a catch-22 that makes them homeless and subject to even greater penalties and legal constraints than other immigrants experience.

In addition, even when boundaries between nations lose their rigidity, smaller boundaries often take on more meaning, as in the case of the intrastate banishments discussed above. As Michael Walzer has observed, "If states ever became large neighborhoods, it is likely that neighborhoods will become little states. Their members will organize to defend the local politics against strangers . . . to tear down the walls of the state is not to create a world without walls, but rather to create a thousand petty fortresses."[41] As Wendy Brown reminds us, globalization has been accompanied, perversely enough, by the increasing prevalence of physical, material barriers in the form of walls between warring nations—such as that between the Palestinians and the Israelis—but also in the form of barriers to mobility, in the form of checkpoints or Jersey barriers that prohibit vehicular access to buildings of national importance.[42] In such a world banishment seems to have achieved a measure of normalcy that even the Puritans at the height of their banishment frenzy could not claim.

In addition to smaller and smaller groups putting up physical walls, metaphysical boundaries now surround us. For example, while we speak of a global order and the unbundling of national boundaries, we note the rise of religious divisions that even as they defy national boundaries often supplant them. One of the biggest problems for the Puritans was their aspiration to make their geographical identity isomorphic with their religious identity. This brought the rules about how to govern a geographically united community into conflict with the rules about how to do the same for a religiously united one. Of the two, the religious community was by far the more exclusionary, given to strict decisions about who could or could not be a member that put pressure on but ultimately gave way to more ambiguous rules within the law. With certain notable exceptions, this aspiration—to map a religiously bounded community onto a geographically bounded one—has become less common, and yet the clash of religious and legal rules about community membership has not. If religious communities now often span more than one nation or continent because their members have been the victims of large-scale, diasporic migrations, they do not always or perhaps ever offer a denationalized or deterritorialized alternative to community formation; rather they either assert a sovereignty all their own or have that sovereignty ascribed to them, as in the war that the West is fighting against terror.

Still, diasporic communities, religiously inflected or not, may hold out some promise for thinking through the ends of banishment, for when they are at their best, diasporic communities position themselves as transcending the territorial borders of the nation-state. Indeed diasporic communities have come closer than any others to using banishment as a narrative provocation and thus to producing a literature that might be examined, alongside the banishment narratives of the seventeenth century, for evidence of new, nonnational communities imagined in new, nonhomogenous ways. Of course much of this literature treats diaspora as a form of exile that vacillates between a nostalgia for the homeland that leads to a sense of nonbelonging and an antipathy for the homeland that leads to an overzealous sense of belonging in the new land. Most recently we see versions of these narratives in the explosion of postcolonial literature from India, Pakistan, and many countries in Africa and the Middle East. But there may be versions of these narratives that have escaped our notice, perhaps because they are essentially nonnarrative and thus do not tell stories of exile or even engage in the rhetorical kinds of arguments that characterized the banishment narratives studied here. Indeed the rhetoric of law that made the reconception of community possible in the early American narratives under consideration here is arguably no longer available to the banished, who cannot call upon a legal language—beyond the limited language of human rights, perhaps—that was shared across borders and that was primarily concerned with community-making.

In the babel of tongues that marks the current, international deportation regime, in other words, opportunities for putting the rhetorical structure of the common law to work in the area of banishment are few and far between. Yet there have been occasions, increasingly evident in trial testimony culled from recent deportation hearings, suggesting that at least some of the force of the rhetoric we saw in the early American context has been recaptured. I am referring here to the rhetorical use of the law by deportees to call on others to respond or, more specifically, to recognize or acknowledge them.[43] Given the absence of a shared language, this rhetorical demand is often pithy in the extreme; many of these statements amount to little more than affirmations of the deportee's presence in the new territory; "I am here" is the form most of these statements take.[44] Pithy as they are, they nevertheless contain the requirement of all rhetorical statements: that they be persuasive. In the articulation of their presence, the deportees not only affirm that presence for themselves but also demand that others hear and respond to them, even if, as is too often the case, those responses take the form of nonresponses or denials. Moreover, pithy as they are, these statements meet the additional requirement that they be neither nostalgic nor overly identificatory, about neither nonbelonging nor overbelonging. Captured in the simple phrase "I am here" is the legal version of Esperanto, an ability to set in motion the legal mechanisms of all laws about community and social exclusion.

In these simple phrases, with which so many reports about deportation and asylum are populated, we witness the third way in which many of the banished today are replicating what the banished in seventeenth-century New England seem to have accomplished: they are not silent. Like their early American counterparts, they are taking their banishments seriously; hailed by the law, they are responding to the law in kind and thus turning their forcible transfers from one place to another from just another means of social exclusion inflicted on them into a limit case of what exclusion can do to them and why the law should not be used to fuel division but rather to disseminate it. This then, in a world in which boundaries and borders will continue to prevail, might provide a glimpse into the future of banishment and the ends to which banishment might more profitably be put.

Notes

INTRODUCTION

1. Peter Goodrich, "Antirrhesis: Polemical Structures of Common Law Thought," in *The Rhetoric of Law*, ed. Austin Sarat and Thomas R. Kearns (Ann Arbor: University of Michigan Press, 1994), 83.

2. Charles Tilly, *Identities, Boundaries, and Social Ties* (Boulder: Paradigm, 2005), 174.

3. Banishment statutes are still on the books in many American states. See Michael F. Armstrong, "Banishment: Cruel and Unusual Punishment," *University of Pennsylvania Law Review* 111.6 (1963): 758–86. See also Peter D. Edgerton, "Banishment and the Right to Live Where You Want," *University of Chicago Law Review* 74.3 (2007): 1023–55.

4. Because court records from this period are fragmentary, these numbers are far from exact, but if we assume that the percentage of those banished from the population in the first decade of white settlement remained relatively constant over the fifty additional years of concern to us here, this guesstimate seems reasonable. In addition to the celebrated cases of banishment covered here, of course, there were others, including those of John Wheelwright, Samuel Gorton, and dozens of family members who accompanied Anne Hutchinson out of the Bay Colony, whom I did not include because the records generated by those controversies were not as relevant to my discussion. If we also take into account the frequency of those crimes for which banishment was a common penalty, including fornication, lewd or lascivious behavior, vilifying authorities, stealing, and Lord's Day violations, we can begin to see what a staggering number of banishments there must have been. For charts substantiating some of these figures, see Edwin Powers, *Crime and Punishment in Early Massachusetts 1620–1692: A Documentary History* (Boston: Beacon Press, 1966), 210, 404–8.

5. William Bradford, *Of Plymouth Plantation: 1620–1647*, ed. Samuel Eliot Morison (New York: Alfred A. Knopf, 2002), 150.

6. Nathaniel B. Shurtleff, ed., *Records of the Governor and Company of the Massachusetts Bay in New England*, vol. 1, *1628–1641* (1854; repr., Memphis: General Books, LLC, 2010).

7. Why certain crimes were punishable by banishment and others, for example witchcraft, were not remains something of a mystery, but the fact that banishment was considered a relatively lenient punishment may help to explain why it was not imposed in capital cases.

8. See Edgar J. Mcmanus, *Law and Liberty in Early New England: Criminal Justice and Due Process, 1620–1692* (Amherst: University of Massachusetts Press, 1993), 55; and Stephen Innes, *Creating the Commonwealth: The Economic Culture of Puritan New England* (New York: W. W. Norton, 1995), 44.

9. Charles M. Andrews, *The Colonial Period of American History: The Settlements*, vol. 1 (New Haven: Yale University Press, 1934), 468.

10. Mcmanus, *Law and Liberty in Early New England*, 202.

11. Adding to the confusion created by the variety of offenses that could be punished with banishment was the erratic way in which the punishment was meted out. One colonist, George Haskins reports, who threatened to take an appeal to an English court and thus committed a crime similar to Walford's and Ratcliffe's, was not banished but merely sentenced to the bilboes. See George Haskins, *Law and Authority in Early Massachusetts: A Study in Tradition and Design* (New York: Macmillan, 1960), 28. There was even a law passed in York County, Maine, then under the territorial control of the Bay Colony but often at odds with it, that ordered all men and women whose spouses were still in England to leave the colony "because they were guilty of immoral conduct and loose living and given to contracting bigamous marriages" (Andrews, *Colonial Period of American History*, 1:468).

12. Hutchinson was banished by the General Court in 1637, but the church court in Boston conducted a separate trial in March 1638. Hutchinson finally left the colony after this trial ended in her excommunication.

13. Andrews, *Colonial Period of American History*, 1:469–70.

14. Ibid.

15. John Winthrop, "A Modell of Christian Charity," *The Winthrop Papers*, 5 vols. (Boston: Massachusetts Historical Society, 1929–47), 2:291.

16. René Girard, *Violence and the Sacred*, trans. Patrick Gregory (New York: Continuum, 2005), 84.

17. Michel de Certeau, *The Certeau Reader*, ed. Graham Ward (Oxford: Blackwell, 2000), 103.

18. See Perry Miller, *Errand into the Wilderness* (1956; repr., Cambridge, Mass.: Harvard University Press, 2000); and Matt Cohen, *The Networked Wilderness: Communicating in Early New England* (Minneapolis: University of Minnesota Press, 2010).

19. Philip F. Gura, *A Glimpse of Sion's Glory: Puritan Radicalism in New England, 1620–1660* (Middletown, Conn.: Wesleyan University Press, 1984), 5. On this matter Knight quotes Winthrop, who said that "two so opposite parties [meaning the orthodox and the so-called spiritists] could [not] continue in the same body without apparent hazard of ruin to the whole" (Janice Knight, *Orthodoxies in Massachusetts: Rereading American Puritanism* [Cambridge, Mass.: Harvard University Press, 1994], 28).

20. Louise A. Breen, *Transgressing the Bounds: Subversive Enterprises among the Puritan Elite in Massachusetts, 1630–1692* (New York: Oxford University Press, 2001), 17–19; Jonathan Beecher Field, *Errands into the Metropolis: New England Dissidents in Revolutionary London* (Hanover, N.H.: Dartmouth College Press, 2009), 6.

21. Martha Nussbaum, *Liberty of Conscience: In Defense of America's Tradition of Religious Equality* (New York: Basic Books, 2008), 65.

22. Schmitt aligned himself with the Nazis and the state of exception their government ushered in, while Agamben maintained a more critical attitude about the state of exception, despite picking up on many of Schmitt's theories about it.

23. Carl Schmitt, *Political Theology: Four Chapters on the Concept of Sovereignty* (Chicago: University of Chicago Press, 2006).

24. Giorgio Agamben, *Homo Sacer: Sovereign Power and Bare Life* (Stanford, Calif.: Stanford University Press, 1998).

25. Alison Games, "Atlantic History and Interdisciplinary Approaches," *Early American Literature* 43.1 (2008): 187–90.

26. David Delaney, *Territory: A Short Introduction* (Oxford: Blackwell, 2005), 95.

27. A battle is raging in the social sciences between those who privilege what is called a dispositional reading of social processes and those who prefer more empirical or transactional readings of them. I do not take sides in this dispute but use both approaches to help us understand how communities in the New and Old Worlds came into being.

28. See Liah Greenfield, *Nationalism: Five Roads to Modernity* (Cambridge, Mass.: Harvard University Press, 1992), 1–17. See also Liah Greenfield, *The Spirit of Capitalism: Nationalism and Economic Growth* (Cambridge, Mass.: Harvard University Press, 2001), 2.

29. See Benedict Anderson, *Imagined Communities* (London: Verso, 1983); Peter Sahlins, *Boundaries: The Making of France and Spain in the Pyrenees* (Berkeley: University of California Press, 1989); and Anthony D. Smith, *National Identity* (Reno: University of Nevada Press, 1991).

30. Tilly, *Identities, Boundaries, and Social Ties*, 3–8.

31. Saskia Sassen, *Territory, Authority, Rights: From Medieval to Global Assemblages* (Princeton, N.J.: Princeton University Press, 2006).

32. Ibid., 2.

33. Ibid., 278.

34. For a breakdown of general religious differences by generation, see, for example, David D. Hall, *The Faithful Shepherd: A History of the New England Ministry in the Seventeenth Century* (Chapel Hill: University of North Carolina Press, 1972); and Knight, *Orthodoxies in Massachusetts*. For a more specific rendering of millennialist attitude according to generation, see Theodore Dwight Bozeman, *To Live Ancient Lives: The Primitivist Dimension in Puritanism* (Chapel Hill: University of North Carolina Press, 1988). For more of a focus on cultural and political differences, see, for example, Roger Thompson, *Mobility and Migration: East Anglian Founders of New England, 1629–1640* (Amherst: University of Massachusetts Press, 1994); and Breen, *Transgressing the Bounds*.

35. James Stoner does a good job of explaining the practices of seventeenth-century common lawyers and the differences between them and today's common lawyers: "He begins from the case before him and searches out its precedents in cases decided in the past. If the precedents are honestly read, the result is not necessarily dyslexic. Still the case by case search for precedents, which comprises so much of Coke's historical work, does rest on

certain assumptions that modern historians understandably question—it assumes that the whole while in principle changeable has remained constant." See James R. Stoner, Jr., *Common Law and Liberal Theory: Coke, Hobbes, and the Origins of American Constitutionalism* (Lawrence: University of Kansas Press, 1992), 64.

36. See Aristotle, *Rhetoric*, trans. W. Rhys Robert (New York: Dover, 2004).

37. Cicero, *On the Orator*, ed. James M. May and Jakob Wisse (New York: Oxford University Press, 2001), 157.

38. James Boyd White, "Law as Rhetoric, Rhetoric as Law," *University of Chicago Law Review* 52.3 (1985): 684–702, 690–91.

39. Francis J. Mootz III, *Rhetorical Knowledge in Legal Practice and Critical Legal Theory* (Tuscaloosa: University of Alabama Press, 2006), 126.

40. Kieran Dolin, *A Critical Introduction to Law and Literature* (Cambridge: Cambridge University Press, 2007), 11. See also the classic studies of the law and literature movement, including Robert Ferguson, *Law and Letters in American Culture* (Cambridge, Mass.: Harvard University Press, 1987); and James Boyd White, *Heracles' Bow: Essays on the Rhetoric and Poetics of the Law* (Madison: University of Wisconsin Press, 1989).

41. For the idea of talking the world into being, see Leigh Hunt Greenshaw, "'To Say What the Law Is': Learning the Practice of Legal Rhetoric," *Valparaiso University Law Review* 29.2 (1995): 861–96. For law as one of many normative discourses, by contrast, see Robert M. Cover, "Foreword: Nomos and Narrative," *Harvard Law Review* 97.4 (1983).

42. In her study of Shakespearean exiles, for example, Jane Kingsley-Smith notes that "[b]anishment effect[s] the removal of a character beyond civic or national limits and in that moment redefine[s] the exile, depriving him of origins, language and a name." Indeed far from "being removed to the margins of the English-speaking world," those banished from the Puritan jurisdictions typically started in the colonial margins and from there often moved to other English colonies in the New World, including Jamaica and Barbados, or back to England. But the other, perhaps more significant, reason for the contrast between Shakespeare's silenced exiles and the more voluble exiles represented here is the difference made by the common law. Unlike the Shakespearean exiles and their real -life counterparts, those banished by the Puritans were banished in the terms made available by the common law—terms that created rhetorical opportunities for new understandings of state, territory, and membership within it. See Jane Kingsley-Smith, *Shakespeare's Drama of Exile* (New York: Palgrave, 2003), 1.

43. Edward W. Said, *Reflections on Exile and Other Essays* (Cambridge, Mass.: Harvard University Press, 2002).

44. Paul Tabori, *The Anatomy of Exile: A Semantic and Historical Study* (London: Harrap, 1972); Christopher D'Addario, *Exile and Journey in Seventeenth-Century Literature* (Cambridge: Cambridge University Press, 2007).

45. D'Addario, *Exile and Journey*, 3.

46. Nico Israel defines "literary exile" in precise terms as an ironic distance from nationalism; see Nico Israel, *Outlandish: Writing between Exile and Diaspora* (Stanford, Calif.: Stanford University Press, 2000).

47. Norval Morris and David J. Rothman, eds., *The Oxford History of the Prison: The Practice of Punishment in Western Society* (New York: Oxford University Press, 1998).

48. Marjorie McIntosh, *Controlling Misbehavior in England, 1370–1600* (Cambridge: Cambridge University Press, 1998), 88–107.

49. Ibid., 39. See Powers, *Crime and Punishment in Early Massachusetts 1620–1692*, 210, 334.

50. On vagrancy at the time, see A. L. Beier, *Masterless Men: Vagrancy Problem in Britain, 1560–1640* (London: Methuen, 1985); and Ruth Wallis Herndon, *Unwelcome Americans: Living on the Margin in Early New England* (Philadelphia: University of Pennsylvania Press, 2001).

51. Based on the ancient ritual of frankpledge, in which every member of the community was required to help every other member in the event of hardship, warnings were given to newcomers whose presence threatened to tax the community's financial well-being. In many cases "warned out" individuals were obvious troublemakers, jobless vagrants, or loiterers. But in others they might be upstanding individuals whom the town council had decided for one reason or another it did not want to support. If "warned out," of course, the individual in question could try the next town with impunity. See Josiah Henry Benton, *Warning Out in New England, 1656–1817* (Boston: Press of Geo. B. Ellis Co., 1911). See also Cornelia Drayton and Sharon Salinger, "Searching for the English Origins and Puritan Roots of New England's Practice of Warning Out Strangers," paper delivered at the Symposium on Comparative Early Modern Legal Discipline in the Early Modern Atlantic World, The Newberry Library, Chicago, October 6, 2006.

52. Edward Coke, *The Selected Writings and Speeches of Sir Edward Coke*, ed. Steve Sheppard, vol. 2 (Indianapolis: Liberty Fund, 2003), 848ff.

53. See Kingsley-Smith, *Shakespeare's Drama of Exile*, 10–12.

54. On jurisdiction and the history of jurisdiction in general, see Richard T. Ford, "Law's Territory (A History of Jurisdiction)," *Michigan Law Review* 97 (1999): 843–930; and Shaun McVeigh, ed., *Jurisprudence of Jurisdiction* (New York: Routledge-Cavendish, 2007). On some interesting theoretical approaches to jurisdiction, see, for example, Perry Dane, "Jurisdictionality, Time, and the Legal Imagination," *Hofstra Law Review* 23.1 (1994): 1–136; and Lauren Benton, "Colonial Law and Cultural Difference: Jurisdictional Politics and the Formation of the Colonial State," *Comparative Studies in Society and History* 41.3 (1999): 563–88. For more specific accounts of jurisdictional formations in the early American colonies, see Christopher Tomlins, "The Legal Cartography of Colonization, the Legal Polyphony of Settlement: English Intrusions on the American Mainland in the Seventeenth Century," *Law & Social Inquiry* 26.2 (2001): 315–72.

55. For information on the differences between territorial and personal kinds of jurisdiction, see, for example, Arthur M. Weisburd, "Territorial Authority and Personal Jurisdiction," *Washington University Law Quarterly* 63.3 (1985): 377–432; and Lea Brilmayer, "Introduction: Three Perennial Themes in the Law of Personal Jurisdiction," *Rutgers Law Journal* 22.3 (1991): 561–68.

56. Hannah Arendt, *The Origins of Totalitarianism* (New York: Harcourt, Brace, Jovanovich, 1973), 278.

57. Although the distinction between the courts and the legislature came to be hotly contested in the colonies, the early years in both Plymouth and Massachusetts Bay saw an unprecedented blending of the two. In 1630 the General Court and the Court of Assistants were given the power to adjudicate cases and to issue legislation at the same time, which meant that banishment in the colonies remained within the realm of the common law.

58. See Richard J. Ross, "The Career of Puritan Jurisprudence," *Law and History Review* 26.2 (2008): 227–58, 242. For additional lucid accounts of the complexity of the early legal system in the New England Puritan colonies, see James S. Hart and Richard J. Ross, "The Ancient Constitution in the Old World and the New," in *The World of John Winthrop: Essays on England and New England, 1588–1649*, ed. Francis J. Bremer and Lynn A. Botelho (Boston: Massachusetts Historical Society, 2010); and Richard J. Ross, "Puritan Godly Discipline in Comparative Perspective: Legal Pluralism and the Sources of 'Intensity,'" *American Historical Review* 113.4 (2008): 975–1002.

59. Michael Zuckerman, "The Fabrication of Identity in Early America," *William and Mary Quarterly* 34.2 (1977): 183–214, 197; Ross, "Puritan Godly Discipline in Comparative Perspective," 975–1002.

60. David Cressy, *Coming Over: Migration and Communication between England and New England in the Seventeenth Century* (Cambridge: Cambridge University Press, 1987), 192.

61. On these nonstandard traffic patterns, see, for example, Thompson, *Mobility and Migration*; Carla Gardina Pestana, *The English Atlantic in an Age of Revolution, 1640–1661* (Cambridge, Mass.: Harvard University Press, 2004); and Alison Games, *Migration and the Origins of the English Atlantic World* (Cambridge, Mass.: Harvard University Press, 1999).

62. Andrew Delbanco, "Looking Homeward, Going Home: The Lure of England for the Founders of New England," *New England Quarterly* 59.3 (1986): 358–86, 362.

63. See William J. Scheick, "The Captive Exile Hasteth: Increase Mather, Meditation, and Authority," *Early American Literature* 36.2 (2001): 183–200.

64. Delaney, *Territory*, 90.

65. Charles Taylor, *Modern Social Imaginaries* (Durham, N.C.: Duke University Press, 2004), 23.

66. Yi-Fu Tuan, *Space and Place: The Perspective of Experience* (Minneapolis: University of Minnesota Press, 1977); Edward W. Soja, *Postmodern Geographies: The Reassertion of Space in Critical Social Theory* (London: Verso, 1989); Edward S. Casey, *The Fate of Place: A Philosophical History* (Berkeley: University of California Press, 1998).

67. Tim Cresswell, *Place: A Short Introduction* (Oxford: Blackwell, 2004), 15.

68. Delaney, *Territory*, 12. If Delaney's definition makes it clear that place and territory share an emphasis on human experience, these concepts, like those of space and place, also need to be differentiated. First, territory, as the following study of various banishments will show, is, unlike place, crucially associated with control. If the paradigm of territory has moved beyond bounded space, in other words, it is still caught up in its problematic and engages in the drawing of boundaries and the making of decisions about inclusion and exclusion at all times. Second, if territory, like place, is implicated "in ways of thinking,

acting, and being in the world," it concerns itself with these things on a much larger scale. Whereas both place and territory are defined in part by the experience of the people within them, in the case of territory that experience revolves largely around questions of membership and affiliation. Put another way, while experiencing a place might entail any number of sensory perceptions or emotions, experiencing a territory tends to revolve around the relationship between the individual and the sovereign—be it the king, governor, judge, or some other legal entity—that has declared the space a legal jurisdiction in the first place.

69. Bradin Cormack, *A Power to Do Justice: Jurisdiction, English Literature, and the Rise of Common Law* (Chicago: University of Chicago Press, 2007), 8.

70. J. G. A. Pocock, *Politics, Language, and Time: Essays on Political Thought and History* (Chicago: University of Chicago Press, 1989), 209.

71. See Daniel Kerman, "Jurisdictional Competition and the Evolution of the Common Law: An Hypothesis," and Anthony Masson, "Introduction," both in *Boundaries of the Law: Geography, Gender and Jurisdiction in Medieval and Early Modern Europe*, ed. Anthony Masson (Aldershot: Ashgate, 2005), 149–68 and 1–6.

72. Max Farrand, Introduction to *The Laws and Liberties of Massachusetts* (1648; repr., Cambridge: Harvard University Press, 1929), vii.

73. As much as they planned to follow the dictates of the common law, the colonists planned to change them as well. Their goal in bringing the common law over with them to the New World was in part to reform the criminal law of England by reducing the severity of a number of capital crimes. See G. B. Warden, "Law Reform in England and New England, 1620 to 1660," *William and Mary Quarterly* 35.4 (1978): 668–90.

74. See, for example, E. P. Thompson, *Customs in Common: Studies in Traditional Popular Culture* (New York: New Press, 1991), 97–184. See also William E. Nelson, *The Common Law in Colonial America*, vol. 1: *The Chesapeake and New England 1607–1660* (Oxford: Oxford University Press, 2008); J. A. Sharpe, *Judicial Punishment in England* (London: Faber and Faber, 1990); and David Konig, *Law and Society in Puritan Massachusetts: Essex County, 1629–1692* (Chapel Hill: University of North Carolina Press, 1981).

75. See Mary Sarah Bilder, *The Transatlantic Constitution: Colonial Legal Culture and the Empire* (Cambridge, Mass.: Harvard University Press, 2004); and Vicki Hsueh, *Hybrid Constitutions: Challenging Legacies of Law, Privilege, and Culture in Colonial America* (Durham, N.C.: Duke University Press, 2010).

76. Robert Sack, *Human Territoriality: Its Theory and History* (Cambridge: Cambridge University Press, 1986), 33.

CHAPTER 1

1. This was not the case for the first settlers of the Plymouth Colony, but the financial requirements for membership there were not high.

2. Julius Goebel, Jr., "King's Law and Local Custom in Seventeenth-Century New England," *Columbia Law Review* 31.3 (1931): 416–48, 428.

3. William Bradford, *Of Plymouth Plantation: 1620–1647*, ed. Samuel Eliot Morison (New York: Alfred A. Knopf, 2002), 44n9.

4. Charles Tilly, *Identities, Boundaries, and Social Ties* (Boulder: Paradigm, 2005), 174.

5. See ibid., 247.

6. Jacques Derrida, *Of Hospitality: Anne Dufourmantelle Invites Jacques Derrida to Respond*, trans. Rachel Bowlby (Stanford, Calif.: Stanford University Press, 2000), 77.

7. See Felicity Heal, *Hospitality in Early Modern England* (Oxford: Clarendon Press, 1990), 2; Olivia Remie Constable, *Housing the Stranger in the Mediterranean World: Lodgings, Trade, and Travel in Late Antiquity and the Middle Ages* (Cambridge: Cambridge University Press, 2003), 2; Catherine Marie O'Sullivan, *Hospitality in Medieval Ireland, 900–1500* (Dublin: Four Courts Press, 2004), 63; Christine D. Pohl, *Making Room: Recovering Hospitality as a Christian Tradition* (Grand Rapids, Mich.: William B. Eerdmans, 1999), 4; and Immanuel Kant, *Toward Perpetual Peace and Other Writings on Politics, Peace, and History*, ed. Pauline Kleingeld, trans. David L. Colclasure (New Haven, Conn.: Yale University Press, 2006), 82.

8. Heal, *Hospitality in Early Modern England*, 3.

9. Cotton Mather, "Nehemias Americanus," in *Magnalia Christi Americana*, vol. 1 (repr., Hartford: Thomas Robbins, 1852), 119.

10. Bradford, *Of Plymouth Plantation*, 149.

11. Derrida, *Of Hospitality*, 156. History and literature are full of hostile hosts; one thinks first perhaps of the unfortunate Duncan, who invited Macbeth into his home only to be murdered by him in his sleep. Georg Simmel underscored these observations about hospitality when he referred to strangers as "wanderers," who enter existing communities, bringing the quality of difference or otherness with them. Strangers, in Simmel's words, are near and far at the same time. "The stranger is close to us," he wrote, "insofar as we feel between him and ourselves common features of a national, social, occupational, or general human nature. He is far from us, insofar as these common features extend beyond him or us, and connect us only because they connect a great many people." For Simmel, additionally, the prototypical stranger is a trader because trade by its nature ushers into a preexisting social sphere commodities and merchants from the outside. The trader, he noted, "intrudes as a supernumerary . . . into a group in which the economic positions are actually occupied." See Georg Simmel, "The Stranger," in *The Sociology of Georg Simmel*, ed. Kurt H. Wolff (New York: Free Press, 1950), 406, 403.

12. J. Hillis Miller, "The Critic as Host," *Critical Inquiry* 3.3 (1977): 439–47.

13. Heal, *Hospitality in Early Modern England*, 122–25. Constable actually claims that the hostels provided from the twelfth through the sixteenth centuries for strangers disappeared in the early modern period and thus provided a consistency to the premodern world that the early modern world lacked. See Constable, *Housing the Stranger in the Mediterranean World*, 3.

14. James's speech is recorded in James I, *The Workes of James . . . King of Great Britain*, ed. James Montague (London, 1616), 567. Even in this speech, however, as Heal suggests, what appears to be an exhortation to restore the ancient custom of hospitality may have

simply been a by-product of the king's more pressing goal: to send the gentry home in order to reduce the overcrowding that was beginning to consume London and Westminster. See Heal, *Hospitality in Early Modern England*, 119.

15. See Maria Moisa, "Debate: Conviviality and Charity in Medieval and Early Modern England," *Past and Present* 154.1 (1997): 223–34, 223.

16. Steve Hindle, "Dearth, Fasting and Alms: The Campaign for General Hospitality in Late Elizabethan England," *Past and Present* 172.1 (2001): 44–86, 80.

17. Heal, *Hospitality in Early Modern England*, 139.

18. John Winthrop, "A Modell of Christian Charity," *The Winthrop Papers*, 5 vols. (Boston: Massachusetts Historical Society, 1929–47), 2:282–95, 289. For a different view, see Hugh J. Dawson, "'Christian Charitie' as Colonial Discourse: Rereading Winthrop's Sermon in Its English Context," *Early American Literature* 33.2 (1998): 117–48. Dawson argues that Winthrop was speaking not only to the people on board the *Arbella* but also to the people left behind. However, my point about the preexisting nature of the New England community still holds.

19. Bruce H. Mann, *Neighbors and Strangers: Law and Community in Early Connecticut* (Chapel Hill: University of North Carolina Press, 1987). Mann's book is about a later period, but he does have some interesting language about neighbors becoming strangers through the operation of the legal system.

20. Goebel suggests as much in "King's Law and Local Custom in Seventeenth-Century New England," 429.

21. Not surprisingly references to hospitality as a rule began to multiply in this period, and if legal discourse did not yet refer to it as a law, paralegal and religious discourse often did. Caleb Dalechamp, for example, preaching in the 1630s, spoke of the abiding obligation that men had to care for strangers as a law. See Dalechamp, *Christian Hospitality: Handled Common-wise in the Chappel of Trinity Colledge in Cambridge* (Cambridge, 1632), 4.

22. Francisco de Vitoria, *Political Writings*, ed. Anthony Pagden and Jeremy Lawrance (Cambridge: Cambridge University Press, 1991), 278.

23. Hugo Grotius, *Commentary on the Law of Prize and Booty*, ed. with an introduction by Martine Julia van Ittersum (Indianapolis: Liberty Fund, 2006), 304.

24. Samuel Pufendorf, *Two Books of the Elements of Universal Jurisprudence* (Indianapolis: Liberty Fund, 2009), 244.

25. Although a somewhat controversial claim, it is generally agreed that human-rights law derives from and is in some sense a continuation of liberal Western democracy. See, for example, Makau Mutuaz, *Human Rights: A Political and Cultural Critique* (Philadelphia: University of Pennsylvania Press, 2002), 40.

26. Micheline R. Ishay, *The History of Human Rights: From Ancient Times to the Globalization Era* (Berkeley: University of California Press, 2004), 3.

27. As the notion of one's rights became decoupled from one's social standing, law became a bastion of rights outside of class status as opposed to the arbiter of rights within them. See Alex Honneth, *The Struggle for Recognition: The Moral Grammar of Social Conflicts*, trans. Joel Anderson (Oxford: Polity Press, 1995).

28. See Richard Tuck, *The Rights of War and Peace: Political Thought and the International Order from Grotius to Kant* (Oxford: Oxford University Press, 1999), 209, for some of the disagreements Kant had with Grotius.

29. Kant, *Toward Perpetual Peace and Other Writings on Politics, Peace, and History*, 82.

30. Winnifred Cockshott, *The Pilgrim Fathers, Their Church and Colony* (1909; repr., Ithaca, N.Y.: Cornell University Library, 209), 107.

31. Daniel Plooij, *The Pilgrim Fathers from a Dutch Point of View* (N.p.: 1932; repr., Native American Books Distributor, 2007), 22.

32. Nathaniel Morton in Alexander Young, *Chronicles of the Pilgrim Fathers* (New York: Cosimo, 2005), 8.

33. Henry Martyn Dexter and Morton Dexter, *The England and Holland of the Pilgrims* (Boston: Houghton, Mifflin, 1906; repr., Boston: Adamant Media Corporation, 2005), 420.

34. Morton in Young, *Chronicles of the Pilgrim Fathers*, 10.

35. Donald F. Connors, *Thomas Morton* (New York: Twayne, 1969), 18.

36. Morton arrived in New England first in 1622 and then again in 1624 as a trader, but he had three periods of prolonged residence punctuated by three banishments from 1628 to 1630. The letters the Pilgrims sent back to England accused him of bad conduct, which included erecting a large Maypole, conducting pagan rituals, and willfully misunderstanding the laws and rights of individual fur traders in the region. After his last banishment, Morton stayed in England for thirteen years, from 1630 to 1643, at which point he returned once again to New England, but this time to the west country in Maine, where the Plymouth Pilgrims would not disturb him. He lived there until his death in 1647. See Connors, *Thomas Morton*, 22–27. See also Thomas Morton, *New English Canaan: Text & Notes*, ed. Jack Dempsey (Scituate: Digital Scanning, 2000), xxii–xxxix.

37. For a concise summary of these scholarly assessments, see Philip Ranlet, *Enemies of the Bay Colony* (New York: Peter Lang, 1995), 14ff.

38. Morton, *New English Canaan*, 9. As a description of the land, this was a far cry from that of the Puritans, who saw the land as relatively harsh, infertile, and inhospitable. Edward Winslow, for example, who wrote a relatively glowing account of New England in his *Good Newes from New England* (1624), cannot help but observe "the mean condition" of the first settlements in Plymouth ([Carlisle, Mass.: Applewood Books, 1996], 19), while Bradford spends most of the opening chapter of his history discussing how while searching for a place of habitation and a good harbor they "ranged up and down all that day, but found no people, nor any place they liked" (69). William Wood too, in his *New England's Prospect*—a work that Morton found particularly misleading and set out to parody in his own volume—spoke disparagingly of the New England land: "Such is the rankness of the ground that it must be sown the first year with Indian corn, which is a soaking grain, before it will be fit to receive English seed"(William Wood, *New England's Prospect* [Amherst: University of Massachusetts Press, 1977],35).

39. Morton, *New English Canaan*, 12.

40. Michelle Burnham, "Land, Labor, and Colonial Economics in Thomas Morton's New English Canaan," *Early American Literature* 41.3 (2006): 405–28, 413.

41. Morton, *New English Canaan*, 205.

42. Ibid., 208.

43. Minor Wallace Major, *Thomas Morton and His New English Canaan* (Ph.D. diss., University of Colorado, 1957), 36.

44. See, for example, John Winthrop's description of the antinomians in "A Short Story of the Rise, Reign, and Ruine of the Antinomians, Familists and Libertines," in *The Antinomian Controversy, 1636–1638: A Documentary History*, ed. David D. Hall (Durham, N.C.: Duke University Press, 1999), 202.

45. It is worth noting in this regard that when Morton finally came back from England after his first banishment, he came with the distinguished agent Isaac Allerton, who not only welcomed him as an ally but also gave him shelter in his own home for months in Boston. See Charles Francis Adams, "The May-Pole of Merrymount," *Atlantic Monthly* 39 (June 1887): 687.

46. Morton, *New English Canaan*, 134–35.

47. The Maypole has been traced back to the folk customs of the French, Germans, and English as well as to those of others in northern European cultures. Its exact provenance is unknown, but James Frazer has described it as an example of an old custom of tree worship. See James George Frazer, *The Golden Bough* (New York: Macmillan, 1963), 141–43. For its significance as an ancient symbol in Morton's community of Mare Mount, at least as reenvisioned by Nathaniel Hawthorne, see John B. Vickery, "The Golden Bough at Merry Mount," *Nineteenth-Century Fiction* 12.3 (1957): 203–14.

48. Matt Cohen, *The Networked Wilderness: Communicating in Early New England* (Minneapolis: University of Minnesota Press, 2010), 27.

49. Morton, *New English Canaan*, 140.

50. From Emery Battis, *Saints and Sectaries: Anne Hutchinson and the Antinomian Controversy in the Massachusetts Bay Colony* (Chapel Hill: University of North Carolina Press, 1962), 36; see 73 for information on Hutchinson's house and how Henry Vane encouraged her to open it to her neighbors.

51. See ibid., 249–86, for the most detailed reconstruction of these meetings, including how many people attended and who they were.

52. This is often read as a rivalry between ministers such as Thomas Hooker and Thomas Shepard, on the one hand, and ministers such as John Cotton, on the other, who greatly influenced Hutchinson's own spiritism but in the end set himself in opposition to it. See Michael J. Colacurcio, "Primitive Comfort: The Spiritual Witness of John Cotton," *English Literary History* 67.3 (2000): 655–96; Janice Knight, *Orthodoxies in Massachusetts: Rereading American Puritanism* (Cambridge, Mass.: Harvard University Press, 1994); and Julie Sievers, "Refiguring the Song of Songs: John Cotton's 1655 Sermon and the Antinomian Controversy," *New England Quarterly* 76.1 (2003): 73–107, for much more information about these issues.

53. Winthrop, "A Short Story of the Rise, Reign, and Ruine of the Antinomians, Familists and Libertines," 207.

54. Lloyd A. Robson, *Anne Hutchinson and Her Neighbors* (1938; repr., n.p.: Hard Press, 2008), 23, my emphasis.

55. Ibid., 30.

56. John Winthrop, "The Examination of Mrs. Anne Hutchinson at the Court at Newtown," in *The Antinomian Controversy, 1636–1638,* ed. Hall, 312.

57. Michael Gorr, "Actus Reus Requirement: A Qualified Defense," *Criminal Justice Ethics* 10.1 (1991): 11–18, 11–12.

58. Winthrop, "The Examination of Mrs. Anne Hutchinson at the Court at Newtown," 312.

59. Ibid., 313, my emphasis.

60. Ibid., 315.

61. Winthrop, "A Short Story of the Rise, Reign, and Ruine of the Antinomians, Familists and Libertines," 204.

62. After the antinomian crisis, John Cotton changed the venues for the conversion narratives of women from public to private ones, effectively banishing their speech.

63. Winthrop, "The Examination of Mrs. Anne Hutchinson at the Court at Newtown," 313.

64. J. H. Adamson and H. F. Folland, *Sir Harry Vane: His Life and Times, 1613–1662* (Boston: Gambit, 1973), 102–8. See also Knight, *Orthodoxies in Massachusetts,* 28.

65. The order passed was "to keep out all such persons as might be dangerous to the commonwealth, by imposing a penalty upon all such as should retain any, etc., above three weeks, which should not be allowed by some of the magistrates; for it was very probably, that they [the antinomians] expected many of their opinion to come out of England from Mr. Brierly his church, etc." See John Winthrop, *The Journal of John Winthrop,* ed. Richard S. Dunn, James Savage, and Laetitia Yeandle (Cambridge, Mass.: Harvard University Press, 1996), 219.

66. "Here came over a brother of Mrs. Hutchinson, and some other of Mr. Wheelwright's friends, whom the governour thought not fit to allow, as others, to sit down among us, without some trial of them. Therefore, to save others from the danger of the law in receiving of them, he allowed them for four months. This was taken very ill by those of the other party, and many hot speechs given forth about it, and about their removal, etc." (Winthrop, *Journal,* 226).

67. Thomas Hutchinson, ed., *A Collection of Original Papers Relative to the History of the Colony of Massachusetts Bay* (1769; repr., Carlisle: Applewood Books, 2010), 68.

68. Ibid., 69.

69. See Jack Greene, "Transatlantic Colonization and the Redefinition of Empire in the Early Modern Era," in *Negotiated Empires: Centers and Peripheries in the New World, 1500–1820,* ed. Christine Daniels and Michael V. Kennedy (New York: Routledge, 2002), 271–72.

70. Hutchinson, *A Collection of Original Papers Relative to the History of the Colony of Massachusetts Bay,* 77.

71. The Council for New England declared the Massachusetts charter void in 1634, redivided its lands in 1635, and asked Morton to file a writ of quo warranto against the Massachusetts Bay Colony for repeal of the colonists' patent, an effort that in 1637 succeeded

formally in the Court of the King's Bench but had no practical effect in the colony and failed to alter the policy on hospitality. Having the actual charter in their possession, the colonists simply refused to give it up and, pretending that they had not heard about its revocation, pressed ahead in their campaign against the antinomians.

72. See Conrad Lashley and Alison Morrison, eds., *In Search of Hospitality* (Oxford: Reed Educational and Professional Publishing, 2000).

73. Conrad Lashley, Paul Lynch, and Alison Morrison, "Ways of Knowing Hospitality," in *Hospitality: A Social Lens*, ed. Conrad Lashley, Paul Lynch, and Alison Morrison (London: Elsevier, 2007), 176.

74. Moisa, "Debate," 223–34, 223.

75. Hindle, "Dearth, Fasting and Alms," 44–86, 47.

76. Erving Goffman, *Interaction Ritual:Essays on Face-to-Face Behavior* (New York: Anchor Books, 1967), 5.

77. Clifford Geertz, *The Interpretation of Cultures: Selected Essays* (New York: Basic Books, 1973), 424.

78. See Matt Cohen, "Morton's Maypole and the Indians: Publishing in Early New England," *Book History* 5.1 (2002): 1–18, 3.

79. Paul Raffield, *Images and Cultures of Law in Early Modern England: Justice and Political Power, 1558–1660* (Cambridge: Cambridge University Press, 2004), 85–86, 93.

80. The Maypole has been cast as a signifier of almost unlimited meaning. See Morton, *New English Canaan*, 192. See also Leah S. Marcus, *The Politics of Mirth: Jonson, Herrick, Milton, Marvell, and the Defense of Old Holiday Pastimes* (Chicago: University of Chicago Press, 1986), 21.

81. Linda Gregerson notes that "the verbal image was thought to be as dangerous as the visual" and that Francis Bacon called words "idols." See Gregerson, *The Reformation of the Subject: Spenser, Milton, and the English Protestant Epic* (Cambridge: Cambridge University Press, 1995), 3, 64.

82. Edith Murphy, "'A Rich Widow, Now to Be Tane Up or Laid Downe': Solving the Riddle of Thomas Morton's 'Rise Oedipeus,'" *William and Mary Quarterly* 53.4 (1996): 755–68.

83. Jack Dempsey, "Reading the Revels: The Riddle of May Day in New English Canaan," *Early American Literature* 34.2 (1999): 289.

84. Daniel Shea has observed that Morton made the ostensibly great readers of texts— namely the Puritan separatists of Plymouth—into really bad readers insofar as they found it impossible to decipher his poem "Rise Oedipus." See Shea, "'Our Professed Old Adversary': Thomas Morton and the Naming of New England," *Early American Literature* 23.1 (1988): 52–69, 61–62.

85. See Amy Schrager Lang, *Prophetic Woman: Anne Hutchinson and the Problem of Dissent in the Literature of New England* (Berkeley: University of California Press, 1989); and Eve LaPlante, *American Jezebel: The Uncommon Life of Anne Hutchinson, the Woman Who Defied the Puritans* (New York: HarperCollins, 2004), to name just two studies with a feminist bent.

86. According to Flaherty, neighborhoods in early New England were odd mixtures of privacy and publicity in which intimacy intermingled with a great deal of mutual interaction, confusing the distinction we understand today between privacy and publicity. See David H. Flaherty, *Privacy in Colonial New England 1630–1776* (Charlottesville: University of Virginia Press, 1972), 90, 97.

87. Bradford, *Of Plymouth Plantation*, 206.

88. John Demos, *A Little Commonwealth: Family Life in Plymouth Colony* (New York: Oxford University Press, 1970).

89. David M. Engel, "Law in the Domains of Everyday Life: The Construction of Community and Difference," in *Law in Everyday Life*, ed. Austin Sarat and Thomas R. Kearns (Ann Arbor: University of Michigan Press, 1995), 126.

90. Simmel, "The Stranger," 402.

91. Patricia Ewick and Susan S. Silbey, *The Common Place of Law: Stories from Everyday Life* (Chicago: University of Chicago Press, 1998), 134.

92. See generally, Richard Ross, "The Commoning of the Common Law: The Renaissance Debate over Printing English Law, 1520–1640," *University of Pennsylvania Law Review* 146.2 (1998): 323–461.

CHAPTER 2

1. C. W. Brooks, *Pettyfoggers and Vipers of the Commonwealth: The 'Lower Branch' of the Legal Profession in Early Modern England* (Cambridge: Cambridge University Press, 2004), 36.

2. Patricia Fumerton, *Unsettled: The Culture of Mobility and the Working Poor in Early Modern England* (Chicago: University of Chicago Press, 2006).

3. Ibid., 4–5.

4. Bryan Reynolds, *Becoming Criminal: Transversal Performance and Cultural Dissidence in Early Modern England* (Baltimore: Johns Hopkins University Press, 2002), 96. See also Linda Woodbridge, *Vagrancy, Homelessness, and English Renaissance Literature* (Champaign: University of Illinois Press, 2001).

5. Jane Newman, "'Race,' Religion, and the Law: Rhetorics of Sameness and Difference in the Work of Hugo Grotius," in *Rhetoric and Law in the Early Modern Period*, ed. Victoria Kahn and Lorna Hutson (New Haven, Conn.: Yale University Press, 2001), 285–317, 297.

6. For a general sense of how the colonists' laws differed from those of the mother country, see George Haskins, *Law and Authority in Early Massachusetts: A Study in Tradition and Design* (New York: Macmillan, 1960); and William E. Nelson, *Americanization of the Common Law: The Impact of Legal Change on Massachusetts Society, 1760–1830* (Cambridge, Mass.: Harvard University Press, 1975).

7. Mary Sarah Bilder, *The Transatlantic Constitution: Colonial Legal Culture and the Empire* (Cambridge, Mass.: Harvard University Press, 2004), 35–38.

8. Christopher D. Felker, "Roger Williams's Uses of Legal Discourse: Testing Authority in Early New England," *New England Quarterly* 63.4 (1990): 624–48.

9. Edward Coke, *The Selected Writings of Sir Edward Coke*, ed. Steve Sheppard, vol. 1 (Indianapolis: Liberty Fund, 2003), 182.

10. See Polly J. Price, "Natural Law and Birthright Citizenship in Calvin's Case (1608)," *Yale Journal of Law and Humanities* 9 (1997): 73–146; Ayelet Shachar, *The Birthright Lottery: Citizenship and Global Inequality* (Cambridge, Mass.: Harvard University Press, 2009), 114. On the question of sovereignty, which preoccupied all of the important legal minds in the first half of the seventeenth century, see also Joyce Lee Malcolm, ed., *The Struggle for Sovereignty: Seventeenth-Century English Political Tracts*, 2 vols. (Indianapolis: Liberty Fund, 1999), 1:xix–lxii.

11. Jacqueline Stevens, *States without Nations: Citizenship for Mortals* (New York: Columbia University Press, 2010), 67.

12. Quoted in Price, "Natural Law and Birthright Citizenship in Calvin's Case (1608)," 74.

13. Bilder, *The Transatlantic Constitution*, 1.

14. Ibid., 1. The ability to choose between jurisdictions was also mixed with a prohibition against bringing colonists who had committed crimes in England back to England to be judged. Nehemiah Wallington, for example, reported that his friend James Cole, who had distributed a dissident pamphlet and was wanted by the courts in England, could no longer be arrested because he had immigrated to Connecticut. See Paul S. Seaver, *Wallington's World: A Puritan Artisan in Seventeenth-Century London* (Stanford, Calif.: Stanford University Press, 1988), 100.

15. See Sir Frederick Pollock and Frederic William Maitland, *The History of English Law before the Time of Edward I*, 2nd ed. (Cambridge: Cambridge University Press, 1923), 3:194.

16. See Patricia Caldwell, *The Puritan Conversion Narrative: The Beginnings of American Expression* (Cambridge: Cambridge University Press, 1985).

17. In "God's Promise to His Plantations," a farewell sermon Cotton gave to Winthrop's company as they left for the New World in 1630, we see how intimately connected Israel and New England were for him. He began with a quote from 2 Samuel 7:10: "Moreover, I will appoint a place for my people Israel, and I will plant them, that they may dwell in a place of their own, and move no more." Having moved to New England, in other words, God's newly chosen people would need to go no further because New England was "appointed," a place not only from which to escape persecution—like the Netherlands—but also a destination, a place invested with the sacral qualities of Israel. To speak of New England as a destination, however, is not to suggest that settling in New England and only New England was the Puritans' destiny. To do so would be, as many scholars have pointed out, to implicate the Puritans in a trajectory of American imperialism and manifest destiny that erroneously took hold in the popular imagination centuries after their arrival. Arguing against such an association, Andrew Delbanco reads the appointment of America in "God's Promise" as random. "The land of promise," he writes, "was a place of intimacy with God" that initially included a variety of appointed places, including Providence Island off the

coast of Nicaragua. But from my perspective, it matters little whether the Puritans ended up in New England or Nicaragua. The important element from the point of view of jurisdiction is that Cotton associated people with place. See John Cotton, "God's Promise to His Plantations" (London: Printed by William James for John Bellamy, 1634); and Andrew Delbanco, *The Puritan Ordeal* (Cambridge, Mass.: Harvard University Press, 1991), 91.

18. Williams argued that he was banished for four things: (1) violating the king's patent; (2) refusing to take the oath of residency; (3) separating from the established church; and (4) mixing civil and spiritual matters. Governor Winthrop had a slightly different list and a slightly different order. He argued that Williams was banished for the following: (1) mixing civil and spiritual affairs; (2) refusing to take the oath; (3) separating from the church; and (4) not giving thanks after the sacrament. See Roger Williams, *The Complete Writings of Roger Williams*, 7 vols. (Paris, Ark.: Baptist Standard Bearer, 2005), 2:40–41n8. Some scholars have gone so far as to claim that the actual reasons for the banishment are of no interest at all. See Henry Bamford Parkes, "John Cotton and Roger Williams Debate Toleration 1644–1652," *New England Quarterly* 4.4 (1931): 735–56, 735.

19. See, e.g., Glenn W. LaFantasie, ed., *The Correspondence of Roger Williams*, vol. 1: *1629–1653* (Providence, R.I.: Brown University Press, 1988), 15; Henry S. Burrage, "Why Was Roger Williams Banished?," *American Journal of Theology* 5.1 (1901): 1–17, 9; Delbanco, *The Puritan Ordeal*; Edmund P. Morgan, *Roger Williams: The Church and the State* (New York: W. W. Norton, 1987); Philip F. Gura, *A Glimpse of Sion's Glory: Puritan Radicalism in New England, 1620–1660* (Middletown, Conn.: Wesleyan University Press, 1984); Louise A. Breen, *Transgressing the Bounds: Subversive Enterprises among the Puritan Elite in Massachusetts, 1630–1692* (New York: Oxford University Press, 2001); Martha Nussbaum, *Liberty of Conscience: In Defense of America's Tradition of Religious Equality* (New York: Basic Books, 2008).

20. Edmund S. Morgan, "Review: Miller's Williams," *New England Quarterly* 38.4 (1965): 518.

21. See Sacvan Bercovitch, "Typology in Puritan New England: The Williams-Cotton Controversy Reassessed," *American Quarterly* 19.2 (1967): 166–91.

22. Jesper Rosenmeier, "The Teacher and the Witness: John Cotton and Roger Williams," *William and Mary Quarterly* 25.3 (1968): 408–31, 410; Gura, *A Glimpse of Sion's Glory*, 43, 47.

23. Teresa Toulouse, *The Art of Prophesying: New England Sermons and the Shaping of Belief* (Athens: University of Georgia Press, 1987), 190n22.

24. Andrew Delbanco, *The Puritan Ordeal* (Cambridge, Mass.: Harvard University Press, 1991), 169–70.

25. There has been some question in scholarly circles about what kind of relationship Williams had with Coke. An early twentieth-century biography by James Ernst asserts, without support, that Williams took down speeches for Coke in the Star Chamber. See James Ernst, *Roger Williams: New England Firebrand* (New York: Macmillan, 1932), 27–28. A later essay reaffirms this relationship by referring to Williams as "court recorder for then chief justice of the Common Pleas." See Felker, "Roger Williams's Uses of Legal Discourse,"

625. I can find no direct evidence that Williams ever worked in an official capacity for Coke, but Coke did serve as Williams's mentor, seemed to have paid for all or part of his education, and may well have used him to "take down speeches" in court.

26. While the impulse behind the common law may have been toward homogenization, the competing discourses between jurisdictions were only thinly veiled. See Peter Goodrich, *Law in the Courts of Love: Literature and Other Minor Jurisprudences* (London: Routledge, 1996).

27. Henry Ainsworth, *La Communion des Saincts* (Lausanne: Giles Thorpe, 1615).

28. Williams deemed the churches of New England to be insufficiently separated from the Church of England, which was, in his view, a place of irremediable religious corruption.

29. See John Winthrop, *The Journal of John Winthrop, 1630–1649*, abridged ed., ed. Richard S. Dunn, James Savage, and Laetitia Yeandle (Cambridge, Mass.: Harvard University Press, 1996), 29.

30. Ibid.

31. See Michael Winship, *Making Heretics* (Princeton, N.J.: Princeton University Press, 2001), 80.

32. See Michael Colacurcio, *Godly Letters: The Literature of the American Puritans* (Notre Dame, Ind.: University of Notre Dame Press, 2006), 517.

33. Williams, *The Complete Writings of Roger Williams*, 3:230.

34. See Edwin S. Gaustad, *Liberty of Conscience: Roger Williams in America* (Valley Forge, Pa.: Judson Press, 1999), 31–38, for one version of these events.

35. Titus Mooney Merriman, *Pilgrims, Puritans, and Roger Williams Vindicated, and His Sentence of Banishment Ought to Be Revoked* (1892; repr., Ithaca, N.Y.: Cornell University Library, 2010), 76.

36. There were simultaneous challenges made in Parliament by Coke to all the patents issued by the king, not only for land but also for the operation of certain trades on the basis that they granted monopolies. These challenges were the first to question the prerogative of the king. See Elizabeth Read Foster, "The Procedure of the House of Commons against Patents and Monopolies, 1621–1624," in *Law, Liberty, and Parliament: Selected Essays on the Writings of Sir Edward Coke*, ed. Allen D. Boyer (Indianapolis: Liberty Fund, 2004), 309. Like the Spanish, the English claimed a monopoly of contact with the regions they intended to occupy. See James Muldoon, "Discovery, Grant Charter, Conquest, or Purchase: John Adams on the Legal Basis for English Possession of North America," in *The Many Legalities of Early America*, ed. Christopher L. Tomlins and Bruce H. Mann (Chapel Hill: University of North Carolina Press, 2001), 42.

37. Merriman, *Pilgrims, Puritans, and Roger Williams Vindicated*, 82.

38. There is a lively if obscure strain of early American criticism whose aim is to associate Williams with forward-looking views of cultural relativism and Cotton with backward views.

39. Nathaniel B. Shurtleff, ed., *Records of the Governor and Company of the Massachusetts Bay in New England*, vol. 1: *1628–1641* (1854; repr., n.p.: General Books, LLC, 2010).

40. Before the Protestant Reformation, papal bulls had typically authorized the

possession by Christians of non-Christian lands; after the Reformation charters took their place and were intended to usher in a new era in which the law of land acquisition would be more suitably modern and secular. As James Muldoon points out, however, the charters often failed to live up to their reputation; see Muldoon, "Discovery, Grant Charter, Conquest, or Purchase: John Adams on the Legal Basis for English Possession of North America," in *The Many Legalities of Early America*, ed. Christopher L. Tomlins and Bruce H. Mann (Chapel Hill: University of North Carolina Press, 2001), 30, 38.

41. Williams, *The Complete Writings of Roger Williams*, 4:80.

42. Theodore Dwight Bozeman, *To Live Ancient Lives: The Primitivist Dimension in Puritanism* (Chapel Hill and London: University of North Carolina Press, 1988), 163.

43. Williams, *The Complete Writings of Roger Williams*, 2:69.

44. Ian Maclean, *Interpretation and Meaning in the Renaissance: The Case of Law* (Cambridge: Cambridge University Press, 1992), 87–88.

45. David Leverenz, *The Language of Puritan Feeling: An Exploration in Literature, Psychology, and Social History* (New Brunswick, N.J.: Rutgers University Press, 1980), 183.

46. Cotton, "God's Promise to His Plantations," 6.

47. Williams, *The Complete Writings of Roger Williams*, 3:232.

48. Maclean, *Interpretation and Meaning in the Renaissance*, 87.

49. Donald R. Kelley, *The Human Measure: Social Thought in the Western Legal Tradition* (Cambridge, Mass.: Harvard University Press, 1990), 169.

50. Williams, *The Complete Writings of Roger Williams*, 3:71.

51. See C. H. Perelman and L. Olbrechts-Tyteca, *The New Rhetoric: A Treatise on Argumentation* (Notre Dame, Ind.: University of Notre Dame Press, 1969), 222.

52. Littleton, who was a justice of the common pleas in the second half of the fifteenth century, wrote a well-known treatise on property law, which Coke took as his foundation.

53. Williams, *The Complete Writings of Roger Williams*, 1:44, 34.

54. Ibid., 1:319.

55. LaFantasie, *The Correspondence of Roger Williams*, 1:33.

56. For Williams, not coincidentally, this statement had other meanings, and he was, as La Fantasie and others suggest, convinced that he had caught Cotton in a verbal slip. Why, after all, had Cotton said that Williams had banished himself from the fellowship *of all* the churches? Even admitting that he had in fact banished himself, why did it necessarily follow that he had banished himself from all the churches as well? With these words, Williams argued, Cotton had admitted that "the frame or constitution of their churches is but implicitly national . . . for otherwise why as I am not yet permitted to live in the world, or Common-weale, except for this reason, that the Common-weale and Church is yet but one, and he that is banished from the one, must necessarily be banished from the other also." (Williams in LaFantasie, *The Correspondence of Roger Williams*, 1:45).

57. Williams, *The Complete Writings of Roger Williams*, 2:58.

58. Ibid., 2:64.

59. Ibid., 2:116.

60. Ibid., 2:61.

61. Ibid., 3:414.

62. Ibid., 3:282.

63. Ibid., 4:87.

64. Christopher D'Addario, *Exile and Journey in Seventeenth-Century Literature* (Cambridge: Cambridge University Press, 2007), 25. D'Addario argues forcefully throughout the book for a transatlantic perspective on the mid-seventeenth-century work on exile.

65. Richard J. Ross, "The Commoning of the Common Law: The Renaissance Debate over Printing English Law, 1520–1640," *University of Pennsylvania Law Review* 146 (1997–98): 323–461, 367.

66. Williams, *The Complete Writings of Roger Williams*, 2:17–18.

67. Ibid., 1:292. At first Cotton blamed Williams for this violation, although Williams denied it in the preface to his reply "to the impartiall reader." Here he wrote that he had found the letter "publike (by whose procurement I know not)." But if the letter circulated a little before Williams got hold of it, we can assume Williams's widely read "Reply" was what made it well known. In the end, of course, it mattered little who published it, but finding it widely known, Cotton finally accused "some other, unadvised christian, who, having gotten a copy of the letter, took more liberty than God alloweth, to draw forth a private admonition to public notice in a disorderly way." Further problems arose in the publication of another discourse—against set forms of prayer—that Williams ascribed to Cotton. On this matter another dispute ensued as to the source of the publication, in which once again Cotton accused Williams of unlawfully publishing his words and Williams denied it. "The truth is," Williams wrote, "I did not publish that discourse to the world, much lesse did I see cause to publish it upon the Grounds he speaketh of" (ibid., 2:39).

68. Ibid., 3:61.

69. Ann G. Myles, "Arguments in Milk, Arguments in Blood: Roger Williams, Persecution, and the Discourse of the Witness," *Modern Philology* 91.2 (1993): 150.

70. Williams, *The Complete Writings of Roger Williams*, 3:61.

71. Ibid., 4:105.

72. Ibid., 2:56–57, 42, 57, 61, 65, 116.

73. Ibid., 2:42.

74. Ibid., 3:xxiv.

CHAPTER 3

1. Most accounts put the number at no more than forty. See Richard Price Hallowell, *The Quaker Invasion of Massachusetts* (Boston: Houghton, Mifflin, 1883).

2. One Bay Colony declaration, for example, justified the Puritan laws against the Quakers as a way to "secure Peace and Order Against their Attempts, whose design (we were well-assured by our own experience as well as by the example of their Predecessors in Munster) was to undermine and ruin the same"; see George Bishop, *New England Judged by*

the Spirit of the Lord: Containing a Brief Relation of the Sufferings of the People Called Quakers (1703; repr., Whitefish, Mont.: Kessinger, 2008), 3.

3. Quoted in Stephen Foster, "New England and the Challenge of Heresy, 1630 to 1660: The Puritan Crisis in Transatlantic Perspective," *William and Mary Quarterly* 38.4 (1981) : 624–60, 647.

4. George Fox, *The Journal of George Fox*, ed. Rufus M. Jones (1908; repr., Richmond, Va.: Friends United Press, 1976), 222.

5. Michael Zuckerman has written about their insistence on personal revelation as suggesting an "encompassing system of discipline and church control with a thoroughness the Puritans never managed," while April Lee Hatfield has spoken of their spiritual affinities with the Indians as challenging the Puritans' idea of the church-state. In addition Philip Gura has focused on their status as religious martyrs, and Carla Pestana has suggested that they attacked congregationalism at every turn. Similarly literary analyses of these early encounters tend to support this religious focus, with Michele Tartar talking about their different form of prayer and Ann Myles pointing out their expression of affective bonds with one another as a basis for their insistence on return to the colony. See Michael Zuckerman, "The Fabrication of Identity in Early America," *William and Mary Quarterly* 34.2 (1977): 183–214; April Lee Hatfield, *Atlantic Virginia: Intercolonial Relations in the Seventeenth Century* (Philadelphia: University of Pennsylvania Press, 2004); Philip F. Gura, *A Glimpse of Sion's Glory: Puritan Radicalism in New England, 1620–1660* (Middletown, Conn.: Wesleyan University Press, 1986); Carla Gardina Pestana, *Quakers and Baptists in Colonial Massachusetts* (Cambridge: Cambridge University Press, 1991); Michele Lise Tartar, "Quaking in the Light," in *A Centre of Wonders: The Body in Early America*, ed. Janet Moore Lindman and Michele Lise Tartar (Ithaca, N.Y.: Cornell University Press, 2001); and Ann Myles, "From Monster to Martyr: Re-Presenting Mary Dyer," *Early American Literature* 36.1 (2001): 1–30.

6. William E. Nelson, *The Common Law in Colonial America, Vol. 1: The Chesapeake and New England 1607–1660* (Oxford: Oxford University Press, 2008), 55.

7. Francis J. Bremer, *The Puritan Experiment: New England Society from Bradford to Edwards* (Hanover, N.H.: University Press of New England, 1976), 140.

8. See Karen Ordahl Kupperman, "Definitions of Liberty on the Eve of Civil War: Lord Saye and Sele, Lord Brooke, and the American Puritan Colonies," *Historical Journal* 32.1 (1989): 17–33, 20.

9. Edwin Powers, *Crime and Punishment in Early Massachusetts 1620–1692: A Documentary History* (Boston: Beacon Press, 1966), 326.

10. See Rufus Jones, *The Quakers in the American Colonies* (New York: Norton, 1966), 35–37, for the sequence of events for these early visits and for the story of Samuel Gorton. See also Philip F. Gura, "Samuel Gorton and Religious Radicalism in England, 1644–1648," *William and Mary Quarterly* 40.1 (1983): 121–24, in which Gura makes the case that though Gorton never became a Quaker officially, he was of their mind in many things, including making women more important in the church.

11. Nathaniel B. Shurtleff, ed., *Records of the Governor and Company of the Massachusetts Bay in New England*, vol. 3, *1644–1657* (1854; repr., Memphis: General Books, 2010).

12. Ibid., 346.

13. Bishop, *New England Judged by the Spirit of the Lord,* 109.

14. David Downes and Paul Rock, *Understanding Deviance,* 5th ed. (Oxford: Oxford University Press, 2007).

15. Quoted in Powers, *Crime and Punishment in Early Massachusetts,* 343.

16. The Quakers may have learned to adopt this posture as a result of their long struggle with the authorities in England, where they were imprisoned in large numbers and yet from prison waged an extraordinarily successful letter-writing campaign that galvanized their supporters and eventually altered the state's treatment of them.

17. J. P. Sommerville, *Politics and Ideology in England, 1603–1640* (New York: Addison-Wesley, 1986), 230.

18. Alan Cromartie, "The Constitutionalist Revolution: The Transformation of Political Culture in Early Stuart England," *Past and Present* 163 (May 1999): 76–120, 98.

19. See Mary Sarah Bilder, *The Transatlantic Constitution: Colonial Legal Culture and Empire* (Cambridge, Mass.: Harvard University Press, 2008).

20. Quoted in Edward Burroughs, *A Declaration of the Sad and Great Persecution and Martyrdom of the People of God Called Quakers* (London: Printed for Robert Wilson, 1661).

21. Francis Howgill, *The Popish Inquisition Newly Erected in New-England* (London: Printed for Thomas Simmons, 1659), 34–35.

22. Hallowell, *The Quaker Invasion of Massachusetts,* 169.

23. Bishop, *New England Judged by the Spirit of the Lord,* 12.

24. On the expression "the law of the land," see Victoria Kahn, *Wayward Contracts: The Crisis of Political Obligation in England, 1640–1674* (Princeton, N.J.: Princeton University Press, 2004), 86.

25. Bishop, *New England Judged by the Spirit of the Lord,* 13.

26. Craig Horle, for example, has pointed out that even in the period of their greatest persecution (1660–88), the Quakers did not rejoice in their sufferings because it made them into martyrs but rather used them to demonstrate the injustice of the legal system; see Craig Horle, *The Quakers and the English Legal System, 1660–1688* (Philadelphia: University of Pennsylvania Press, 1988), 161–86. John Knott summarizes Horle's point: "While he recognizes and describes the violence against Quakers in the period, Horle focuses on Quaker activism in gathering and publishing their 'sufferings' as a way of confronting their persecutors and judges and in developing a legal support system through the Meeting for Sufferings, established in London in 1676"; see John R. Knott, "Joseph Besse and the Quaker Culture of Suffering," in *The Emergence of Quaker Writing: Dissenting Literature in Seventeenth-Century England,* ed. Thomas N. Corns and David Lowenstein (London: Frank Cass and Company, 1995), 126–27.

27. Bishop, *New England Judged by the Spirit of the Lord,* 63.

28. Ibid., 71.

29. Ibid., 76.

30. Howgill, *The Popish Inquisition Newly Erected in New-England,* 6.

31. The provision in the charter of the Massachusetts Bay Colony provided for

"the governors and officers of the said Company, for their special defence and safety, to incoutner, repulse, repell, and resist as well by seas by land, all such person and persons as shall attempt or enterprise the destruction, invasion, detriment or annoyance to the said plantation or inhabitants." The Avalon Project: Documents in Law, History, and Diplomacy (New Haven: Lillian Goldman Law Library, 2008, online source). It is worth remembering, however, that the authority to banish, though granted to the Puritan authorities in the charter of the Bay Company, was of questionable provenance. In England since the time of Queen Elizabeth, only Parliament had the authority to banish. Moreover the banishment law against the Quakers could not be defended as an English borrowing since England, while perfectly willing to imprison them, had neither called for their banishment nor identified their presence in the kingdom as a capital crime.

32. Howgill, *The Popish Inquisition Newly Erected in New-England*, 25.

33. *The Laws and Liberties of Massachusetts,* introduction by Max Farrand (1648; repr., Cambridge, Mass.: Harvard University Press, 1929), A3.

34. Bishop, *New England Judged by the Spirit of the Lord,* 14.

35. John Norton, *The Heart of New-England Rent at the Blasphemies of the Present Generation* (London: Printed for J. H. for John Allen, 1660), 73.

36. From John Noble, *William Leddra the Quaker* (Boston: Colonial Society of Massachusetts, 1906), 335–45, 336.

37. For more on the Petition of Right, see James R. Stoner, Jr., *Common Law and Liberal Theory: Coke, Hobbes, and the Origins of American Constitutionalism* (Lawrence: University of Kansas Press, 1992), 46.

38. Bishop, *New England Judged by the Spirit of the Lord,* 62.

39. Hugo Grotius, *On the Law of War and Peace* (1625; repr., Whitefish, Mont.: Kessinger, 2004), 58.

40. Norton, *The Heart of New-England Rent at the Blasphemies of the Present Generation,* 67–68.

41. Burroughs, *A Declaration of the Sad and Great Persecution and Martyrdom of the People of God Called Quakers,* 12.

42. Norton, *The Heart of New-England Rent at the Blasphemies of the Present Generation,* 73.

43. See Horle, *The Quakers and the English Legal System 1660–1688,* 161–86.

44. Bishop, *New England Judged by the Spirit of the Lord,* 365.

45. Frederick B. Tolles, *Quakers and the Atlantic Culture* (New York: Macmillan, 1960), 23.

46. Henry J. Cadbury, "Intercolonial Solidarity of American Quakerism," *Pennsylvania Magazine of History and Biography* 60.4 (1936): 362–74, 366.

47. John Rous quoted in Humphrey Norton, *New England's Ensigne* (London: Printed by T. L. for G. Calvert, 1659), 89.

48. Bishop, *New England Judged by the Spirit of the Lord,* 35.

49. Bishop quoted in Powers, *Crime and Punishment in Early Massachusetts,* 331.

50. Bishop, *New England Judged by the Spirit of the Lord*, 33–34.

51. Howgill, *The Popish Inquisition Newly Erected in New-England*, 22.

52. Michel Foucault, *Security, Territory, Population: Lectures at the College de France, 1977–1978*, ed. Michel Senellart, trans. Graham Burchell (New York: Palgrave, 2007), 71.

53. Robert David Sack, *Human Territoriality: Its Theory and History* (Cambridge: Cambridge University Press, 1986), 33.

54. Foucault, *Security, Territory, Population*, 71.

55. Jürgen Habermas, *The Inclusion of the Other: Studies in Political Theory* (Cambridge, Mass.: MIT Press, 1998), xxiii.

56. Burroughs, *A Declaration of the Sad and Great Persecution and Martyrdom of the People of God Called Quakers*, 8.

57. *The Laws and Liberties of Massachusetts*, 49.

58. Ibid., 35.

59. Foucault, *Security, Territory, Population*, 44.

60. Carl Schmitt, *The Concept of the Political*, trans. George Schwab (Chicago: University of Chicago Press, 1996), 26–27.

61. Meredith Baldwin Weddle, *Walking in the Way of Peace: Quaker Pacifism in the Seventeenth Century* (Oxford: Oxford University Press, 2001), 89.

62. See Jody Greene, "Hostis Humani Generis," *Critical Inquiry* 34.4 (2008): 683–705, 693.

63. Richard Tuck, *The Rights of War and Peace: Political Thought and the International Order from Grotius to Kant* (Oxford: Oxford University Press, 1999), 78.

64. Norton, *New England's Ensigne*, 89.

65. By a strange twist, it may be possible that the Puritans were pursuing an argument in the alternative that finds its justification in Grotius's theory of punishment in *The Rights of War and Peace*, which justifies war not only on the part of a state against another state but also on the part of nonstate actors against other private individuals—*inimici* in Grotian terms—who do not have the power invested by civil jurisdiction. It is not the case, in other words, that war was justified only when "he who undertakes it be injured in himself, in his State, or that he has some Jurisdiction over the person against whom the War is made." See Grotius, *The Rights of War and Peace*, 3 vols., ed. with an introduction by Richard Tuck (Indianapolis: Liberty Fund, 2005), 1:xvii.

66. Howgill, *The Popish Inquisition Newly Erected in New-England*, 49.

67. Weddle, *Walking in the Way of Peace*, 78.

68. Pestana, *Quakers and Baptists in Colonial Massachusetts*, 72.

69. Howgill, *The Popish Inquisition Newly Erected in New-England*, 42.

70. George Edward Ellis, *The Puritan Age and Rule in the Colony of the Massachusetts Bay* (Cambridge: University Press, 1888; repr., Lenox, Mass.: Hard Press, 2008), 459.

71. Peter Hallward, *Badiou: A Subject to Truth* (Minneapolis: University of Minnesota Press, 2003), 87.

72. Kenneth Reinhard, "Toward a Political Theory of the Neighbor," in Savoj Žižek, Eric L. Santner, and Kenneth Reinhard, *The Neighbor: Three Inquiries in Political Theology* (Chicago: University of Chicago Press, 2005), 67.

73. Grotius, *The Rights of War and Peace*, 3 vols., ed. with an introduction by Richard Tuck (Indianapolis: Liberty Fund, 2005), 2:555.

74. Hallowell, *The Quaker Invasion of Massachusetts*, 55. These and other expressions of legal protest ultimately led King Charles II to condemn the executions, which in turn led the Puritans to divest the General Court of its power to enforce the law and finally in 1661 to repeal it altogether.

75. See Robert G. Pope, *The Half-Way Covenant: Church Membership in Puritan New England* (Princeton, N.J.: Princeton University Press, 1969).

CHAPTER 4

1. Jean M. O'Brien, *Dispossesion by Degrees: Indian Land and Identity in Natick, Massachusetts, 1650–1790* (Cambridge: Cambridge University Press, 1997).

2. Stuart Banner, *How the Indians Lost Their Land: Law and Power on the Frontier* (Cambridge, Mass.: Harvard University Press, 2005), 191.

3. Nathaniel B. Shurtleff, ed., *Records of the Governor and Company of the Massachusetts Bay in New England*, vol. 5, *1674–1686* (1854; repr., Memphis: General Books, 2010), 57. On the Deer Island banishment in general, see James D. Drake, *King Philip's War: Civil War in New England, 1675–1676* (Amherst: University of Massachusetts Press, 1999), 87–88; Yasuhide Kawashima, *Igniting King Philip's War: The John Sassamon Murder Trial* (Lawrence: University Press of Kansas, 2001), 146; Jill Lepore, *The Name of War: King Philip's War and the Origins of American Identity* (New York: Vintage Books, 1999), 138–45; Jean M. O'Brien, *Dispossession by Degrees: Indian Land and Identity in Natick, Massachusetts, 1650–1790* (Lincoln: University of Nebraska Press, 2003), 61–62, 67–68; and Jenny Hale Pulsipher, *Subjects unto the Same King: Indians, English, and the Contest for Authority in Colonial New England* (Philadelphia: University of Pennsylvania Press, 2005), 143–47.

4. The hostile Indians, a category that included all the Indians fighting against the English in King Philip's War, were not implicated in this deterritorialization. They remained associated with their land, but in a way that provoked their ultimate annihilation.

5. Justin Winsor noted that when the Indians were moved to Deer Island, the island was already owned by an individual: "And by another vote, Eliot's colony of Praying Indians at Natick were removed to Deer Island in Boston harbor, with the consent of Mr. Shrimpton who owned it." See Winsor, *The Memorial History of Boston, Including Suffolk County, Massachusetts 1630–1880* (Boston: James R. Osgood and Company, 1880), 320–21.

6. The singularity of the Deer Island banishment is reinforced by the history of the events that immediately preceded it. This history included numerous failed efforts on the part of the Puritans to dispose of the Indians from the praying towns in response to outbreaks of extraordinary hostility on the part of English soldiers and inhabitants of towns nearby. Most of these initial efforts failed because the accommodations that were chosen for sequestering the Indians, usually townhouses or private homes, were too small or too vulnerable to mob violence, and authorities feared that the Indians would be killed. Deer

Island was unique in being sufficiently large and remote to contain all the Christian Indians from Natick as well as many from the other praying towns. See George Madison Bodge, *Soldiers in King Philip's War, Containing Lists of the Soldiers of Massachusetts Colony Who Served in the Indian Wars from 1620–1677* (Boston: Printed for the author, 1906), 397.

7. Stephen Saunders Webb, *1676: The End of American Independence* (Syracuse, N.Y.: Syracuse University Press, 1995), 222.

8. Stephen Foster, *The Long Argument: English Puritanism and the Shaping of New England Culture, 1570–1700* (Chapel Hill: University of North Carolina Press, 1991), 178.

9. For a clear explanation of this phenomenon, see ibid., 60–64.

10. See ibid., 178n8, for the increased frequency after the Half-Way Covenant.

11. Richard White, "'Although I Am Dead, I Am Not Entirely Dead. I Have Left a Second of Myself': Constructing Self and Persons on the Middle Ground of Early America," in *Through a Glass Darkly: Reflections on Personal Identity in Early America*, ed. Ronald Hoffman, Mechal Sobel, and Fredrika J. Teute (Chapel Hill: University of North Carolina Press, 1997), 410.

12. See Peter Karsten, *Between Law and Custom: 'High' and 'Low' Legal Cultures in the Lands of the British Diaspora—The United States, Canada, Australia, and New Zealand, 1600–1900* (Cambridge: Cambridge University Press, 2002); and Donald R. Kelley, *The Human Measure: Social Thought in the Western Legal Tradition* (Cambridge, Mass.: Harvard University Press, 1990), for illuminating discussions of custom in culture and law.

13. Using Englishness as a basis for denying the Indians status as common-law agents may come as a surprise to those who recall the European debates about whether the Indians could be considered human in the first place. But this question had for the most part been decided in the Indians' favor, so the authorities who sought to exclude them from the legal arena had to look elsewhere, at which point nationality presented itself.

14. J. G. A. Pocock, The *Machiavellian Moment: Florentine Political Thought and the Atlantic Republican Tradition* (Princeton, N.J.: Princeton University Press, 1975), 341.

15. See, for example, James Axtell, "Some Thoughts on the Ethnohistory of Missions," *Ethnohistory* 29.1 (1982): 35–41; Kristina Bross, *Dry Bones and Indian Sermons: Praying Indians in Colonial America* (Ithaca, N.Y.: Cornell University Press, 2004), 21–28; Craig White, "Praying Indians' Speeches as Texts of Massachusetts Oral Culture," *Early American Literature* 38.3 (2003): 437–67; and Hilary E. Wyss, *Writing Indians: Literacy, Christianity, and Native Community in Early America* (Amherst: University of Massachusetts Press, 2003), 19–21.

16. See Joshua David Bellin, "John Eliot's Playing Indian," *Early American Literature* 42.1 (2007): 1–30; Sarah Rivett, "Empirical Desire: Conversion, Ethnography, and the New Science of the Praying Indian," *Early American Studies: An Interdisciplinary Journal* 4:1 (2006): 16–45; James P. Ronda, "'We Are Well as We Are': An Indian Critique of Seventeenth-Century Christian Missions," *William and Mary Quarterly* 34.1 (1977): 66–82; Daniel Mandell, "'To Live More Like My Christian English Neighbors': Natick Indians in the Eighteenth Century," *William and Mary Quarterly* 48.1 (1991): 552–79; and Pulsipher, *Subjects unto the Same King*, 136–37.

17. Ronda, "We Are Well as We Are," 67.

18. Alice Nash, "Antic Deportments and Indian Postures," in *A Centre of Wonders: The Body in Early America,* ed. Janet Moore Lindman and Michele Lise Tartar (Ithaca, N.Y.: Cornell University Press, 2001), 169.

19. Daniel R. Mandell, *Behind the Frontier: Indians in Eighteenth-Century Eastern Massachusetts* (Lincoln: University of Nebraska, 2000); Jenny Hale Pulsipher, *Subjects unto the Same King: Indians, English, and the Contest for Authority in Colonial New England* (Philadelphia: University of Pennsylvania Press, 2006); James Ronda, "'We Are Well as We Are': An Indian Critique of Seventeenth-Century Christian Missions," *William and Mary Quarterly* 34.1, 66–82.

20. Matt Cohen, *The Networked Wilderness: Communicating in Early New England* (Minneapolis: University of Minnesota Press, 2010), 93.

21. Anne Marie Plane, "Legitimacies, Indian Identities, and the Law: The Politics of Sex and the Creation of History in Colonial New England," *Law and Social Inquiry* 23.1 (1998): 55–77, 56–57. On the Indians' highly developed legal and political systems, see Kathleen J. Bragdon, *Native People of Southern New England, 1500–1650* (Norman: University of Oklahoma Press, 1999), 14–155; and O'Brien, *Dispossession by Degrees,* 19–21. On Indian status in colonial law as landowners, see Peter S. Leavenworth, "'The Best Title That Indians Can Claime': Native Agency and Consent in the Transferral of Penacook-Pawtucket Land in the Seventeenth Century," *New England Quarterly* 72.2 (1999): 275–300; Christopher W. Hannan, "Indian Land in Seventeenth-Century Massachusetts," *Historical Journal of Massachusetts* 20.2 (Summer 2001): 1–12; James Warren Springer, "American Indians and the Law of Real Property in Colonial New England," *American Journal of Legal History* 30.1 (1986): 25–58; and Banner, *How the Indians Lost Their Land,* 10–48. Additional studies include Yasuhide Kawashima, "Legal Origins of the Indian Reservations in Colonial Massachusetts," *American Journal of Legal History* 13.1 (1969): 42–56, which examines the legal basis of the reservation system; and Kathleen J. Bragdon, "Crime and Punishment among the Indians of Massachusetts, 1675–1750," *Ethnohistory* 28.1 (1981): 23–32, which discusses the Indians' status in criminal law cases.

22. Julie Stone Peters, "Legal Performance Good and Bad," *Law, Culture, and the Humanities* 4.2 (2008): 179–200.

23. See Joseph Roach, *Cities of the Dead: Circum-Atlantic Performance* (New York: Columbia University Press, 1996), which links performance to the law but does not focus on mundane actions specifically. Roach describes law as "a cultural system dedicated to the production of certain kinds of behaviors and the regulation or proscription of others . . . [which] functions as a repository of social performances, past and present" (55).

24. For a discussion of the social and legal flexibility afforded to members of colonial militias, see John W. Shy, "A New Look at Colonial Militia," *William and Mary Quarterly* 20.2 (1963): 175–85; and Richard R. Johnson, "The Search for a Usable Indian: An Aspect of the Defense of Colonial New England," *Journal of American History* 64.3 (1977): 623–51.

25. William Wood, *New England's Prospect* (1634; repr., Amherst: University of Massachusetts Press, 1993), 75.

26. To say that the Indians were recognized as territorial inhabitants is not to say that

this was necessarily on their own terms; they often altered their own territorial practices to conform to the English understanding of land. *See* David J. Silverman, "'We Chuse to Be Bounded': Native American Animal Husbandry in Colonial New England," *William and Mary Quarterly* 60.3 (2003): 511–48.

27. Kelley, *The Human Measure, 171.*

28. In 1634 the General Court passed its first law regarding the purchase of Indian lands: "and it is Ordered, that no person whatsoever, Shall henceforth buy land of any Indian without License first had and obtained of the General Court, and if any offend herein, such Land so bought shall be forfeited to the Country" (quoted in O'Brien, *Dispossession by Degrees*, 71n22).

29. The best example of such a treaty is the one drawn up by Massasoit, King Philip's father, with Plymouth Colony's governor in 1621. This treaty referred to the Indians as "friends" and specified reciprocal duties and privileges in most things. See *Mourt's Relation: A Journal of the Pilgrims at Plymouth* (1622; repr., Bedford, Mass.: Applewood Books, 1963), 57.

30. Kawashima refers to this period in which the Indians ruled over their own people as one of peaceful coexistence. This may have been partly because the Indians had such an efficient and personality-based legal system that the English felt it was all right to leave it all up to them. See Yasuhide Kawashima, *Puritan Justice and the Indian: White Man's Law in Massachusetts, 1630–1763* (Middletown, Conn.: Wesleyan University Press, 1986), 230. See also Alfred A. Cave, *The Pequot War* (Amherst: University of Massachusetts Press, 1996), 166–67.

31. Katherine Hermes, "Jurisdiction in the Colonial Northeast: Algonquian, English and French Governance," *American Journal of Legal History* 43.1 (1999): 52–73, 52. Kawashima notes too that "Indian criminal law [which was not distinguishable from civil law] was based upon personality, not on territoriality, which was the basis of the white man's law" (Kawashima, *Puritan Justice and the Indian,* 230). See also Kathleen Joan Bragdon, "Crime and Punishment among the Indians of Massachusetts, 1675–1750," *Ethnohistory* 28.1 (1981): 23–32, 23–25.

32. The details of this story are murky. John Sassamon, a praying Indian who maintained close ties to King Philip and served off and on as his translator, was killed, allegedly by three of Philip's men who had discovered Sassamon's intention to alert the governor of the Plymouth Colony of Philip's plans to form an intertribal army to attack English settlements. Apprehending the three men accused of killing Sassamon, the English, without consulting Philip and in violation of treaty law authorizing Philip to adjudicate the crime himself, proceeded to bring the three men to trial. While six jury members were Indians, historical accounts strongly suggest that they were coerced to vote with the white jury, and so the three Indians were convicted and hanged. For specifics about the clash between English and Indian jurisdictions, see Yasuhide Kawashima, *Igniting King Philip's War: The John Sassamon Murder Trial* (Lawrence: University Press of Kansas, 2001), 62.

33. Richard Hooker, *Of the Laws of Ecclesiastical Polity* (Cambridge: Cambridge University Press, 2002), 93.

34. New Plymouth Colony, *Records of the Colony of New Plymouth, in New England: Laws, 1623–1682*, 12 vols. (Charleston, S.C.: Nabu Press, 2010), 11:259.

35. Pocock, *The Machiavellian Moment*, 8.

36. In discussing this impulse in the context of the mixed jury—an adjudicative body comprised of people from a variety of places put in place specifically to overcome inherent inequity—Marianne Constable links this practice with an acknowledgment of the legal agency of the defendant on the part of the dominant authority. We should also note, however, that while Indians may have been nominally present in certain juries, they were never wholly incorporated and were usually barred from participating in the rendering of verdicts. See Marianne Constable, *The Law of the Other: The Mixed Jury and Changing Conceptions of Citizenship, Law, and Knowledge* (Chicago: University of Chicago Press, 1994).

37. See George Lee Haskins, *Law and Authority in Early Massachusetts: A Study in Tradition and Design* (New York: Macmillan, 1960), 101.

38. Anyone who has looked at the business of the Indians in the Puritan courts will note their appearance there for the most part as criminals, a status that considered their actions but only from the perspective of their deviance. In addition, as Erikson and Abrams suggest, characterizations based on deviance lack the status of those based on positive actions and fall far short of them; see Kai T. Erikson, *Wayward Puritans: A Study in the Sociology of Deviance* (New York: Macmillan, 1966); and Philip Abrams, *Historical Sociology* (Ithaca, N.Y.: Cornell University Press, 1983).

39. Laura M. Stevens, *The Poor Indians: British Missionaries, Native Americans, and Colonial Sensibility* (Philadelphia: University of Pennsylvania Press, 2004), 20.

40. The praying Indians of Natick were examined three times from 1652 to 1659; only in 1660 did the Puritan elders finally sanction full communion, and then only for eight confessors. Nor did these eight ever achieve the status that English Christians enjoyed. See O'Brien, *Dispossession by Degrees*, 51.

41. Rivett accounts differently for such hesitation, reading it as evidence of the effort on the part of Eliot and others to bring out the atavistic or primitive nature of the Indians' conversion. But even in her account, these repeat performances suggest the insufficiency of the Indians' conversion; see Rivett, "Empirical Desire," 41.

42. John Eliot, *Tears of Repentance, or A Further Narrative of the Progress of the Gospel amongst the Indians in New England* (1653; repr., Whitefish, Mont.: Kessinger, 2001), 13.

43. Ibid., C, my emphasis.

44. Ibid., B2.

45. Robert James Naeher, "Dialogue in the Wilderness: John Eliot and the Indian Exploration of Puritanism as a Source of Meaning, Comfort, and Ethnic Survival," *New England Quarterly* 62.3 (1989): 346–68, 367.

46. Eliot, *Tears of Repentance*, 33.

47. The historical status of the military also facilitated the transition of the Indian into common-law agency. At the heart of the common law but simultaneously an alternative to it, the military was often a place for the rootless to establish themselves. At the same time the early colonial militia—the body of civilian volunteers from which the fighting army

was gathered—represented a strangely democratic institution in a society where democracy did not reign. For more on the social and legal flexibility afforded to members of colonial militias, see Shy, "A New Look at Colonial Militia," 175–85; Johnson, "The Search for a Usable Indian," 623–51; Louise A. Breen, "Religious Radicalism in the Puritan Officer Corps: Heterodoxy, the Artillery Company, and Cultural Integration in Seventeenth-Century Boston," *New England Quarterly* 68.1 (1995): 3–43; S. T. Ansell, "Legal and Historical Aspects of the Militia," *Yale Law Journal* 26.6 (1917): 471–80; Timothy Breen, "English Origins and New World Development: The Case of the Covenanted Militia in Seventeenth-Century Massachusetts," *Past & Present* 57.1 (1972): 74–96; and Kyle F. Zellner, *A Rabble in Arms: Massachusetts Towns and Militiamen during King Philip's War* (New York: New York University Press, 2009). For a theory of the democratic militia, see especially Morrison Sharp, "Leadership and Democracy in the Early New England System of Defense," *American Historical Review* 50.2 (1945): 244–60.

48. William Hubbard, *A Narrative of the Indian Wars in New-England, from the First Planting Thereof in the Year 1607, to the Year 1677* (1814; repr., Whitefish, Mont.: Kessinger, 2005), 117, 170, 185.

49. Ibid., 152–54. Very occasionally Hubbard mixed praise for the Indians' faithfulness with brief mentions of their courage. For example, he wrote, "It is worth the noting what faithfulness and courage some of the Christian Indians, with the said Captain Pierce shewed in the fight" (152). At such moments, however, he was careful to qualify the Indians' courage: "many of them have proved not only faithful, but very serviceable and helpful to the English; they usually proving good seconds, though they have not ordinarily confidence enough to make the first onset" (155).

50. Benjamin Church, *Diary of King Philip's War, 1675–76*, tercentenary ed. (Guilford, Conn.: Pequot Press, 1975), 128.

51. Daniel Gookin, *Historical Account of the Doings and Sufferings of the Christian Indians in New England in the Years 1675–1677* (1836; repr., Whitefish, Mont.: Kessinger, 2005), 55.

52. Ibid., 486, 488.

53. Ibid., 436, my emphasis. Though several witnesses perceived the injustice of sending the Indians to Deer Island, Gookin alone complained about the continued injustice of sending those who had performed valiantly in battle back to their prison after they returned from the field.

54. Gookin, *Historical Account of the Doings and Sufferings*, 445, 447, my emphasis.

55. Ibid., 477.

56. Ibid., 453.

57. See Robert Nozick, *Anarchy, State, and Utopia* (New York: Basic Books, 1974), 152–53. See also Stephen M. Best, *The Fugitive's Properties: Law and the Poetics of Possession* (Chicago: University of Chicago Press, 2004), 221–24, for how this kind of language plays out in the context of landmark Supreme Court race cases of the twentieth century.

58. After the war these restrictions were lifted at the May 1677 session of the General Court, and movement on pain of death was made void. An amnesty of sorts was given to those Indians who surrendered after the capture of King Philip, but the vast majority of

these were sent out of the jurisdiction and sold into slavery in the West Indies. Some remained as servants, although a law barred any servants over the age of twelve from living in Boston. The remaining Indians—most of them the praying Indians who were released from Deer Island—were put into four remaining praying towns—Natick, Punkapoag, Hassanesmesit, and Wamesit—and were allowed to move about without being accompanied by an Englishman, although each needed to carry a certificate.

59. Jenny Hale Pulsipher, "'Our Sages Are Sageless': A Letter on Massachusetts Indian Policy after King Philip's War," *William and Mary Quarterly* 58.2 (2001): 431–48, 440.

60. Many of these documents are held by the Mormon Church.

61. Gookin, *Historical Account of the Doings and Sufferings*, 524.

62. Ibid., 525.

63. Ibid., 524.

64. This is not to say that these petitions were always successful. Several of the Indians who fought in the war on the side of the English petitioned to save loved ones, but the council often rejected those pleas. See ibid., 528.

65. See the records at the end of Bodge, *Soldiers in King Philip's War*, 484–86, for English soldiers invoking such precedents well into the eighteenth century.

66. Quoted in O'Brien, *Dispossession by Degrees*, 66.

67. Daniel Mandell, *Behind the Frontier: Indians in Eighteenth-Century Eastern Massachusetts* (Lincoln: University of Nebraska Press, 2000), 25. See also Daniel R. Mandell, *King Philip's War: Colonial Expansion, Native Resistance, and the End of Indian Sovereignty* (Baltimore: Johns Hopkins University Press, 2010).

68. Pulsipher, "Our Sages Are Sageless," 441. For more on the emergence of a racialized discourse about the Indians after King Philip's War, see Kawashima, "Legal Origins of the Indian Reservations in Colonial Massachusetts," 42–56; and James P. Ronda, "Red and White at the Bench: Indians and the Law in Plymouth Colony, 1620–1691," *Essex Institute Historical Collections* 110.3 (1974): 200–215. See also Lyle Koehler, "Red-White Power Relations and Justice in the Courts of Seventeenth-Century New England," *American Indian Culture and Research Journal* 3.4 (1979): 1–31.

69. Philip J. Deloria, *Playing Indian* (New Haven, Conn.: Yale University Press, 1998).

70. For more on the ways in which the Indians interacted with the common law after the war, see Colin G. Calloway, ed., *After King Philip's War: Presence and Persistence in Indian New England* (Hanover, N.H.: Dartmouth University Press, 1997), 208ff.

CONCLUSION

1. *Trop v. Dulles*, 365 U.S. 86, 102 (1958).

2. Ibid., 101.

3. It is something of a tragic irony that the concept of birthright, though challenged in this early period, is seen today as a seemingly ineluctable way of organizing membership in the nation. See Jacqueline Stevens, *States without Nations: Citizenship for Mortals* (New

York: Columbia University Press, 2010); and Ayelet Shachar, *The Birthright Lottery: Citizenship and Global Inequality* (Cambridge, Mass.: Harvard University Press, 2009).

4. Robert G. Pope, *The Half-Way Covenant: Church Membership in Puritan New England* (Princeton, N.J.: Princeton University Press, 1969).

5. For varying degrees of one or the other view, see George Lee Haskins, *Law and Authority in Early Massachusetts: A Study in Tradition and Design* (New York: Macmillan, 1960); David Thomas Konig, *Law and Society in Puritan Massachusetts: Essex County, 1629–1692* (Chapel Hill: University of North Carolina Press, 1981); William E. Nelson, *The Common Law in Colonial America*, vol. 1: *The Chesapeake and New England 1607–1660* (Oxford: Oxford University Press, 2008); and Bradley Chapin, *Criminal Justice in Colonial America, 1606–1660* (Athens: University of Georgia Press, 2010).

6. Mary Sarah Bilder, *The Transatlantic Constitution: Colonial Legal Culture and the Empire* (Cambridge, Mass.: Harvard University Press, 2008).

7. Jacques Rancière, *Disagreement: Politics and Philosophy* (Minneapolis: University of Minnesota Press, 2004), 55.

8. For Rancière, this is what ultimately brings politics and aesthetics under the same umbrella, but I invoke Rancière here only to help us see how the rhetoric of and around banishment, a rhetoric of the law, made it possible to undo and redo the boundaries of seventeenth-century New England and to facilitate travel between them.

9. Frederick Jackson Turner, *The Frontier in American History* (1921; repr., Whitefish, Mont.: Kessinger, 2010), 39.

10. Ibid., 41.

11. William Blackstone, *Commentaries on the Laws of England: In Four Books*, vols. 1–2 (Philadelphia: Geo. T. Bisel Co., 1922), 125.

12. As Abbot Emerson Smith has pointed out, however, transportation was a relatively common practice even in the seventeenth century; see Smith, "The Transportation of Convicts to the American Colonies in the Seventeenth Century," *American Historical Review* 39.2 (1934): 232–49.

13. A. Roger Ekirch, *Bound for America: The Transportation of British Convicts to the Colonies, 1718–1775* (Oxford: Clarendon Press, 1990), 132.

14. As Smith wrote, "An important change in legal procedure took place about 1655, when the first convicts were transported with conditional pardons under the great seal. This method became standardized for all crimes until 1718, and for major felons until the nineteenth century" (Smith, "The Transportation of Convicts to the American Colonies," 237).

15. Ekirch argues otherwise; he concludes that transportation from the time of the passage of the 1718 act to about 1785 was instituted solely to remedy the upsurge in crime in England and to restore social order after the conclusion of the War of the Spanish Succession in 1713; see Ekirch, *Bound for America*, 232–33.

16. See Ruth Wallis Herndon, *Unwelcome Americans: Living on the Margin in Early New England* (Philadelphia: University of Pennsylvania Press, 2001), for an excellent discussion of transportation and several other popular mechanisms for social exclusion in eighteenth-century America.

17. See Lee H. Bowker, "Exile, Banishment and Transportation," *International Journal of Offender Therapy and Comparative Criminology* 24.1 (1980): 67–80.

18. Saxe Bannister, *On Abolishing Transportation, and on Reforming the Colonial Office, in a Letter to Lord John Russell* (London: Effingham Wilson, 1837), 10.

19. See Frank Lewis, "The Cost of Convict Transportation from Britain to Australia, 1796–1810," *Economic History Review* 41.4 (1988): 507–24, for a convincing argument that while the cost of actual transportation was high, the net profit from the labor by the convicts and their progeny far outweighed the cost.

20. The act, for instance, has been frequently invoked in the detention proceedings at Guantanamo Bay.

21. See Daniel Kanstroom, *Deportation Nation: Outsiders in American History* (Cambridge, Mass.: Harvard University Press, 2007), 110.

22. The nation's naturalization law, which had extended the residency requirement for immigrants from five years to fourteen in the first of the four alien and sedition bills, had until that time been the normal route for evaluating an immigrant's status.

23. In *Fong Yue Ting v. United States*, 149 U.S. 698, 707 (1893), which upheld key provisions of the 1892 Exclusion Act, the Supreme Court wrote, "The duty to exclude carries the right to expel" (46). For a discussion of the impact of this language in the postreconstructionist context, see Brook Thomas, "Reconstructing State and Federal Jurisdiction in *A Fool's Errand* and *The Clansman*," *English Language Notes* 48.2 (2010): 80.

24. Allegra M. McLeod, "The U.S. Criminal-Immigration Convergence and Its Possible Undoing," *American Criminal Law Review* 49 (forthcoming 2012): 22, 23.

25. For the recent history of banishment in the United States and arguments against it, see Matthew D. Borrelli, "Banishment: The Constitutional and Public Policy Arguments Against This Revived Ancient Punishment," *Suffolk University Law Review* 36.1 (2002): 469; and Peter D. Edgerton, "Banishment and the Right to Live Where You Want," *University of Chicago Law Review* 74.3 (2007): 1023.

26. On August 21, 1993, in Gordon County Superior Court in Georgia, Jerry Tipton was sentenced to twenty years for the brutal assault of an elderly woman, fifteen of those years to be served in prison and the remainder to be served on probation. As a condition of his probation, Tipton was to be banished from the state of Georgia. This was contrary to the Constitution of the State of Georgia, which expressly forbids banishment. When this fact was brought to the attention of the trial judge some three years later, the judge banished Jerry Tipton from every county in the state except Ware County, a remote, sparsely populated area in southern central Georgia. The Supreme Court of Georgia, in *State v. Collett*, determined that this attempted circumvention of Georgia constitutional law was valid.

27. Angela R. Riley, "Good (Native) Governance," *Columbia Law Review* 107.5 (2007): 1049, 1105.

28. Ibid., 1107.

29. Katherine Beckett and Steve Herbert, *Banished: The New Social Control in Urban America* (Oxford: Oxford University Press, 2010), 8.

30. Kanstroom, *Deportation Nation*, 3.

31. Ibid., 4–6.

32. For an excellent discussion of the implications of this process, see T. Alexander Aleinikoff, "Citizens, Aliens, Membership, and the Constitution," *Constitutional Commentary* 7.1 (1990): 9; and T. Alexander Aleinikoff, "Sovereignty Studies in Constitutional Law: A Comment," *Constitutional Commentary* 17.2 (2000): 197.

33. See William Garth Snider, "Banishment: The History of Its Use and a Proposal for Its Abolition under the First Amendment," *New England Journal on Criminal & Civil Confinement* 24.2 (1998): 455–509.

34. See Martha Minow, *Making All the Difference: Inclusion, Exclusion, and American Law* (Ithaca, N.Y.: Cornell University Press, 1990), 148–56, for a discussion of the ways in which the constitutional rights discourse can be exclusionary.

35. Kwame Anthony Appiah, *Cosmopolitanism: Ethics in a World of Strangers* (New York: W. W. Norton, 2006), 71.

36. Yasemin Nuhoglu Soysal, *Limits of Citizenship: Migrants and Postnational Membership in Europe* (Chicago: University of Chicago Press, 1995), 1.

37. Seyla Benhabib et al., *Another Cosmopolitanism: Hospitality, Sovereignty, and Democratic Iterations*, ed. Robert Post (New York: Oxford University Press, 2006).

38. Edward Casey, "A Matter of Edge: Border vs. Boundary at La Frontera" (unpublished paper delivered at the NEH Summer Institute "Mapping and Art in the Americas," Newberry Library, Chicago, Summer 2010).

39. For one of the earliest notions of what a borderland might be, see Gloria Anzaldúa, *Borderlands/La Frontera: The New Mestiza* (San Francisco: Aunt Lute Books, 2007).

40. Nicholas de Genova and Nathalie Peutz, eds., *The Deportation Regime: Sovereignty, Space, and the Freedom of Movement* (Durham, N.C.: Duke University Press, 2010).

41. Michael Walzer, *Spheres of Justice: A Defense of Pluralism and Equality* (New York: Basic Books, 1983), 39.

42. Wendy Brown, *Walled States, Waning Sovereignty* (New York: Zone Books, 2010).

43. Countless deportation cases rely on a basic appeal to the government for recognition, sometimes of a lengthy residence preceding deportation and sometimes of a brief one. See, for example, *Arrellano-Mendoza v. Holder*, 391 F. Appx. 683, WL 3157185 (2010).

44. Statements of this sort can often be found in immigrant or exile testimony recorded in many of the Board of Immigration Appeals (BIA) cases, some of which have been published in *Federal Reporters* and some of which have not. See, for example, *Lopez v. Attorney General of the United States*, 383 F. Appx. 189, WL 2292314 (C.A. 3 2010). I have elsewhere written about how the language of this case conforms to the kind of illocution increasingly offered by immigrants and exiles; see Nan Goodman, "The Illocutions of Exile," *Law, Culture, and the Humanities* (forthcoming).

Index

Acknowledgments

The stories I tell in this book—of banishment and social exclusion—bear no resemblance to the story of what it was like to write it. Over the course of the many years it took to research and write this book, I experienced a sense of inclusion—of making new friends and connecting in new ways with old friends—that exceeded my wildest expectations. Sally Gordon, Hilary Schor, and Robin West deserve special thanks not only for taking the time to talk with me about my work on many different occasions, but also for making it possible for me to air some of my ideas in friendly but rigorous settings. At the West Coast Conference on Law and Literature at the University of Southern California, I had the good fortune to receive detailed critiques of an early version of my argument from Gary Rowe and Clyde Spillenger and invaluable feedback from Cynthia Herrup, Heather James, Rebecca Lemon, Peter Mancall, and Hilary Schor, among others. At the McNeil Center for Early American Studies at the University of Pennsylvania, I benefited from the comments of Elaine Crane, Sally Gordon, Daniel Richter, and Richard Ross, among others. At Georgetown University Law Center, I had the privilege of leading a faculty seminar on law and humanities in which I assigned some of my work in progress and benefited from insightful and engaged responses from Martha Ertman, Heidi Feldman, Karen Knop, Allegra MacLeod, Naomi Mezey, Shari Motro, Michael Seidman, Mortimer Sellers, Jerry Spann, Adrienne Stone, Adam Thurschwell, Philomila Tsoukala, and Robin West, among others.

Many people at the University of Colorado also helped me work through issues of interest to me. I had a conversation with Marjorie MacIntosh only two or three weeks into my research for the book, which helped me pinpoint banishment within the context of English criminal law and spared me much aimless searching. Only a little later, conversations with Valerie Forman, David Glimp, Elizabeth Robertson, William Kuskin, Richelle Munkhoff, and Katherine Eggert greatly enriched my understanding of the late medieval and early modern worlds in England, which were for my subjects just a stone's throw away in time and space.

Other friends and colleagues, including Pompa Banerjee, Céline Dauverd, Anne Lester, Deepti Misri, Sue Zemka, Michael Zimmerman, and other members of the 2009–10 Center for Humanities and the Arts Seminar on Migration read portions of my work and asked illuminating questions about it. I want especially to thank Jane Garrity and Karen Jacobs, who commented on selected pieces of the book, listened to me talk about banishment even when they would rather have been sleeping, shared endless meals with me, and made me feel at home when home seemed far away. Karen Jacobs was especially helpful in clarifying big-picture ideas and rendering the logic of my introduction and conclusion legible. Two visiting scholars to the University of Colorado helped me, almost certainly without their knowing it, orient myself with respect to the law under consideration: Harry Berger Jr. gave an eye-opening talk in the spring of 2007 on Shakespeare's *Henry V*; and Victoria Kahn, with Lorna Hutson, conducted a fascinating two-day workshop in the spring of 2009 on early modern English common law.

My greatest thanks, however, go to one person in particular, who shaped this work in ways that mark its overall spirit as well as each of its pages. Teresa Toulouse guided my efforts at every stage, from pointing me to previously unknown source materials, to asking me generous yet trenchant questions, to commenting on draft after draft until her fingers were cramped from writing. In countless conversations over coffee, tea, wine, and the occasional frozen yogurt, she shared her vast knowledge of and insights into early America and its denizens—their habits of mind, their deepest concerns, their many contradictions—until the seventeenth century came alive with the power that the reconstructed villages of Sturbridge, Mystic, and Plymouth once held for me as a child. Talking with and learning from Terry about this period and its texts were among the greatest pleasures I have known.

An interdisciplinary work at its core, *Banished* also benefited from the many conversations I had with scholars on the legal side of the interdiscipline. Emily Calhoun helped me sort through many legal issues pertinent to the book in the course of team teaching a class with me on legal rhetoric. Martha Umphrey read pieces of various chapters and always made stunning suggestions. Naomi Cahn and Martha Ertman made it possible for me to present a portion of my chapter on hospitality at a meeting of the Feminist Legal Reading Group in Washington, D.C. I am also grateful to Katherine Franke, Austin Sarat, Simon Stern, and Nomi Stoltzenberg for making comments that were often delivered casually but turned out to be earth-shattering for me.

Many other people lent their support to me and to this project in various ways. Elliott Urdang, M.D., and Erik Urdang read very early drafts and hunted down useful information. Sacvan Bercovitch gave wise counsel, as always. Brad Alpert, Laurie Bullock, Stefan Bullock, Silva Chang, Ingrid Creppell, Ted Fishman, my father Norman, mother Ruth, and sister Susan Goodman, Rob Gross, Kerry Palmer, Hollis Robbins, Edie Rosenberg, Michael Sonnenfeld, Nina Stern, Sara Stern, Cara Stiles, and Betty Symington showed me kindness at every turn and continued to ask me about the book even when they were, I suspect, afraid of the answer. Anne and Tom Lyons saw to it that I had shelves enough to accommodate the excess of books that had taken up residence on my office floor.

Several institutions provided me with funds that allowed me to carry out my research and to devote myself to writing. The University of Colorado was especially generous, awarding me a Faculty Fellowship in 2007, a LEAP Associate Professor Grant in 2008, a CHA Fellowship in 2009, and a Eugene M. Kayden Grant in 2010. The National Endowment for the Humanities gave me a Summer Stipend Fellowship in 2010. I am very grateful for all of these infusions.

At the University of Pennsylvania Press, I have had the great good fortune to work with Jerry Singerman, Senior Humanities Editor, who provided the impetus for me to finish the project, endorsed its purpose, and shepherded me through the initial phase of publication with a deftness, precision, and good humor that amazed me. I am also grateful to Patricia Coate, my meticulous copy editor at the press, and Erica Ginsburg, associate managing editor, and I especially want to thank my previously anonymous but now unmasked readers, Stephen Carl Arch and Robert Ferguson, whose criticisms were measured, detailed, and always constructive. This book is far better because of them.

My children grew up hearing stories of banishment—not exactly the typical childhood fare—and endured them with great patience. My son, Sam, took an interest in the subject early on, read portions of the manuscript, simplified many of my overwrought sentences, and brainstormed with me about possible book titles. My daughter, Q, kept abreast of my progress, asked me penetrating questions, and found the image that now adorns the cover of the book. Both of them kept me going with their love and made me laugh when it could just as easily have gone the other way. This book is dedicated to them.

Portions of Chapter 2 were published as "Banishment, Jurisdiction, and

Identity in Seventeenth-Century New England: The Case of Roger Williams" in *Early American Studies* 7.1 (Spring 2009): 109–39; and portions of Chapter 4 were published as "'For Their and Our Security': Jurisdictional Identity and the Performance of the 'Poor Indian' on Deer Island," in *Native Acts: Indian Performance in Early North America*, ed. Joshua Bellin and Laura Mielke (Lincoln: University of Nebraska Press, 2011). I am grateful for permission to reprint them here.